JUDAS SON OF SIMON

A Novel

-

Books by Daniel Molyneux:

The Angel of Antioch

Elias' Proverbs

יהודה

JUDAS SON OF SIMON

A Novel

Daniel Molyneux

מ

moriah books

First Edition March 2017

Published by Moriah Books
PO Box 1094
Casper, WY 82602
www.moriahbook.com
Derek Hansen Publisher
dhansen@moriahbook.com

This book is a work of fiction Any reference to historical events, real people, or real places are used fictitiously. Other names characters, places and events are the product of the author's imagination and any resemblance to actual events or places or persons, living or dead, is entirely coincidental.

All biblical quotations translated and/or paraphrased by author.

Library of Congress Control Number: 2016947374
ISBN 978-1543110463

Printed in the United States of America

LIBRARY EDITION

Cover illustration: Caravaggio's *The Taking of Christ*

To all who believe their sins are unforgiveable.

Table of Contents

Preface

Judas Iscariot is the most hated figure in human history. And yet, the name "Judas" was revered among first-century Israelites. It and Jude are versions of the name given to Jacob's fourth son, Judah, whose descendants became the most prominent of Israel's twelve tribes, the tribe of King David and Jesus. Judas Maccabees was a hero of Israelite nationalism. Judas the Galilean founded the Zealot movement. Another of Jesus' twelve disciples was named Judas (son of James, Luke 6:16). One of Jesus' brothers was named Judas (Mathew 13:55), and Jude is the name of a New Testament book. Even the term "Jew" is derived from Judah.

Judas is not the only betrayer in the pages of the Bible. Jesus' was surrounded by violence, conspiracies, cowardice, and betrayal. When he was arrested, his disciples fled and hid. Peter denied him three times. When Jesus stood trial before Pilate, where were his disciples? Only a few female relatives, Mary of Magdala, and one of the Twelve appear to have been present at his crucifixion.

Simon Peter shares striking similarities with Judas. Both were important members of Jesus' inner-circle. Peter was the closest spiritual disciple, while Judas was the group's treasurer (John 12:6, 13:29). Jesus said to Peter, "Get behind me Satan" (Matt. 16:23). Whereas, Luke 22:3 says, "Then Satan entered Judas."

There is a critical difference between the two men. Peter did not despair to the point of suicide. But Judas surrendered to the ultimate expression of guilt. Peter's betrayal was forgiven, allowing him to became the most important leader of Jesus' Church. If Judas had not ended his life, he too may have been restored to his place with the other apostles.

Suicide frequently happens near the end of troubles. This was true for my grandfather, a farmer. Following seven years of crop failure, he killed himself in a fit of despair. The next season, his family produced a bumper crop. Peter lived to see the abundant harvest planted by Jesus, but Judas did not.

Judas is torn between faithfulness to Jesus, and loyalty to his family and party. Plots swirl in the palaces of Pilate, Antipas, and Caiaphas, as they struggle to maintain their tenuous grip on power. In *Judas Son of Simon,* you will see Jesus and Roman-dominated Israel through new eyes - those of a questioning and double-minded young man torn by competing priorities and demands. Judas' actions will surprise and disturb you, move you to tears, and rage.

The Christian and Hebrew Scriptures provide the foundation for this novel, aided by the writings of first-century Israelite/Roman historian, Flavius Josephus, and many additional historical and archeological sources.

Join Judas, and Jesus' disciples, on their deeply perplexing spiritual journey. As you do, you will gain new insight into Jesus and his ministry, transforming your faith and your understanding of the Gospel.

Daniel Molyneux

List of Characters

Judas' Family

Simon Bar-Levi: Judas' father, Treasurer of the Temple
Rachel: Judas' wife, Caiaphas' daughter

Jesus' Followers

Judas Bar-Simon (Iscariot): Treasurer for the Twelve
Simon Bar-Jonah: fisher, Andrew's brother, one of the Twelve
Andrew Bar-Jonah: fisher, Simon's brother, one of the Twelve
James Bar-Zebedee: fisher, John's brother, one of the Twelve
John Bar-Zebedee: fisher, James brother, one of the Twelve
Nathaniel Bar-Tholomew: one of the Twelve
Philip the Hellenist: one of the Twelve
Thomas the Twin (Didymas): one of the Twelve
Levi Bar-Alpheus (Matthew): tax-collector, one of the Twelve
James Bar-Alpheus: Levi's brother, one of the Twelve
Judas Bar-James (Thaddaeus): one of the Twelve
Simon the Zealot: one of the Twelve
Mary from Magdala: Jesus' closest female follower
Chuza: Minister of Finance (Chief Steward) for Antipas
Joanna: a female supporter of Jesus, Chuza's wife
Lazarus: friend of Jesus, brother of Martha and Mary
Martha and Mary: friends of Jesus, Lazarus' sisters

Jesus' Family

Jesus the Nazarene (the Branch of David): son of Mary
Zechariah the Priest: father of John the Baptizer, Jesus' uncle
Elizabeth: mother of John the Baptizer, Jesus' aunt
John Bar-Zechariah: the Baptizer, Jesus' cousin
Mary: Jesus' mother, Joseph's wife
James Bar-Joseph: Jesus' eldest brother

Political and Religious Leaders

Annas Bar-Seth: High Priest 6–15AD, Caiaphas' father-in-law
Ishmael Bar-Fabus: High Priest 15-16AD
Eleazar Bar-Annas: High Priest 16-17AD, Annas' son
Simon Bar-Camithus: High Priest 17-18AD
Joseph Bar-Caiaphas: High Priest 18-36AD, Annas' son-in-law
Malchus: Captain of the Temple Guard, Levite, Caiaphas' aide
Herod the Great: Rome's puppet-king of Israel 37-4BC
Antipas Bar-Herod: Tetrarch of Galilee and Perea 4BC-39AD
Herodias: Antipas' wife and niece, formerly his brother's wife
Philip Bar-Herod: Tetrarch of Iturea 4BC-34AD, Antipas' brother
Archelaus Bar-Herod: Tetrarch of Judea 4BC-6AD, Antipas' bro.
Pontius Pilate: Roman Prefect of Judea 26-36AD
Tiberius Caesar: Emperor of Rome 14-37AD
Sejanus: virtual co-emperor of Rome from 26 -31AD
Jesus Bar-Abbas: Zealot guerilla leader in Judea

NOTE ON NAMES: Aramaic, a Semitic language closely related to Hebrew, was the day-to-day language in Judea and Galilee. Greek was the language of trade, commerce, and education, across the Roman Empire, particularly in the Eastern half.

First century names in Israel may appear in their Greek, Hebrew, or Aramaic forms. Example: Jesus is from the Greek. Joshua is the same name, but from the Hebrew.

"Bar" is the Aramaic equivalent of the Hebrew "Ben" - both mean "son of." Men are referred to as "Bar" or by other distinguishing characteristics, such as: Jesus the Nazarene, or Levi the Tax-collector.

Woman are often differentiated by the town they are from, or who they are related to, such as: Mary from Magdala, or Martha the sister of Lazarus.

PART 1
JUDAS' FAMILY

ש

Chapter I: Armageddon

Armies of good and evil will meet in a final cosmic battle, at a pass on the Via Maris named Megiddo. Some call it Armageddon.

Simon Bar-Levi was returning to Jerusalem from Damascus. He stopped for the night at an inn built on the site of ancient Megiddo.

The sun had set. Simon was drowsy, weary from a long days' journey. He retired for the night. But restful sleep was allusive. Feeling as though he were still bouncing up and down on his horse, his was a fitful slumber of turning and tossing.

In early morning, he fell into a deep sleep and began to dream. A bright morning star appeared in the sky above. Descending towards the earth, it transformed into a lightning bolt. Striking in front of Simon with a loud crack, making the ground quake, the smell of burnt grass entered his nose. In front of Simon, the lightening congealed into human form. The figure stood there, glowing white-hot, a light so bright, it was like staring at the sun, the creature's eyes ablaze with fire.

The figure spoke, "My name is Azazel, the most powerful of all angels, possessing glory and power second to none," his voice sounding like thunder. "Simon Bar-Levi, I have come to give you a word."

Simon shook with fear. Sadducees do not believe in angels…or demons. Whenever a Pharisee or Essene had told him of an angelic appearance, Simon ridiculed the teller, calling them "gullible simpletons ignorant of Plato, Aristotle and scientific truth." But

Greek philosophy and science give little comfort when confronted by an entity able to burn a man to ashes with a single breath.

Simon said, "What do I have to do with…"

"Silence," demanded Azazel, "do not speak when you should listen," anger in his voice.

Simon fell on his knees before the figure. With face to the ground he said, "I am your servant. Speak. Your servant hears."

Azazel said, "Your wife is now four-weeks pregnant."

"Pregnant?"

"In eight-months-time she will deliver you a firstborn son. You will name him Judah."

"How can this be?" Simon said, facing the ground, not daring to look up. "My father's name was Levi, and my name is Simon. The baby should be named Levi Bar-Simon."

Eyes flaring, the blazing figure said, "You will name the child Judah. The glory and honor given to him, will fall upon many of his people. The afflictions and pain that come to him, will also be suffered by many sons and daughters of Judah."

"How can I be certain what you say is true?"

"This will be a sign to you, Sadducee," said the being. "When you return home, your wife will meet you at the door. She will tell you the news - that she is with child. As a further sign to you, she will say, 'The boy is to be named Judah, for the glory and honor that come to him, will also be visited upon many in Judah.'"

Years earlier, Simon had heard stories of Zechariah the Priest. It was said, an angel appeared to him while serving in the Temple's sanctuary. The angel told him his wife would soon bear a child, but Zechariah did not believe. So, the angel made him mute until the baby's birth and dedication. Simon had dismissed the tale as the superstitious prattling of an old priest. But the story now seemed all too real. Not wanting to suffer a fate worse than Zechariah's, Simon answered the figure, "May it be as you say."

Φ

Simon then awoke, morning sunlight starting to shine into the room. Rising, he washed, straightened his hair, dressed, and put on his sandals. He walked out of the inn, grabbing his wineskin on the way out. Walking towards the ridge overlooking the valley, Simon bought a loaf of freshly baked flatbread from a merchant. Finding a large rock to sit on, he ate breakfast. He washed the bread down with unmixed wine from the wineskin, while contemplating the joyous prospect of having a son, a precious and long awaited child.

Taking deep breaths, smelling the fresh ionized scent that lingers after a spring thunderstorm, the joy of God's creation filled Simon's heart. A grass carpet covered the valley below. Birds sang in the trees and bushes. He said to himself, "How odd this glorious place should have such a notorious past."

Looking across the Jezreel Valley, Simon could see the village of Nazareth. Nearby, the white-stone buildings of Sepphoris, Galilee's capital, reflected brightly in the morning sunlight.

Looking at the Via Maris, Simon thought about all the gold, frankincense, myrrh, and precious goods that had traveled through Megiddo, during the past thousand years, going back to the time before King David. This was the main trade route connecting the empires of Mesopotamia and Egypt.

King Solomon stationed a garrison of chariots at Megiddo. Anyone holding the city and the road, controlled untold wealth and power. Whether Britannia, Spain, Holland, America, or the ancient empires, trade has always been the key to power and wealth. Whomever controls trade, rules the world.

Solomon had taxed all goods passing through the kingdom, making him wealthy beyond imagination, and providing the money to construct Jerusalem's grandiose Temple. Employing 200,000 men for seven-years, Solomon built God's House on Mt. Moriah, just above his palace.

Even before the Israelites arrived in the Land of Canaan, Megiddo had long been an important city. It was also a mecca for worshiping the Canaanite god, Moloch.

Solomon did not want to alienate the local population. Swayed by his wives who also worshiped Moloch, Solomon permitted Megiddo's priests to continue sacrificing infants to the idol. As they did so, the scent of burning human flesh and sound of baby screams, floated up as pleasing aromas and a melodic symphony to the Canaanite god.

If this were not enough, in the Valley of Hinnom just outside Jerusalem, Solomon erected altars to Moloch and other idols, providing a place of worship for his wives.

Solomon did this, even though the God of Moses had commanded in Leviticus 20, "Any Israelite or foreigner living in Israel who sacrifices their child to Moloch is to be put to death… If the people close their eyes, when a man sacrifices his child to Moloch, and do not put him to death, I will turn my face against them and their families, and will cut them off from my people, together with all who join in bowing down to Moloch."

When Solomon died, a unified Israel perished with him. The Northern Tribes of Israel broke away from Judah and Jerusalem, forming the Northern Kingdom. Joining Megiddo in its worship of Moloch and the pantheon of Canaanite gods, the Northern Tribes of Israel stopped worshiping at Jerusalem's Temple.

Ω

Simon looked left at the western end of the Jezreel Valley, seeing Mt. Carmel twenty-miles away. It was there the prophet Elijah confronted Baal, and his 450 prophets.

Elijah prepared a sacrifice for YWVH, while Baal's prophets prepared a sacrifice for their god. The deity who sent fire from the heavens to consume their prophets' sacrifice, would be declared the victor.

Baal was commonly depicted as a warrior, his right-arm cocked to throw a lightning bolt - a fitting image for a god of wind. rain, storms, and fertility.

Mt. Carmel was a high-place for the worship of Baal. And lightning was the deity's weapon of choice. But YWVH's Temple was in Jerusalem, a three-day's journey south. It should have been easy for Baal to throw a spear of white-light, with its accompanying crash of thunder. Instead, it was Elijah's God who consumed his prophet's sacrifice, sending down a bright flash of fire from the sky, along with the resounding crackle that follows.

Being a fertility god, Baal's preferred sacrifice was the offering of public sex in his temples. Frantic indiscriminate intercourse was performed in front of the pagan god - carnal acts of polyamorous passion, shared between Baal's priests, temple prostitutes (male and female), and common worshipers. The idol watched with blind eyes, while ecstatic screams entered his stone-deaf ears, and scents floated like smoky incense into his non-existent nostrils.

This provided Baal stimulation, enticing him to copulate with his female consort, the goddess Asherah. Their heavenly union brought rain to the fields, fertility for the crops, and an increased number of livestock births - or so the idol's worshipers believed.

Unwanted babies conceived by such promiscuous worship, were returned to the Canaanite idols as burnt offerings, earning additional favors from Moloch, Baal, and the other pagan gods. But such practices were an abomination to the God of Moses, earning only YHVH's wrath.

When the Hebrews were in the Sinai wilderness, they too reverted to such evils. When Moses was delayed on Mt. Sinai, the Children of Israel constructed a graven image, a golden calf. They offered similar sensuous sacrifice to the idol. The golden calf represented Apis, an Egyptian god. But Baal was also frequently depicted and worshiped as a virile bull or calf. Centuries and millennia come and go, borders are drawn and redrawn, but human behavior remains remarkably the same.

λ

Ignoring YWVH's Laws given to Moses on Mt. Sinai, the Northern Kingdom oppressed the poor, widows, orphans, foreigners, and slaves. Injustice, dishonesty, and self-gratification reigned supreme, as they continued to worship their idols with human sacrifice and orgies. Numerous prophets of YWVH warned of impending doom. But the Northern Tribes remained unrepentant, continuing their abominations for the next two-hundred years.

Then the rumble of chariots shook Israel's hills, announcing the arrival of Assyrian invaders. Swooping down the Via Maris like locusts, they blackened the hills of Galilee and Samaria. Megiddo was one of the first cities to fall. Like Sodom and Gomorrah, the Northern Tribes of Israel were wiped clean from the earth. Instead of fire falling from the sky as in Sodom, or a torrent of water drowning the people as in Noah's day, the Northern Kingdom was swept away in a deluge of human devastation.

Swinging severed human limbs like party streamers, the Assyrian soldiers sang victory songs, dancing in delight at Israel's defeat.

The invaders relished public "hangings" as fine entertainment, but not hanging from the neck by a rope. The Assyrians erected pikes. Impaling their foes upon them, they watched as their victims writhed on the poles for hours, like worms. Wagers were placed on which would happen first – death or the victim's bowels spilling onto the ground. Countless severed heads were hung on the walls of each Israelite town. Thousands were crucified or impaled, bodies left to rot, a warning to all who dare oppose Assyrian might.

Survivors had rings pierced through their noses and lips. By them, they were led to Assyria as slaves, as though the God of Moses were saying, "from slavery in Egypt I saved you – into slavery in Assyria you shall return." Thus, the Northern Kingdom became known as the "Lost Tribes of Israel."

An Assyrian king erected a monument near the Tigris River. It bragged, "Their men, young and old, I took prisoners. Of some, I cut off their feet and hands. Of others, I cut off their noses, ears and lips. Of the young men's ears, I made a heap. Of the old men's heads, I made a minaret. In front of their city, I exposed their heads as a trophy. Their children, male and female, I burnt in flames, and burned the city, consuming it with fire in utter destruction."

Everything not taken as spoils, the Assyrians destroyed in a holocaust. Cleansed of Israelite identity, Megiddo then became the capital of a new Assyrian province.

Π

To Simon's relief, Moloch's murderous worship was now a faded memory. But to the shame and embarrassment of devout Israelites, Greco-Roman deities had replaced the Canaanite gods. Roman sexual practices were no better than those who worshiped Baal. Roman Bacchanalia, and the worship of Pan, were particularly odious to the Children of Israel. But at least Greek and Roman idols did not require the sacrifice of human life. The Greco-Roman gods had a taste for pork chops, pig's blood oozing down the sides of their altars.

Temples to the Greek gods were first built in Israel when Alexander the Great conquered the land.

A century-and-a-half later, the Seleucid Greek ruler, Antiochus Epiphanes, tried to eradicate worship of YWVH through forced Hellenization. Antiochus desecrated the Jerusalem Temple, by erecting a statue of Zeus in the Holy-of-Holies, and had pigs sacrificed on YWVH's altar. Burning all Israelite Scriptures, he could find, Antiochus executed Jews who continued to circumcise their infant sons, killing both parent and child.

When Pompey's Roman Legions invaded the Land of Israel, Rome continued the process of Hellenization, but used a less draconian approach. Confident in the alluring appeal of Roman might, culture, religion, and prosperity, they believed all people, even Israelites, would eventually succumb to the fleshly and monetary benefits of Roman rule.

Greco-Roman temples were built in Caesarea Marittima, the Decapolis, Sepphoris, Caesarea Philippi, and across the Promised Land.

Γ

Simon watched as a squad of Roman soldiers marched down the Via Maris, their weapons and armor clanging in harmonious rhythm. Charged with protecting trade caravans, Roman business interests, and tax-collection, they vigilantly watched for Galilean Zealots. Rebels lurked near the highways and roads, looking for an opportunity to strike. The Zealots were also a problem in Judea. But it was in Galilee that the movement was born and enjoyed the support of the masses. The Pharisees were overwhelmingly dominant in Galilee. And since the Zealots were little more than an extreme expression of Pharisee theology, the Pharisees were sympathetic to Zealot goals. The term Pharisee means "to separate." The Zealots wanted to separate Israel from Roman and Hellenistic influence. They pursued this goal by separating Roman travelers from their riches and lives, severing Roman heads from their bodies, and spilling Roman intestines on the ground. Using hit-and-run tactics, Zealots ambushed Romans, and those who collaborated with them, including Sadducees. The confiscated goods were used to fund the Zealots' continued resistance to Roman rule.

Simon hated Zealots almost as much as the Romans did, because they endangered all that had been gained under Roman rule. He muttered to himself, "I don't like the Romans...but, being a Sadducee, a member of the Sanhedrin, and treasurer of the Temple, I can appreciate the benefits Roman rule and culture have brought to our land.

"Before Roman rule, civil war raged between the various Hasmonean claimants to Israel's throne. And Israel suffered continuous conflict with neighboring kingdoms. Even worse, the empires of Egypt, Assyria, Babylonia, Persia, and Greece had waged many devastating conquests to gain control of the world's most lucrative trade route.

"After the Romans brought peace (the Pax Romana), the Land of Israel has enjoyed increasing economic prosperity. Since King Herod built the harbor at Caesarea, twenty-years ago (in 15 BC), Israelite crops and goods are shipped across the Empire.

"Magdala's dried fish go to Rome. Untold amphorae of olive oil and wine are shipped to many cities. The Salt Sea (Dead Sea) is the Empire's primary source for salt. Tar is also produced at the Salt Sea. Egypt and Israel are the Empire's "bread basket," supplying wheat and barley to the Roman masses. Israel has a virtual monopoly on balm, the fragrant sap. Fine Israelite wool is shipped to Syria and Asia Minor, where it is dyed and manufactured into fine cloth. Truffles from Judea are world renowned, as are dates from Jericho, not to mention Israelite plums, figs, honey, sheep, goats, and cattle. The Promised Land is truly a land flowing with milk and honey.

"Now that Rome has improved our roads, expanded shipping, increased security for transportation, and established an extensive banking system, the Promised Land is a place where fortunes are made. If you are a Roman citizen, banker, tax-collector, Sadducee, or Herodian, riches flow into your purse, like a river. We Sadducees have learned well the lessons of the Roman system, where money and position determine everything."

Rome's oligarchy numbered no more than ten-thousand, ruling an Empire of one-hundred-million. Membership in the Senate required a personal fortune of at least 250,000 denarii (approximately 25 million US dollars). If a sitting senator's wealth dropped below the minimum, they summarily lost their seat. The most exclusive class was the Patrician, descendants of Rome's most ancient ruling families. Next were the Equestrians, Roman knights who provided cavalry to the legions. Roman prefects, like Pontius Pilate, were Equestrians, which required a minimum fortune of 100,000 denarii (approximately 10 million US dollars).

The rest of Rome's subjects: tradesmen, merchants, the plebian masses, and slaves, did not enjoy the same privileges, or prosperity. But the Emperor and oligarchs placated the unruly mases with government assistance programs, and free public entertainment. It was similar in Judea and Galilee.

Simon continued to contemplate the changes Roman rule had brought to the Promised Land, saying to himself, "As for the Israelite masses - few go hungry, and public entertainment is freely available. Athletic contests and spectacles are held in the great hippodromes of Jerusalem and Caesarea.

"Theatres are so popular, the favorite insult today, is to call someone a hypocrite (the Greek word "hypokrities" means actor).

"Roman aqueducts have been built. Several of our cities now have running water and indoor plumbing. Bath houses, with gymnasiums and public toilets, are in cities across the land, improving the hygiene, health, and physical strength of countless Jews. They also facilitate education in mathematics, philosophy, and science, to those Jews openminded enough to take advantage of them.

"Caesar's servant, King Herod the Great, undertook a building program surpassing anything in Israelite history. Greatly expanding the Jerusalem Temple, he made it the largest and most ornate temple in the world. Herod built Caesarea Marittima into a thriving world-class Roman city and port. He also constructed numerous fortresses and opulent palaces across his Kingdom. During Herod's reign, he built more grandiose public projects, than the rest of the Roman Empire combined. This produced full-employment and a booming economy across Israel."

When Herod died, the Emperor split his kingdom between Herod's three sons, Archelaus, Antipas, and Philip. They also undertook large building projects in: Jericho, Sepphoris, Tiberias, and Caesarea Philippi.

"The thing to remember about Roman rule - they are the ultimate pragmatists, their concern limited to a few key interests. Rome required taxes, the maintenance of peace and order, that roads be free of robbers, and that profitable business enterprises be allowed to function without interference from local authorities. Apart from these few items, the Romans allow provincial peoples to govern themselves with little interference."

But Roman authorities were perplexed by the Jews, their invisible God, and rejection of all idolatry in its various forms. The Romans could not get their minds around this, often demonstrating a profound hatred for Jews and their religion.

"Yes," said Simon, "Roman justice is stern, but to some extend fair."

Slaves, however, were viewed as little more than walking furniture, having no more rights than a table or chair. Horses were frequently more valued and better treated. The Emperor Caligula made his horse a senator. Masters could use or abuse their slaves in whatever manner they wished, without scandal or public ostracism. Raping or killing a slave, of any age or gender, was acceptable in aristocratic and genteel Roman society.

Romans felt no shame in using or abusing anyone. Public disgrace only came if one were used or mistreated by someone else. Being an abuser was honorable and good. But being counted among the abused, this resulted in everlasting shame and dishonor. The rule: Do unto others, before they do unto to you.

Remember another Roman rule: It doesn't matter how you play the game - its whether you win or lose that counts. Athletic games and sporting events bore this out. Accolades were given only to the winner. There was no prize for second place. To finish second, no matter the effort or reason, was to be a loser. And losers deserve death.

In the provinces, almost all legal cases were handled by local courts. Only a few capital punishment cases, those involving sedition or treason, were handled directly by Roman authorities. The exception was for the lucky few who were Roman citizens, a small percentage of the people living in the Empire. Citizens of Rome were accorded all honor, respect, and due process. If a citizen objected to being tried by a local authority, they could appeal to the Emperor, and have their case heard personally by him.

The key to an Israelite avoiding Rome's cruelty…don't cause trouble, or rock the boat. If you stirred unrest or endangered the collection of taxes, the Romans would overreact, indiscriminately butchering those involved, crucifying the survivors as an object lesson.

"Yes," Simon said to himself, "Roman rule has much to recommend it. My fortunes have greatly improved in recent years, and my son's future is bright…if we can just keep those damned Zealots from antagonizing the Romans."

Having finished the bread, Simon felt buzzed from the wine. Mounting his horse, he began the three-day journey back to Jerusalem. Kicking the animal in the ribs, it trotted. Catching up to the Roman patrol, he followed the soldiers to the next town, then continued toward Jerusalem.

Λ

Arriving home, all happened just as Azazel had said. Delilah was pregnant. When the baby's delivery drew near, the couple traveled twenty-miles south of Jerusalem, to their hometown Kerioth, to be with family. On the 8th day of Av, Delilah's contractions began.

ר

Chapter II: Firstborn Son

Delilah's labor started in early morning and lasted through the day. Sabbath would begin at sunset. The female family members attending her became concerned. They called Simon to come into the room and comfort his wife.

The crown of the baby's head became visible. When his head fully emerged, the delivery's progress stopped. The umbilical cord was wrapped tightly around the child's neck, chaining him inside his mother's womb.

Simon bent down and kissed Delilah on the cheek. He whispered encouraging words into his wife's ear, "Just a little longer, my love. Don't give up now. Soon you will be holding our precious child."

Exhausted and covered in sweat, Delilah motioned for Simon to bend his ear near. She said, "May this son of yours afflict you with as much pain and heartache as he has given me," the ends of her mouth turning up into a weak smile.

Simon tried to smile back, "Always the joker. That's what I love about you," he said tenderly.

Delilah's muscles tightened in a convulsive spasm, but it was not a labor contraction. Moments later, tension left her body, and breathing became shallow. Simon heard a slight rattle from her chest. The air left Delilah's lungs. Her body went limp and breathing stopped. Delilah died. Muscles relaxing in death, the stench of vacated bowel and emptied bladder filled the room.

"Rest quietly in Sheol, my love," Simon muttered. "We will soon be reunited in death," not believing his own words, but pessimistically hoping for such a reunion.

Looking down at the baby's head, it was purplish blue. Simon grabbed a knife. Hurriedly, he tried to severe the umbilical cord and save the baby's life. Careful not to slit the baby's throat, at last the primal connection between mother and child was cut. Grabbing the baby's head, Simon pulled hard, trying to free the child with all his might. With a squirt, the baby was freed from its mother's fleshly tomb, coming out with a "plop." A mixture of goo, blood, and afterbirth, flowed close behind, in a gush. Holding his child for the first time, the baby's face was black, showing no sign of life. Simon's firstborn son had joined its' mother, in the shadowy realm of Sheol.

Hugging the child tightly, sobbing, he mourned the loss of wife, son, family, and a thousand dreams near to fulfillment, only moments before. Guttural throbbing sobs, groans and cries, came from Simon's chest, throat and mouth - not human utterings, more like those of a wounded animal whose leg has been snapped in a trap. Then Simon paused and blurted out, "What was that?"

The child drew a large breath. Simon held its tiny body at arm's length, watching as the baby's face transformed from black to purple, then to pink. Face now scrunched in an angry frown, a cry came from his itsy-bitsy mouth, a piercing scream that appeared able to wake the dead.

Simon said, "Truly this is a miraculous child! Momentous events are sure to follow him all the days of his life."

η

Simon returned to Jerusalem with his new son, bringing with him a shoestring relative to serve as wet-nurse.

The baby's head had emerged from the womb before sunset. But his body was not born until after dark. The Law of Moses requires that sons be circumcised and named on the eighth-day. But which is the eighth, when a child's birth takes place on two different days?

On the ninth-day after the baby's head first entered the world, Simon took his son to the Temple. He circumcised his firstborn son, naming him Judah, or as is said in Greek - Judas.

Firstborn sons belong to the Lord, and must be redeemed by a sacrifice. Simon sacrificed a lamb at the Temple. The animal was perfect, without blemish...on the outside. But when its blood was spilled, an overwhelming stench choked the priests. When the carcass was cut open, a pervasive cancer was found inside.

Δ

Growing up, Judas was a son beyond compare, sharp minded, mature in personality, likeable, and responsible. He was zealous for God, the Law, and the Temple. Simon could not have been more proud of his only son.

As the Temple's chief treasurer and a Sadducee, Simon trained his son in his faith, profession, and duties. Judas excelled here too, showing himself to have an exceptional aptitude for figures, memorization, and language. Judas became a skilled accountant, and had memorized the Torah. He was fluent in Aramaic, Hebrew, Greek, and knew a little Latin.

Even though young, Simon decided it was time for Judas to marry. He carefully considered prospective brides, pondering which would be the best match for his beloved son. Simon preferred the bride be from their tribe, the Tribe of Levi, and that she be from a Sadducee family.

Judas might seem a prized groom for any prospective bride. But being a Sadducee, this severely limited the list of possible matches. The Sadducee party was small and hated. The most Hellenistic of all Israelites, Sadducees appreciated Greek culture, and the financial prosperity Rome had brought to the Promised Land. The Sadducees were Rome's Israelite lapdogs. Their biggest pet was the High Priest - and his extended family. Living in Jerusalem's largest and most luxurious mansions, wealth and pleasure was theirs. Pharisee and Essene fathers would not marry their daughters to a Sadducee. And don't even mention the Zealots. A Zealot father would rather stab Simon and Judas with a dagger to the gut, than let his daughter marry into a Sadducee family.

The calculation for Simon was quite simple. Judas' best match was Rachel, the only daughter of Joseph Bar-Caiaphas, the High Priest. Not only did Rachel belong to the most powerful and wealthy Israelite family, she was also a beauty. Possessing dark eyes and shimmering black hair, she was nobody's fool. Caiaphas was not content to have a daughter trained in the usual wifely duties. He had taught Rachel the Torah, and Greek classics. Lounging after dinner, Caiaphas loved to have Rachel recite Homer to him.

Most girls Rachel's age were betrothed or married. But she also had limited prospective mates. Her father's exacting standards made a match even more challenging. Caiaphas would not allow his daughter to marry below her station.

Rachel was now fifteen-years old. A girl not betrothed by sixteen became questionable. After that age, prospective families would wonder, "Is there a hidden blemish or defilement that has caused other families to pass her by?"

The next morning, Simon sent word to the High Priest requesting a meeting. He was told to come for dinner.

Arriving that evening, Simon entered the High Priest's insula. The only private home in Jerusalem equaling its size and opulence was the home of Joseph's father-in-law, Annas.

Entering Caiaphas' palace, a servant washed the dust from Simon's feet. Another brought a basin of water to wash his hands and face.

Caiaphas greeted Simon warmly, inviting him to recline and break bread with him. Simon greeted his friend with all the respect due a fellow Israelite, Levite, Sadducee, and High Priest. Then raising his hands, forming the Hebrew letter "Shin" for Shaddai (Almighty), Simon blessed Caiaphas, "'The Lord bless you and keep you; the Lord make his face to shine upon you and be gracious unto you; the Lord lift up his countenance upon you and give you His peace.'"

The table was set, with savory dishes laid upon it. The two men enjoyed roasted lamb, fresh baked bread, figs, olives, nuts, and several glasses of the finest Israelite wine - mixed with water, as was the custom to reduce its strength.

Near the end of the meal, Simon addressed the reason for his visit, "Joseph, you have a daughter who needs a suitable husband. My only son, Judas, is in need of a suitable wife. Let us agree on the bride-price and sign the contract."

The High Priest was surprised. Joseph assumed the meeting was to discuss the Temple's treasury and income.

Caiaphas had known Judas since he was a child. He had always been impressed by him, but had never thought of Judas as a prospective husband for his daughter. He had thought him too young to become a husband. Caiaphas was in his mid-twenties when he married Rachel's mother. Likewise, he desired older suiters for his daughter - those whose youthful follies have begun to fade away. More importantly, a man in his mid to late twenties is well established in his profession, and better able to provide for his wife and family.

Caiaphas did not answer immediately, carefully considering Simon's proposal. Caiaphas said to himself, "Judas is more mature than many men ten-years his senior. He is sharp-witted, well-educated, and a Sadducee. He's even well established in his profession at the Temple treasury."

Simon grew impatient waiting for the High Priest's response, tapping his finger on the table. Finally, he said, "Well?"

Caiaphas calculated whether there were other prospective grooms with better positions or greater wealth. There were none. Caiaphas became convinced. Judas was the best groom for his daughter. Silently Caiaphas said a prayer, "Thank you, Lord, for providing a husband for my little lamb." But he still did not answer Simon. Being the owner of a precious commodity, he was not going to appear eager to close the deal. Caiaphas was not going to give Simon the superior position in the negotiation by speaking first.

The room was silent for several more minutes. Simon finally said, "Well, Joseph, are you going to wait all night? What is your answer?"

Caiaphas said with a hesitant tone, "Judas is very young…"

"People are not like wine. They do not improve with age," said Simon.

"You are right, of course," said Caiaphas. "Still…I do need to consider my daughter's rank, position, and wealth. She is the most prized girl in all of Judea."

"True," said Simon, "but I doubt Pharisee, Essene, or Zealot fathers will line up at your door to pay her bride-price. Nor would you allow such fathers to cross your threshold, set foot beyond your door, or enter into the hospitality of your home - let alone permit such families to take away your precious daughter."

"Yes, once again, you are right," said Caiaphas. "Still… Rachel is our only daughter, and is precious to her mother and me. It will break my wife's heart to send her from our home to another."

"Would you prefer she stay in your home for the rest of her life, sucking on your riches like a mother's tit, depleting your wealth, but never birthing grandchildren?" said Simon. "Come Joseph, I have known you too long. Stop your delays and set a price."

"Very well," said Caiaphas, "you are one of my oldest and dearest friends, Simon. Even so, it will not do for the High Priest's daughter to go cheaply."

"A price," Simon insisted.

"Shall we agree upon two-talents of gold?"

"And where, do you think I can get two-talents of gold? Do you imagine I have hidden a fortune under my home, or discovered lost treasure in a field? Or do you expect me to rob our own Temple treasury to pay for your daughter? All of us are not as wealthy as King Solomon, like our High Priest."

"You really go too far, Simon. Yes, it is true, God has blessed me and my family with wealth…"

"I can give you one-half talent, Joseph. That is a sum worthy of King Solomon's daughter."

"One-half talent? That seems more an insult than an offer. Are you going to cry poverty while trying to obtain my daughter? If you are so impoverished, perhaps your family is too poor for my daughter."

"And perhaps you should tell me the names of the other suiters you are considering," replied Simon. "I do not recall seeing other fathers at your front door, or in the courtyard as I waited for an audience with you."

"Simon, dear friend, let's not bargain with one another as though we were common merchants or money-changers. I am sure to regret it in the morning…The wine is probably clouding my thoughts and leading me to a poor decision…But if you will pay one-talent of gold, we will make the contract."

The High Priest was known for his ambition, love of money, and shrewd business dealings. Caiaphas knew the value of his daughter, and was not going to let her go at a discount.

Simon said, "A robber, that's who we have for High Priest, a thief who steals from the purses of his best friends and closest associates…" Simon knew Caiaphas would come down only so far.

One-talent of gold would substantially deplete the family's wealth. But there is no substitute for marrying well, and no greater curse than marrying an unsuitable spouse. "Alright Joseph," said Simon, "I will pay the extortion, one-talent it is."

In a few weeks, the bride-price was paid, and the betrothal period began.

Ω

Then, as is the custom, Judas began to build a new addition onto the family insula - the couple's new home. Whatever time it took to build the honeymoon house would be the couple's engagement period.

When it was finished, Judas gathered his friends before sunrise, and the groom's party traveled to Caiaphas' home. Grooms try to surprise their brides, coming at a time they do not expect. When the groom arrives, the bridal party processes together to the groom's family insula, to celebrate and consummate the marriage. Rachel and her bridesmaids, being wise young women, were well prepared and ready for Judas' arrival. Lighting their lamps, the party processed to Simon's home, where the wedding feast began.

When it came time for the couple to retire and consummate their marriage, the groom's designated friend stood guard near the wedding chamber, listening for the groom's voice. As is the custom, immediately after the couple's romantic interlude was finished, Judas shouted to his friend, "It is done, my friend. We are truly married. We have become one flesh." Then, as is also the custom, the friend went and reported this joyous fact to all the guests still celebrating, that the deed had been done, and the marriage consummated.

Following the wedding feast, lasting a week, the guests returned to their homes. Judas and Rachel then began their yearlong honeymoon, when couples are excused from most pubic duties and obligations. Judas was excused from his duties at the Temple's treasury, so that the couple could truly become united and emotionally inseparable. In several months, Rachel was pregnant.

Σ

Thirty-years earlier, a Levitical priest and Pharisee named Zechariah, prophesied in the temple, "God will soon reveal himself as one like a Son of Man, in human flesh."

This was not a surprising statement to Pharisees and Essenes - those who trusted the prophesies of Daniel, Isaiah, and Ezekiel. But Sadducees do not believe in prophets, angels, heaven or hell. Their focus is on the Temple and Torah, and the worldly advantages of Greco-Roman culture. But Essenes and Pharisees despised Roman rule, desiring to be free of pagan oppression. This is the reason Rome gave control of the Temple to the Sadducees, even though they were small in comparison to the other parties.

Rome took direct control of Judea, following the brief and unsuccessful rule of Herod's son, Archelaus. In Galilee, a Pharisee scholar named Judas, led a revolt against the Roman census. Part of the Roman crackdown, was to replace the Temple's High Priest, Joazar, putting Annas Bar-Seth in the office. The Roman governor ordered the new High Priest to take firm control of the Temple and Sanhedrin, and quash resistance against Roman rule. He told Annus, "Joazar was too weak. He had no stomach for controlling the rebels in your midst. If you also fail to maintain order among your kinsmen and race, you too will be replaced."

Annus had always regarded Zechariah a troublemaker. He became an even bigger problem, after his child was miraculously born. Zechariah opposed the Sadducees at every turn, stirring unrest among the Pharisee members of the priesthood and Sanhedrin.

The High Priest set in motion a plan to fix the problem. Annus called a secret meeting of the Sanhedrin, notifying only to Sadducee members, excluding the Pharisees. They met at the High Priest's palace, instead of council chambers. At the meeting, Zechariah was tried in absentia, and found guilty of blasphemy.

When it was Zechariah's appointed time to serve at the Temple's altar, Annas arranged for only Sadducees to be present with him in the courtyard. Zechariah was walking to the altar. Between it and the sanctuary, the Sadducees stoned him to death, in the Temple's inner court. The coup-de-grace was delivered by Annas' son-in-law. Taking a large rock weighing several pounds, Caiaphas raised his arms and crushed Zechariah's head. Zechariah's blood ran down, mixing with the blood of animals that had been sacrificed on the altar.

Annas' five sons: Eleazar, Jonathan, Theophilus, Matthias, and Ananus, also took part in the stoning. Each would one day become High Priest. Annas' son, Jonathan, was High Priest when Stephan became the first Christian martyr, and was also High Priest when the first of Jesus' Twelve-disciples was martyred. The last of Annas' five sons, Ananus, presided as High Priest over the martyrdom of Jesus' step-brother, James the Just, the first bishop of the Jerusalem Church. They took James to the top of the Sanctuary. There, Ananus demanded he deny faith in his brother, Jesus. When James refused, he was thrown down onto the pavement stones, several stories below. But the fall did not kill him. Ananus and the other priests then stoned James to death, near the spot where Zechariah had also been slain.

When word of Zechariah's death reached his wife, Elizabeth fled Jerusalem with their young son, John. She feared for her son's safety, because the Sadducees had heard the prophesies concerning him. Zechariah had prophesied in the Temple about his newborn son, "You, child, will be called a prophet of the Most High, and will go in front of the Lord to prepare the path for him, to give his people a knowledge of salvation, through the forgiveness of their sins."

The angel Gabriel had told Zechariah about his son, "He will be great in the sight of the Lord. Having a lifelong nazarite vow, he will never drink wine or other strong drink, but will have the Holy Spirit upon him, even while in his mother's womb. He will bring back many of the Children of Israel to the Lord their God. And he will go in front of the Lord, in the spirit and power of Elijah, turning the hearts of parents to their children, and turning sinners to holiness, preparing the people for the Lord's arrival."

Elizabeth left Jerusalem with her child, having little but the clothes on their backs. They traveled down the winding and narrow road to the oldest city in the world, Jericho. Continuing into the Judean wilderness, they drew near the Salt Sea. Coming to the caves and springs of En-gedi, where David hid from King Saul, it was here Elizabeth and John made their home, in an empty cave.

Others lived in nearby caves that dotted the area - Essenes. Many were Levitical priests who had forsaken the Jerusalem Temple, believing the High Priest and Sadducees to be corrupt tools of Satan.

As John grew in age and stature, he was accepted into the Essene community. Belonging to the Tribe of Levi, a Zadok priest like his father before him, the Essenes instructed John in the full width and breath of Hebrew Scriptures. The scriptural prophesies about the Messiah, the battle between the forces of light and darkness, and the coming of God's Kingdom, were given special emphasis.

John was instructed in the finer points of Mosaic Law and ancient Temple rituals. The Essenes trained him as an untainted and holy priest, preparing him for the day when God would cleanse the Jerusalem Temple, when God would establish a new and holy priesthood, replacing the Sadducees who now controlled it. Progressing through the stages of instruction, John excelled.

When his thirtieth birthday arrived, John was no longer a student of the Scriptures, but became a teacher - a rabbi.

It was then, the Word of God came to John in a personal revelation. Fully trained, equipped, and having received a revelation for God, John left Qumran. YHVH had instructed him to go above the Salt Sea, to the Jordan River. There, John preached the Word of God, and began to gather a band of disciples.

In the wilderness, next to the Jordan, he cried out, "Change your ways. God's kingdom will soon be established. Be prepared for the arrival of the King."

PART 2

JUDAS' LAST TESTAMENT

א

Chapter III: The Baptizer

My dearest son:

I began to record these notes many months ago. At first it was to pass the information along to your grandfather, Joseph. As time passed, I increasingly took the notes for my own benefit, to better decipher the truth. When events began to spin out of control, it was then I decided to write down everything that has transpired, and give it to you, that you might know the truth, and be warned not to follow a similar path.

As I write this, you are just a baby, unable to know or comprehend what I, your father, have done. But I leave this testimony for you, so that when you are old enough, you may learn and fully understand.

By the time you read this, you may have gained a vague awareness of what I have done, and the events that took place. It is my prayer that you will live a better, more honorable, and holier life than your father. My greatest prayer is that you will learn from your family's sins, and help lead the Children of Israel into all truth, and along the righteous path.

My only request, my dear son, is that you read this account from beginning to end, even though it will be painful and hard. God rewards those who persevere. But he punishes those who stray from his straight and narrow path.

Your loving father,
Judas

α

Six-months into our honeymoon, a message came from Caiaphas. He asked me to attend a meeting at the High Priest's chambers. If anyone else had made the request, I would not have responded, because it was still our honeymoon. But one does not refuse the High Priest and chairman of Jerusalem's Sanhedrin, Judea's highest governing body, second only to the Roman prefect, Pontius Pilate.

Rachel was not happy. She tried to stop me, saying, "With my father, everything is business. If you don't show up, he'll find someone else to do his dirty work. He always does. Don't go, love. He'll only entangle you in some sticky matter with the Sanhedrin. It's better to show him you are your own man, and not available at his beckon call. It would be good to show him that now, at the beginning of our marriage."

I said, "But love, he's the High Priest…"

"Yes, and I'm Cleopatra."

"I want to get along with your father, love."

"You'll get along better if you put your foot down, at the beginning."

To my everlasting regret, I did not listen to your mother. Arriving at the Temple, I was shown into Caiaphas' presence. Annas, your great-grandfather, was also there.

Annas had been High Priest years before. But the Roman Prefect of Judea at the time, Valerius Gratus, expected Annas to maintain better control, not only of the Temple, but of Jerusalem as-a-whole. The High Priest and Sanhedrin were the highest governing officials in Jerusalem. But Gratus ruled from Caesarea, a three-day's journey northwest. Gratus was dissatisfied with Annas' inability to keep the unruly Israelite parties from causing problems. So, Gratus deposed Annas and appointed a new High Priest. Each year brought another High Priest, none finding favor in the Prefect's eyes. Then, Caiaphas was appointed High Priest, Annas' son-in-law. Caiaphas pleased Gratus, and his successor, Pontius Pilate. In their view, Caiaphas had the right combination of cunning, diplomacy, and brutality. Using Annas' power, wealth and influence, behind the scenes, Caiaphas proactively dealt with "problem people" before the problems got out of hand.

Many Israelites still regarded Annas as the rightful High Priest, deferring to him as much as to Caiaphas. The Law of Moses established the office of High Priest as a lifelong office, not subject to replacement by pagan rulers. Since Caiaphas was Annas' son-in-law, the two functioned in tandem, like co-high priests. Caiaphas was the outward ceremonial figurehead. Annas was the power behind the throne.

Caiaphas greeted me warmly, "Shalom, Judas. Welcome," he said while hugging me and greeting me with a kiss. "You know my father-in-law, Annas. We have a special mission for you. After careful consideration, we think you are the best man for a very sensitive task."

I was foolishly eager, and said, "As always, I am here to serve the Temple, the Sanhedrin, and our God."

Caiaphas continued, "Please understand, ordinarily I would not request this of a newlywed, especially my own son-in-law. But I want you to know, Annas and I have big plans for your future. You have married into the most powerful, wealthy, and important family in all of Israel. We must work together, support one another, and make sure nothing endangers our family, Temple, or nation. I'm sure you agree." I nodded yes. "You know the methods these Romans use to enforce their will, caring little for our people, or traditions. They are like Antiochus Epiphanes. If given an excuse, they too will try to destroy our religion. It is our solemn responsibility to protect our traditions, the Temple, and our people. Don't you agree, Judas?"

"I am your servant. But what is it you want me to do?"

"Have you heard about this wild man, John Bar-Zechariah, who is gathering large crowds in the wilderness?"

"Yes, many believe he is a prophet. I am told he is from a priestly family."

"He is the son of a Pharisaical priest, but is teaching and performing cleansing rituals in Essene territory. Instead of using a mikveh for the cleansings, he is washing people in the Jordan. As a Sadducee, you know we have a rather skeptical view of prophets, especially self-appointed ones who may start a revolt.

"Have you heard the rumors, Judas? Some suggest this John is the so-called 'Messiah.' The ignorant and foolish masses pray that God will raise up a Jewish Alexander the Great, a king who will deliver them from poverty, taxes, tooth aches, receding hairlines, and Roman rule. Tell us your opinion, Judas. How will the Romans react, if Israelites follow this wild man, take up arms, and crown him as King David's successor, God's Anointed One?"

"It will not end well."

"Why not, my son Judas? Tell me your analysis. Give me your wisdom."

"No ruler or army long prevails against Rome's legions. To revolt against Rome is suicide."

"But aren't you a patriot, Judas? Don't you believe in miracles? Perhaps this John is God's anointed king, the Son of David. By God's power, the Messiah David, defeated Goliath and the Philistines. Perhaps this new Messiah will miraculously defeat the Roman behemoth."

I said to Caiaphas, "Miracles are one thing, childish fantasies another. We all know the story of Judas the Galilean. He revolted before I was born. The Emperor's "anointed ones" crushed him and all who opposed Roman authority. Using Rome's legions, the Zealots involved were killed. Anyone who revolts against Rome is slaughtered. Herod murdered his own wife and sons, when they plotted against him. He killed the babies of Bethlehem, simply because Zoroastrian priests told him a star announced the birth of a new King of Israel. Pilate is brutal and cruel, like Herod. If John proclaims himself the new Israelite king, God's Messiah, Rome will not stand idly by." Annas looked at Caiaphas with an approving nod.

I continued, "Young children can believe in fairytales and follow crazy men in the desert. But those entrusted with God's House - the Temple, must protect it and our nation, using all the wisdom, wiles, and powers they can muster. Otherwise the Romans will destroy the Temple, our priesthood, and Judea. Our nation's fate cannot be endangered by children's stories and fantasies. Roman might is today's one undeniable reality. It cannot be defeated by our small nation. But with wise leadership, Roman power can be deflected and used to our own ends."

Caiaphas said to Annas, "See, I told you we selected the right man." Turning to me he said, "Simon has taught you well, young Judas. I am proud to have such a wise and pragmatic son-in-law.

This is why I sent for you. We need someone of your caliber, loyalty, and discretion. We have a difficult task for you to undertake. If you accept this mission, Annas and I want you to know, we have our eyes on you. We have great plans for you, my son. One day, you too may occupy the office of High Priest, just as we have. Ours is a tight-knit family, and the high priesthood remains within the clan of Annas."

Caiaphas words excited me. It had never occurred to me, that one day I could be High Priest. Such an honor was beyond my wildest dreams. But my imagination is what Caiaphas intended to stimulate, the desire for position, power, prestige, and money. His words made me malleable clay in his hands. He was the potter, and I the clay. At that moment, I was willing to do anything he asked, no matter how hard or strenuous the mission might be.

"This is what we ask of you, young Judas. Go to the Jordan, where this John is preaching. Observe the man. Take note of his words and doctrine. Evaluate whether he intends to raise up the people in revolt. Investigate what party he is aligned with. Is he a Pharisee, like his father? Has he been radicalized to the violent extreme, and become a Zealot? Perhaps he has become an Essene. Or maybe he is just a crazy loner preaching to snakes and lizards, driven mad by the desert. Whatever he is, we need to know his plans and intentions. This task calls for a sharp mind and fine evaluative skills, Judas. Don't simply report facts to us. We want insightful analysis. How much of a danger does this man present? What sort of people are following him? Who does he associate with? Do we need to be concerned about him? And if we do, tell us the best way to counteract the influence he wields over his followers.

"Don't just go and listen, hidden in the crowd. You are a personable and persuasive young man - affable, pleasant to be around, and able to bring people into your confidence. Find an opportunity. Get close to this John and befriend him. If possible, enter his inner circle and become one of his students. It may take some time. We realize this is a sacrifice, for you to be taken away from your beloved wife during your honeymoon year. But, as soon as this danger is eliminated, you may return to your home and wife."

Annas asked, "Will you accept such a charge, Judas?"

I said with pride and eagerness, "I would not do this for anyone else, other than the high priests. Nor would I accept such a task, if I did believe it was crucial. But yes, I will do everything you ask of me. It is my honor to be of service to the chief priests of our people." Both Caiaphas and Annas embraced me, sending me away with a kiss.

δ

When I returned home, and told Rachel the news, she would not speak to me. Following hours of silence, she blurted out, "And what am I supposed to do while you are gone? This is supposed to be the happiest time of our lives. Are you going to be back in time for the baby's delivery?"

"My precious lamb…I don't know...I hope so."

"Hope so? she repeated with dismissive disgust. "And what is the matter with my father? Of all people, he should know better than to ask such a thing from his own daughter and son-in-law."

"My sweet, he is only thinking of you and our child. We live in perilous times. Your father and the Sanhedrin are referees in a wrestling match to the death, trying to keep the Zealots and Romans from killing one another, and destroying our nation."

I hugged Rachel. At first she was resistant, not wanting to hug. Then she relinquished, and we embraced for a long time. Finally, she said, "If you must, you must. But I don't like it." Pulling back and looking into my eyes she said sternly, "You be careful, Judas. Do you hear me?"

"Yes, love, I hear you. I'll be careful."

"And promise me, at the first sign of trouble, you will come home."

"Yes, my lamb, I promise."

ζ

Walking the narrow and winding road down to Jericho, the heat increased with each step. Drawing nearer to the Salt Sea (Dead Sea), I could smell its pungent scent. Continuing past Jericho, I arrived at the Jordan River, just above where it pours into the Sea, the lowest place on the face of the earth (1400 feet below sea level).

Arriving late in the day, John Bar-Zechariah was concluding his afternoon teaching. Making camp with other Jerusalem pilgrims that had come to hear John, I spoke to many of them that evening. Some were curiosity seekers, looking for an entertaining diversion. Others were seekers of the truth, devout Israelites on a spiritual pilgrimage.

Some were partisans - Pharisees, Sadducees, and Zealots, less interested in whether John spoke the truth, than trying to determine whose side he was on. No matter which party they belonged to, all of them were confident and arrogant, sure that their party was right and all the others wrong. Self-satisfied with their own wisdom, superior education, and holiness, they were an irritating lot. The thought that I might be numbered among them offended me. All of them were dressed in distinctive garb, displaying which faction each belonged to. Parroting party-line platitudes, they recited their parties' doctrines by rote, each promising their words were "God given," "pure," and of course, non-negotiable. If I ignored their words and fashions, focusing only on their mannerisms, modes of speech, and cock-sure self-righteousness, all of them appeared remarkably the same, regardless of party. It became difficult for me to see them as people. In my mind's eye, they had transformed into a conspiracy of ravens or a murder of crows. Black in spirit and dower, mean and angry, the scavengers constantly pecked away at their victims, until each carcass was picked clean. At that moment, I desired a God-given prophet, longed for a true Messiah, to deliver me from these cackling crows of contention.

The common people camped nearby. Many appeared to have been there for some time. Their lifestyle was primitive and rough, like John's. Some appeared to be Essenes, notable for their white garments, like the priestly robes worn in the Temple. But these robes were mostly tattered, because Essenes wear them until they are little more than rags. Worn as their cloths may be, they were clean, spotless. No one, on the face of this earth, either Jew or Gentile, focuses on cleanliness like the Essenes, both physical and spiritual.

The next morning, I was rudely awakened with a start. "Repent. For God's Kingdom is near. Make straight and holy, the crooked path of your life. Straighten your crooked ways, for the Messiah will soon arrive."

Groggily I asked the person nearest me, "What time is it? Do you know?"

"Time for the Temple's morning sacrifice. John speaks at the same times each day – when the sacrifices are being offered in the Temple."

To John, being the son of a priest and himself a member of the Kohanim (priesthood), it seemed fitting to teach and pray at the appointed times of the Temple sacrifice, the third and ninth hours each day. John knew the time by using a special pendant he wore around his neck, a portable sundial that is popular among travelers in the Empire.

η

When John finished teaching that morning, the Pharisees and Sadducee began to question him, "What do you claim about yourself?"

John said, "I am not the Messiah."

The Pharisees asked, "Who are you then? Are you Elijah, who is to come before the Messiah?"

"Judge for yourself. You know the Scriptures."

"Are you a prophet?"

"I am the voice of one crying in the wilderness. As the prophet Isaiah said, 'Straighten the path of your life, in preparation for the coming of the Lord.'"

The Sadducees said, "Are you a Zealot or an Essene?"

"I am a partisan for God."

The Sadducees pressed him, "Tell us who you are, so that we can report to the Sanhedrin. What do you say about yourself? If you do not claim to be a prophet or someone of importance, why are you performing ceremonial washing?"

John answered them, "I wash with water. But there is one standing among you - one you do not know. He is the anticipated one, the one who has been prophesied, who will come after me. I am not worthy to untie his sandals."

They continued to question him, trying to determine which party John belonged to, but with little success. John claimed no party, and showed little sign of hidden allegiance.

Not getting satisfactory answers, the Sadducees tried to trap John in his own words, to have a criminal charge to bring against him, if it proved necessary.

Bureaucrats belonging to Antipas' court, were listening. They had also come to investigate John. Although most people coming to John were from Judea, he spent most of his time on the eastern shore of the River, in Perea, part of Antipas' domain. So, Antipas also wanted a report on the Baptizer's activities.

When it came time for the afternoon sacrifice, John spoke once again. He explained, "When I turned thirty, the Word of God came to me saying, 'You shall take on the mantle, spirit, and ministry of the prophet Elijah. You will live and preach in the places he lived and taught. Remove the white Essene garment, and put on cloths like Elijah's, made of camel's hair. Fasten a leather belt around your waist, like Elijah. Go to the wilderness, and north along the Jordan. Just as I provided manna for the Hebrews, and gave miraculous provisions to Elijah, I will provide desert food for you - locusts and wild honey. In the wilderness, near the roads that pass by the Jordan, call the Israelites to repent of their sins, prepare for the coming of the Son of Man, and be cleansed of iniquity. There, wash the people with a purification in the waters of the Jordan.'"

I had come to the wilderness expecting to see a wild man, a Zealot rebel, or an Essene preacher made half-crazy by the desert. Instead, John's words spoke to me and touched my heart.

Those passing on the roads nearby, heard John's call. Turning aside, they listened. His words pierced through their armor, slicing through their objections. Like a sharp and double-edged sword, his words entered their hardened hearts. Overcome by grief and sorrow, for the sins each had committed, and for the many sins of Israel, they freely confessed their wrongs, begging for God's forgiveness.

John's words did the same to me. My spirit was slain. I shed many tears in repentance, resolved to change my life. Joining the others, I was washed in the Jordan, the outward sign of being cleansed from all uncleanness.

Following our washings, John gave us additional instructions and encouragements. Most continued on their journeys, as transformed Children of Abraham.

Some lingered with John in the desert, adding to the growing number who sat at his feet, learning from the Baptizer.

More Sadducees and Pharisees came, sent by the Sanhedrin. John said to them, "Sons of poisonous snakes, who warned you to flee from the coming judgement? Produce fruit that proves you have turned away from sin and evil. Don't say to yourselves, 'Abraham is our father.' I tell you, God can raise up children for

Abraham from these stones. The axe is already at the root of the trees. Every tree that does not produce good fruit, will be cut down and thrown into the fires of Gehenna."

The crowds cried out to John, "What is it we must do?"

"Anyone who has two coats should give one to someone who has none. Anyone who has food, must do the same."

Tax-collectors also came to be washed, and asked John, "Rabbi, what should we do?"

"Take nothing more than you have been ordered to collect by the Romans."

Soldiers asked, "What should we do?"

John told them, "Don't harass, intimidate, or falsely accuse anyone. Be satisfied with your wages. And do not take spoils, or steal the belongings of others."

Even though he had denied it, the people still hoped John was the Messiah. But not the Sadducees. The Sadducees believed in none of it, messiahs, heavenly bliss, or prophets.

But what was I? Was I still a Sadducee? Had I also been hypnotized by this modern-day prophet? All I knew - for the first time in my life, I was no longer in bondage to the cynical Sadducee worldview that had been drilled into me by my father. It was a strange feeling to value hope and faith, more than money, power, or position. It was through the promise of money, power and position that Caiaphas convinced me to spy on John. Now, all that seemed unimportant and far away. It seemed almost insane – at least from a Sadducee viewpoint. I was baptized in the Jordan. It wasn't a cynical deception, to gain John's trust. I did it out of a real spiritual desire. Descending below the waters of baptism, my old self died, as though buried in a tomb. Arising up out of the water, a new man emerged, unlike the one before. Was the desert making me crazy, like John? I don't know. But if insanity brings this much peace and happiness, then number me among the mad.

As the days passed, John continued to preach, "I cleanse you with water. But there is one coming, who is more powerful than I am, whose sandals I am not worthy to untie. He will cleanse you with the Holy Spirit and with cleansing fire. The rake is in his hand. He will thoroughly rake and toss, shifting the harvest to separate the wheat on his threshing-floor, gathering the grain into the grain bin, but burning the chaff with unquenchable fire."

ϒ

I listened to John's preaching for a week. At the end of the eighth day, I followed him across the river to the far bank. He was staying in Perea that night, because the Judean and Temple authorities were a greater danger to him than the authorities in Perea. Antipas had not yet become too alarmed by John's preaching, or the crowds he gathered. After all, most were Judeans, not Antipas' subjects. The Judeans were Pilate's and Caiaphas' concern, not his.

I drew near and blended into the group of John's followers, listening carefully to his every word. It was easy to understand how he had gathered such an enthusiastic group of supporters and admirers.

Around the campfire that night, John taught his band of students (disciples), speaking in a gentle whisper, quite a contrast to the loud and angry public preaching he did each day. His words suggested no Zealot leanings, or loyalty to any party. But it was clear why John made the Temple authorities nervous. He did not preach armed rebellion, but harshly criticized all those in authority. His teachings were clearly not those of the Pharisees or Zealots. Some of his words sounded Essene - but not quite. His was a universal indictment of Israelite society, condemning the compromises Jews had made with the pagan world. John's message was strict and austere, like the Essenes. But Essenes preach monastic separation, and isolation from the outside world. Whereas, John preached radical engagement and confrontation against the secular world - not militarily, but spiritually. John's message called for radical change, beginning with each person's spiritual transformation through repentance and cleansing. But John was not content with individual purity alone. His message was expansive and comprehensive, envisioning the transformation of Israelite society, the Roman Empire, and even the whole world. To that end, he specifically and pointedly condemned the sins of all authorities and principalities.

I needed to get closer to him. Was I a Sadducee spy, or merely wanting to get close to John for my own spiritual growth? I can't say with certainty. My mind was in a fog. At that moment, I wanted to be a faithful follower of John. But in the back of my mind, I also had a deep sense of loyalty, desiring to fulfill my obligation to my father-in-law, Caiaphas, and longing to return to my dear wife and not-yet-born baby. To fulfil either, or both of these competing desires, I needed to get closer to John, to hear his private conversations and secret thoughts.

I approached John the next evening, while he was eating supper. "Rabbi," I said, "I wish to bear the full yoke of your teaching, and become like you. I want to follow the paths of righteousness, to walk in your footsteps, and to have your dust remain on me as your student (disciple)."

John asked, "What is your name, and who is your father?"

"I am Judas Bar-Simon, of Kerioth, belonging to the Tribe of Levi."

"Welcome Judas. I am John Bar-Zechariah. I also belong to the Tribe of Levi, like my father before me, a priest." He paused for a moment, "A Levite, you say. Are you a Sadducee, Judas?"

"Yes, I serve in the Jerusalem Temple. But my heart has been strangely warmed by your teachings."

Taking a bite out of a large fried locust, John said, "You are dressed in fine clothes, Judas. In the City of David, your life must be easy and filled with luxuries. Are you certain you wish to forsake all the pleasures Jerusalem has to offer, to follow me?"

"It is true. I have enjoyed every advantage life has to give. But ease and riches mean nothing apart from God."

"Are you willing to follow me in the wilderness, to eat what I eat, wear what I wear, and sleep under the desert sky?"

"Yes, rabbi. I will go where you go, eat what you eat, fast when you fast, and lay my head wherever you lay yours."

"Tell me Judas, why would you exchange a life of luxury and privilege, for poverty in the wilderness?"

"The Children of Abraham left the fleshpots and grandeur of Egypt to follow the prophet Moses into the wilderness. Egypt was rich. But the Hebrews were in chains there. I am rich, but also in chains. God is worth more than all the riches the world has to offer. Anyone who has God, has wealth beyond compare. I wish to be rich in the ways of God."

"Well said, Judas." He paused for a moment, deep in thought, playing with his food. Then John said, "You are welcome to be my disciple."

We stood. He hugged me. I kissed him, then bowed at his feet, and kissed the tassel of his shawl.

I had become John disciple, his student. The strange thing is, I uttered no lie to John, telling him only the truth, and meaning every word. I had been sent to spy on the Baptizer by the High Priest. But while in John's presence and listening to his words, Jerusalem and the Temple seemed a far-away, a half-forgotten memory, almost as though my earlier life belonged to another person, or that it was a dream fading away in the morning light. I gladly and freely followed John, sitting at his feet, living an austere life in the desert.

θ

The next day, a man came to John for baptism. When he saw the man approach, it was clear from John's expression that he knew the man, and was surprised to see him. When the man spoke, his accent indicated he was from Galilee. John began to disagree with the man, refusing to wash him, saying "I should be baptized by you. And yet you come to me for baptism?"

ו

Chapter IV: The Stranger

The Galilean said to John, "Let it be this way for now. I must complete every holiness, and fulfill all that has been prophesied."

John relented. When the man emerged from the water, without saying a word, the stranger walked alone into the wilderness.

That evening, John told his disciples, "When Jesus came to me at the Jordan, the heavens opened and I saw the Spirit of God come down on him, like a dove. A voice from heaven said to me, 'This is my dear Son. I am very pleased with him.'"

Six-weeks later, I saw the same man return from the wilderness. He had been in the desert the entire time. When John saw him, he said, "Look, it is the Lamb of God, who will remove all sin from the world. This is the one I was talking about when I said, 'A man is coming after me who is greater than I am, because he existed before me.' I did not know who the Messiah would be ahead of time, but that at the right time, God would reveal him to me and to Israel. It is for his sake I called the people to repentance and to be cleansed from sin. He who sent me to wash with water said to me, 'On whomever you see the Spirit descend and remain, this is the one who will bring cleansing, not with water, but with the Holy Spirit.'

John said, "It is my testimony to you - this is the Son of Man that has was prophesied about, the one who is to come into the world."

Near evening the following day, John, Andrew (another of John's disciples) and I were standing beside the Jordan. When Jesus walked by, John said, "Look, the Lamb of God, who takes away the sin of the world." We gazed intently at the man, but he paid us no mind. John said to Andrew and me, "You have been my faithful disciples. But my mission will soon end. Then all who follow me will be scattered to the four winds. Happy are those who choose to leave the lesser light to follow the greater."

Giving our rabbi a hug, Andrew and I left John at the Jordan. Catching up to Jesus, we followed a short distance behind him. He turned and asked, "Are you looking for something?"

I said, "The man John told us about."

Andrew asked, "Rabbi, where are you straying for the night?"

Jesus said, "Come and see." We followed him to a small oasis, made camp there, and remained with him that night.

ϰ

Sitting near the fire I asked Jesus, "What were you doing in the desert?"

He said, "The Spirit led me into the wilderness."

"But what were who doing there for such a long time? What did you eat?"

"I fasted for forty-days."

Skeptical I said, "But that is the limit of human endurance. How could you last so long without food?"

"It was my time of testing. If one has faith in God, He will provide all you need. My Heavenly Father led Moses and the Hebrews into the desert, testing to see if they would trust in His provision for them. Even though God provided water, manna, and quail, and preserved their lives, they failed the test.

"But I passed the test, fasting for forty-days, mastering this human body with all its fleshly desires. After fasting for forty-days, I was hungry. The Tempter came to me and said, 'If you truly are the Son of Man, command these rocks to become loaves of bread.'

"I said to him, 'It is written in the Torah, 'Man shall not live only on bread, but on every word, that comes from the mouth of God.''' (Deut. 8:3)

"Then Satan took me to Jerusalem, placed me on top of the Temple and said, 'If you are truly the Son of Man, jump off. The Scriptures say God will command his angels to save you. On their arms, they will carry you, so that the Son of Man will not even stub his toe on a rock.''' (Psalm 92:12)

"It is also written in the Torah, 'Do not put the Lord, your God, to the test.''' (Deut. 6:16)

"Then Satan took me to a very high mountain. He showed me all the kingdoms of the world and their majesty. Then he said to me, 'I will give you all of this, if you will bow down and worship me.'''

"I said, 'Be gone with you Satan. It is written in the Torah, 'You shall worship the Lord your God, and Him only shall you serve.' (Deut. 6:13) Then the Devil left me."

I shuttered with a chill. There was something that disturbed me about the story. It was eerily familiar, reminding me of one my father had told.

Andrew asked Jesus, "Rabbi, may we follow you?"

He answered, "If you are willing to go with me into the desert, even to the Gates of Hell (Hades), walking on scorpions and snakes, confronting Satan in all his might, then you are welcome to follow me."

I said, "But Rabbi, don't you want to examine us, to determine if we are worthy of you?"

Jesus said, "No sinful human being is worthy of God's truth or His salvation. God's mercy does not depend on worthiness. If you were acceptable to John, then you are welcome to follow me."

The next day Jesus sent us away, telling us to spend the Sabbath with your families, while he prayed alone in the wilderness. He told us, "Return to me again, on the first day of the week."

Ω

Andrew went to the place where John was ministering, to find his brother Simon, who had recently come from Galilee. He too had come to be washed by John, and to hear his teaching.

I walked the fifteen-miles back to Jerusalem. Arriving late in the afternoon, before the start of Sabbath, I immediately went to Caiaphas' house. It was my duty to report everything to him. I did not regard this as a betrayal of John or Jesus. The High Priest is the leader of God's people, and mediator between God and Israel. Besides, if it were not me, Caiaphas would send someone else to do his spying, someone not as sympathetic as I was.

I reported to Caiaphas, "John told his disciples that his ministry would soon end. He sent another of his disciples and me, to follow a man John called 'the greater light.'"

Shaking his head Caiaphas said, "We are surrounded by rabbis, magicians, Zealots, and Essenes. They are behind every corner, and under every rock. The production of religious teachers is Israel's largest and least profitable industry. The wilderness is filled with them. Galilee is overrun by them. We must be careful, or all their heresy's will soon be brought into the Temple, creating unrest here in Jerusalem. We all know how the Romans react to unrest, riots, and rebellion. There is never a shortage of vagabond teachers and violent troublemakers to cause trouble."

I protested, "Your honor, these two men are different, unlike other rabbis. We should not put them in the same category as other teachers."

"Yes, yes, each one is unique, gathering their own particular group of fools and hangers on."

"No, you must not think John and Jesus are like the others."

"What...are you tempted to follow these vagabonds too, my son? Surely not."

"I am the same as always, your servant. But it is a mistake to underestimate one's opponent." It was a lie. I now felt as much loyalty to Jesus and John as to Caiaphas. Don't ask me why. Maybe I was afflicted with desert delirium. Or maybe it was John's and Jesus' sincerity that swayed me. Perhaps it was the spiritual conversion I had felt. Whatever the reason, my mission had changed. I was now as concerned about protecting Jesus and John, as informing on them. But I also hoped to be true to the Sadducees, as well as to my two itinerate rabbis. This was my dilemma.

I continued, "John says Jesus is greater than he ever was. He said this man's importance must increase, but his must decrease. John clearly told his disciples that Jesus is the Messiah."

Caiaphas huffed, "Messiah indeed! The poor and uneducated see Messiahs behind every corner...What did you say this man's name is?"

"Jesus."

"Where is he from, and what are the credentials that recommend him?"

"He is said to be from Galilee, from a small village near the former capital of Sepphoris."

"Galilee...no doubt another Galilean Zealot."

"No, your honor. He does not seem a Zealot at all. Some of the doctrines Jesus and John teach are similar to what the Essenes believe. But at other times they appear to agree with the Pharisees. Unlike the Pharisees, however, they have a conservative view of God's Law, like Sadducees. Jesus and John clearly reject the Pharisees' oral traditions in interpreting God's Law. And they are clearly not Zealots, because there is a gentleness, love, and acceptance of others, lived out in their everyday lives. This is especially true for Jesus, who manifests a love for others, entirely unlike any Zealot. Jesus is said to be a builder, rather than a scholar. But he has an utterly unique dignify and stately authority, I have seen in no other man... except, of course, our high priests." A little flattery is always wise when dealing with Caiaphas, or any of the chief priests.

"What did you say this man's profession is, and his religious qualifications?"

"He is a builder by profession."

"A builder? Does he plan to construct an independent Kingdom of God with his own two hands? King Herod was the greatest builder in the history of Israel. But even he did not lay the stones himself. Tell me, has this Jesus been a disciple of a prominent rabbi or scribe?"

"No, I don't believe so, your honor. He has a close connection to John. But their relationship is not one of teacher and student. John has willingly placed himself below Jesus in importance, taking on the position of student rather than teacher."

"What form of yoke does this Jesus place upon his students' shoulders? Is it like John's?"

"That I cannot say. I have just recently become familiar with the man."

"This greatly disturbs me, Judas – to hear of a second John, one who may have messianic pretentions. We are already overrun with conflict in Judea, having far too many troublemakers. We don't need another. As you know, maintaining order in the Temple and Jerusalem is a constant challenge. This man could make the whole nation erupt in revolution against Roman rule. A single small spark could engulf Israel in flames, consuming us all - not just our party, but even the Temple and the whole nation."

"I agree, your honor," I said.

"My son, this is what I want you to do. Follow this man, Jesus. I will send others to keep an eye on John. Your new task is to watch this Jesus. Discover his intentions. Follow him wherever he goes, even if it requires you to go with him to Galilee, or beyond. As you are able, return and keep me informed. I perceive this man is an even greater threat than John."

"But what of my wife and family, your honor. I have spent little time at home."

"Do not worry, my dear Judas. Look around you, at the splendor of my home. You are well familiar with the large sums of money we collect in the Temple, through the Temple tax and tithes, not to mention the profits from money-changing, and the sale of sacrificial animals. You and your family will be richly rewarded for your faithful service. While you are away from home, I will generously provide for your wife and child.

"When you return from this assignment, I promise you a place of prominence in our party, and a seat on the Sanhedrin. Never forget, someday you too could fill the office of High Priest. Here Judas, take this purse as a down payment on my promise to you. I will send a similar purse to Rachel, each week, for the maintenance of your household."

"If I may be so bold as to ask, how much is in the purse?"

"Thirty pieces of silver."

A chill went through my body. I am sure it was unintended by Caiaphas. Sadducees pay little attention to the writing of the Prophets. But I knew the Prophets, forwards and backwards, and remembered the words in Zechariah, "they paid me thirty-pieces of silver. And the Lord said to me, 'Throw it to the potter' - this handsome price they valued me! So, I took the thirty-pieces of silver and threw them to the potter in the House of the Lord." (Zechariah 11:12-13) I returned to Jesus.

µ

When Andrew found his brother Simon, he told him, "We have found the Messiah." So, Simon returned with Andrew, to meet Jesus for himself.

Jesus gave him a nickname, "Simon Bar-Jonah, from now on I will call you Rock (Peter/Cephas)."

The next day, we set out for their home province of Galilee. We met one of Andrew's and Peter's friends there, Philip, who was from their home town of Bethsaida. Jesus invited Philip to join us on our journey.

Philip went to Nathanael and told him, "We have found the one Moses and the Prophets wrote about, Jesus Bar-Joseph, from Nazareth.

Nathanael skeptically replied, "Can anything good come from the tiny Essene village of Nazareth?"

Philip told him, "Come, and judge for yourself."

When Jesus saw Nathanael walking towards him, he said, "Look, now this is a true Israelite, a blunt and honest man. In him there is no falsehood."

"Where do you know me from?" asked Nathanael.

Jesus said, "Before Philip called you, I saw you siting under the fig tree."

"How did you…rabbi…you are the Messiah, the King of Israel?"

Jesus said, "Are you amazed because of me saying, 'I saw you underneath the fig tree?' If you join me, you will witness far greater things than this. You will see the skies open wide, with angels coming down on the Son of Man and going up again."

ν

One of Jesus' relatives was getting married. We went with him to Cana. His mother, Mary, joined us. It was the first time any of us had met her. We were all impressed. She was obviously a devout woman of great inner strength. Jesus' brothers and sisters also attended.

The wedding banquet had only gone on for a short time, when Mary came to Jesus. She was accompanied by several wedding attendants. Mary said to Jesus, "They have run out of wine."

Annoyed, Jesus said, “Mother, why do you involve me? I am only a guest. And it is not yet time for my ministry to begin.”

Ignoring Jesus’ words, Mary said to the attendants, “Do whatever he tells you.”

Nearby were six stone water jars, used for ritual cleansing. Each jar held about thirty-gallons.

Jesus told the attendants, “Go fill the jars with water”.

I rushed to help fill the jars, even though it was not my responsibility, wanting to see what Jesus had in mind.

When all the jars had been filled, Jesus told the attendants, “Take a pitcher. Dip some water from a jar. Then take it to my cousin, the host of the banquet.”

I grabbed a pitcher, before any of the attendants could act. Dipping it into the nearest jar, it looked like water. I took the pitcher to the host. Handing him a glass, I poured liquid into it. Looking at it, the liquid now appeared red. The host tasted it, not knowing where it had come from. A surprised expression came upon his face. He took the pitcher from me, and pulled the groom aside. Then he poured liquid from the pitcher into the cup, and handed it to the groom. After he had tasted it, the host said, “At a banquet, everyone serves the best wine first. When the guests have had too much to drink, then the cheaper wine is served. But you have saved the best wine till now.”

Grabbing the pitcher out of the host’s hand, I looked into it. No longer clear, the liquid now appeared blood red. Putting the pitcher to my lips, I drank a large gulp. It tasted like sweet red wine.

I rushed to Jesus, poured some into his glass and said, “Take a drink.” He stared at me with his piercing brown eyes, a smile on his face. “Don’t you want to drink?” I asked.

“Those who have faith, have no need to drink. Those who believe, do not need to eat. ‘Human beings shall not live on bread alone…” He paused waiting for me respond.

I replied, "but on every word, that comes from the mouth of God." (Duet. 8:3)

"Remember my time in the desert, Judas. Satan will also test you. But if you have faith in God, He will save you."

A chill went down my spine. I asked, "Me? What would Satan want with me?"

"He already owns you, Judas. But that doesn't mean he can keep you. Satan is not God. Faith is more powerful than evil. The day will come when you drink from the cup of sacrifice with me. When you do, the blood red drink will no longer be sweet, but will have turned to vinegar."

I whispered to myself, "What does Jesus mean? Does he know I am Caiaphas' spy? He couldn't...how could he?

ר

Chapter V: The Branch of David

After the wedding, we went down to the northern end of the Sea of Galilee, in the regions of Zebulun and Naphtali, to Capernaum. The words of Isaiah came to mind, "The lands of Zebulun and Naphtali, above the Jordan and beside the sea, Galilee of the Gentiles: The people who sat in darkness have seen a great light. On those who sat in the shadow of death, light has now dawned."

Peter, James, John, and Andrew, had been born in Bethsaida. But they, and their families, now lived and worked in Capernaum. Located on the Via Maris, Capernaum had good transportation to bring their fish and crops to market. Fish were dried at Magdala, just a couple of miles away. From there, they were shipped across the Empire. Capernaum also had a beautiful synagogue, and fine school, that hosted numerous Pharisee teachers and scholars. Peter and Andrew's house was near the synagogue, beside the sea.

Jesus' mother and brothers came with us from Cana, remaining with us for several days. The family had many friends in Capernaum, from a few years earlier. Being builders, Joseph and his sons had helped construct the synagogue.

One day, I was standing next to Jesus' oldest brother, James. I said, "Mary is an amazing woman. But she seems a little young to be your mother. Are you also her son?"

James said, "She's my mother…now. But it has not always been so. Jesus is the only one she gave birth to."

I said, "Tell me more."

"My father, Joseph, was a widower. The mother who gave birth to me, died a long time ago, while giving birth to our youngest sister.

Having a house filled with children, my father desperately wanted to marry again - to share his life, family, and faith with a wife. But being Essene, prospects were few. Not only that, but he had little money to pay the bride-price demanded by prospective families.

"Being known as a righteous man, my father, Joseph, was approached by Mary's father, Joachim. He said, 'Joseph, you are a good man, a devout worshiper of the Lord, and a dedicated Essene, like my family. I have a proposition for you. You know my young daughter, Mary?'

"'Oh…why…yes…er…of course,' my father answered, surprised because Mary was of prime age to become a bride, a beauty, and very devout, a righteous young woman.

"Joachim asked Joseph, 'What do you think of her?'

"'I…I… think she's…great.'

"My father was a hard worker and a fine builder, but spoke little…except when praying.

"Joachim asked my father, 'Have you contemplated marriage?'

"'Yes,' answered Joseph.

"'Good, I have a proposition for you.'

"'A proposition...oh…a…I must warn you, I…have little money, and many obligations…'

"'Yes, my friend, I am well aware of your circumstances,' said Joachim. "Let me tell you something you may not know. Mary's mother, Anna, and I were childless for many years. The Lord graciously gave us a baby, Mary. At twelve, inspired by the example other devout Essenes, Mary made a life-long vow of chastity and celibacy, dedicating herself to God.

"'This is a difficult dilemma for a father, Joseph. I could have and nullified Mary's vow. It was my right, as her father. But she was so devout and zealous for God. I could see that her vow did not spring from the rashness of youth, nor was it an ill-considered vow. So, I allowed and confirmed her dedication. Now that I am advancing in age, I want to ensure that when her mother and I die,

Mary will have a home that will honor her devotion. I am wondering…'

"'If I would be interested?'

"'Yes, my friend. There are few men who would consent to such a marriage…and agree to honor her vow of celibacy…but I thought…'

"'With a house full of children, and few prospects for a mate…' said Joseph.

"'You might consider such a marriage. What do you think Joseph?'

"'You were right to come to me, Joachim. I will pray about it,' answered devout Joseph.'

James said to me, "Clearly, my father accepted the arrangement, and took Mary as his wife, honoring her vow of celibacy."

I said to James, "But obviously, Mary gave up the vow, since Jesus is her son."

"Well…that is a rather a controversial story, at least in our little hometown," said James.

"Why is that?" I asked.

"According to Mary, the angel Gabriel appeared to her, announcing that she would become pregnant with a baby conceived by God's Spirit, if she consented to such a thing. And that this child would be…special…holy.

"The angel told her, 'If you consent, God's Spirit will come upon you, and the power of God will cover you. The child born to you will be called holy, the Son of Man. He will be great, and will be called the son of the Most High. He will be given the throne of his forefather, David, and will rule over the House of Israel forever. His kingdom will never come to an end.'"

"And you believe this?" I asked, incredulously.

Shrugging, James said, "My father did."

"Really?! How is that possible?"

"The same angel appeared to him in a dream saying, 'Joseph, son of David, do not be afraid to take Mary as your wife. The baby she is carrying was conceived by God's Spirit. You will name him Jesus, for he will save his people from their sins.'"

I asked, "But do you believe this?"

"On days when I am full of faith, yes. At other times…"

"What about after Mary gave birth to Jesus? Did she remain celibate, even after his birth?"

"As far as I know, she maintained her vow of celibacy. So did my father, Joseph, until his death."

"What happened after Jesus' birth?"

"We moved to Egypt for a time."

"Egypt? Is that why your family seems so fluent in Greek?"

"Yes. As you probably know, the Israelite population of Northern Egypt, around Alexandria, is very large, making up half the population. They are Greek speakers, like most Jews who live outside the Land of Israel. Few diaspora Jews know any Hebrew or Aramaic. Even in their synagogues, they read the Septuagint.

"Then, how did your family end up in such a humble Galilean village as Nazareth?"

"After Jesus was born, my father and Mary were concerned about the new baby's safety. Because of the prophesies the angel had said about him - that Jesus would one day occupy Israel's throne. An angel warned them to take the family and flee to Egypt. King Herod would tolerate no competition for Israel's throne. You know how ruthlessly Herod dealt with all the Hasmonean heirs to the throne, even his own wife and children, killing them and sending them to reign in dark Sheol. That is why we moved to Egypt, to escape Herod.

"After the King died, we returned to Israel. But when they heard Caesar had appointed Herod's bloodthirsty son, Archelaus, to rule Judea, they decided to settle our family in Galilee. Rome had also appointed Herod's son, Antipas, to rule Galilee and Perea.

Antipas may be as evil as his brother Archelaus, but his methods are a little less cruel, and more pragmatic.

"While we were in Egypt, Judas the Galilean led a Zealot revolt against the Roman census, taking Galilee's capital. Then the Romans laid siege to the city and destroyed it.

"Afterwards, Antipas set about rebuilding Sepphoris in stately Greco-Roman style, making it the ornament of Galilee, adding many public buildings, including a theatre.

"Members of David's Clan had settled in a village named Nazareth. These kinsmen were Essene, like our family. It was in a growing and prosperous area, situated only three miles from Sepphoris, providing our father construction work that would keep him busy for many years. So, Mary and my father decided to settle the family in Nazareth."

I asked, "Did you and your brothers apprentice under your father as builders?"

"Of course."

"Jesus too?"

"Yes, his passion was the construction of synagogues. That is how we first came to Capernaum. We helped built the synagogue here. Jesus loved to work with the stones. Masonry was his passion."

ϱ

"What was Jesus like as a child?"

"Not so different than now. He was very devout, even at a young age, like his mother. The best story that illustrates what Jesus was like as a child, took place when he was twelve.

"Our family went to Jerusalem for Passover, together with all our clan from Nazareth. Because he had come of age, Jesus was examined by the rabbis at the Temple, testing him for his knowledge of the Torah. Then we celebrated his Bar-Mitzvah.

"We began the return to Nazareth, traveling a day's journey toward home. Then Mary and Joseph realized Jesus was not with our clan.

"They returned to Jerusalem and searched everywhere for him, in the Essene Quarter, at our relatives' homes, and in the neighborhood where Mary was born, near the Bethesda Pools. They even went to the olive press (Gethsemane) owned by one of our relatives. Jesus was nowhere to be found. After searching the city for three days, they found him in the Temple, still discussing the Law with all the rabbis who had questioned him for his Bar-Mitzvah.

"Mary said to Jesus, 'Son, why have you treated us like this? Joseph and I were terribly worried. We searched for you everywhere, but couldn't find you anyplace.'

"He answered her, 'Mother, why were you searching for me? Didn't you know I would be doing my Father's business at my Father's House?'

"One of the teachers said to Mary and Joseph, 'Honor is due to you, for raising such a son. He has great knowledge of the Torah. His understanding is truly amazing for a young man no older than he is.' Motioning to the other teachers he said, 'All of us would like to call him as one of our disciples. How we wish all our disciples had such knowledge.'

"But Joseph said, 'No, ours is a family of builders. Jesus must complete his apprenticeship as a builder.'

"One of the rabbis protested saying, 'But this is a waste, my friends. This boy has an aptitude for God's Law and the Prophets. He could become a great teacher, if trained by one of us.'

"Mary replied, 'This may seem right to you. But God's plans do not always agree with men's. It is not Jesus' time. He must return with us to Nazareth.'

"Jesus obeyed our parents' wishes, returned home, and finished his training as a builder. But all the while, he continued to study and memorize the Scriptures. When dressing stones, he would constantly sing psalms, as though he were in the Temple."

π

The Passover Festival drew near. Being a devout community obedient to the Pharisee school of thought, the residents of Capernaum emptied the town and went up to Jerusalem for the Festival. Jesus, his followers, and family all walked together on the four-day journey to Jerusalem, and to God's House.

Passover's focus on national identity and freedom, always stirred strong emotions. This was especially true among Pharisees and Zealots.

As we neared Jerusalem, the surrounding towns were filled with pilgrims. Tents were scattered across the hillsides, making it appear as though the ancient Hebrews had just come out of the wilderness, and made camp in the Promised Land.

The Holy City has fifty-thousand residents, on a normal day. But during the three most important annual feasts, five-hundred-thousand Jews flood Jerusalem and the Temple. Sojourning from as far away as Spain and India, the largest crowds come at Passover, when Jerusalem swells to almost a million. At those times, every house in the city is filled with guests. Homes in all the surrounding villages are also jammed with visiting relatives, come to join the Temple celebrations. Even the caves that house olive presses become temporary inns, where pilgrims spread out their beds surrounded by the pungent and pervasive scent of olive oil. From Bethany to Bethlehem, all the towns are bloated to several times their normal size.

Each year brings larger crowds to the city. Even though Israelite religion is hated by many pagans, increasing numbers of gentiles are becoming "Godfearers," and then full converts, including Romans. "Godfearers" are gentile's who worship the

Lord, and attend synagogue, but are not yet circumcised, or fully obey the laws of ritual purity. Thousands upon thousands of gentiles now believe in the Lord, study the Scriptures, and seek to obey God's Law.

Ever increasing numbers of Godfearers also come to offer their sacrifices at the Temple. But not being circumcised, they cannot go beyond the Court of the Gentiles. At every entrance leading from the Court of Gentiles to the inner-courts is a large stone sign stating in Greek, "No gentile is allowed into the inner courtyards beyond the wall surrounding the Sanctuary. Any gentile who passes beyond invites his death. And his blood will be upon his own head."

ς

Arriving in Jerusalem, Jesus immediately went into the Temple. The Court of the Gentiles was a deafening din of noise and chaos. Pilgrims bargained loudly with money-changers, trading their "unclean" pagan coins for "ritually clean" Temple money - the required currency for all financial transactions within the Temple, but useless anywhere else.

Roman coins had the images of Emperors and pagan gods engraved upon them, declared idolatrous by the chief priests. Funny though, those same coins were not so grievously idolatrous that they were forbidden from the Temple's Court of the Gentiles, where they were exchanged. I had spent untold hours of my youth counting these "filthy pagan coins" for my father. Requiring the exchange of unholy money for holy, doubled Sadducee profits. We made vast sums on both money exchange, and the sale of sacrificial animals. If pagan coins were ever forbidden from the Temple completely, the Sadducees would lose their lucrative monopoly on money-changing.

Walking past the banking tables, my nose was attacked by the overwhelming scent of manure, decomposing in the hot sun. It was combined with the sweaty smell of livestock, and countless birds jammed into thousands of cages. If this were not enough to make your nose run and eyes burn, the Temple's pavement stones flowed with animal urine everywhere we walked. It splashed generously upon our legs, blotching the bottoms of our robes and staining our tassels.

As a Sadducee, I had never before been in this part of the Court of the Gentiles, confronted by the unpleasant obstacles every pilgrim must face to offer their Temple sacrifices. In the past, I had only looked down on the commotion from an upper window, at a distance, far removed from the din and stench. Sickened by the sorry state of things, I gagged. Not only were pilgrims cheated in their purchases and transactions, but they also had to put up with unbelievable heaps of steaming excrement and other scatological offenses, defiling any baptismal bath just taken in a nearby mikveh, to cleanse oneself before entering God's House.

Turning, I looked at Jesus. His face was red, and there was fire in his eyes. Walking to the animal pens, he grabbed a bunch of cords. Tying them together, he made a whip. Flicking it at the nearest merchants, he began to beat them, shouting, "Get out of here! Stop turning my Father's House into a dung pile of thieving merchants!"

Jesus' righteous anger spread like a contagion, first to me, and then to many others. Grabbing cords or discontent, we joined Jesus in driving out the sellers and setting free their merchandise. Animals began to run across the courtyard, shoving and butting their slave masters, who had placed them on the auction block. The freed birds pelted their previous captors with liquid indignation, taking revenge on them for their planned sacrificial slaughter.

Merchants were in a stampede, seeking shelter from the strife unleased upon them, both human and beastly. With the merchants on the run, Jesus turned his wrath to the money-changers, turning over their tables, and driving them as well. The chiming "ching" of coins striking the stone pavement, rang out like thousands of tiny bells, the sound echoing back and forth from wall to wall. Then the coins rolled en masse, through the urine and excrement. Jesus shouted, "My Father's House is a house of prayer. But you have turned it into a hideout for thieves."

It was then that I remembered the word given by the prophet Jeremiah, "Has this house, which is called by my Name, become a den of robbers in your eyes? Behold, I have seen it, says the Lord." I also remembered the Scripture, "Zeal for your House will consume me."

I too swung a whip. Covered in sweat from the hot noonday sun, moving swiftly through the crowd, I came face to face with… my father. Staring, unblinking, he looked straight at me, his jaw dropping in disbelief, his eyes displaying profound disappointment in his son. For the first time in my life, I had disappointed my father. For the first time, he was embarrassed by his precious boy.

How could I explain that I was doing this for Caiaphas? Then I wondered, was it for the High Priest I was doing this? Or was it for Jesus, or for myself? Was I a Sadducee, or had I become something else…a follower of the prophet from Galilee? At that moment, my feeble mind was in a haze, confused, unknowing and unaffiliated, clouded by Jesus' zeal, and by the events in the Temple that day. It hit me. I had swung the whip because I had become Jesus' follower.

My father, being a top leader in the Temple, confronted Jesus. Not knowing who Jesus was, my father asked him, "By whose authority are you doing such things?" Over Jesus' shoulder, I could see the Temple Guard trying to fight through the crowds, and drawing near. My father continued, "If you claim to be someone important, prove your authority for what you have done."

Jesus answered, "Destroy this Temple, and in three-days, I will raise it again."

"It has taken forty-six years to build this Temple, and you are going to raise it in three-days?"

"I whispered into Jesus ear, 'The Guard is coming. We need to leave, rabbi.'"

We withdrew, leaving the Temple and the City, going out through the Eastern Gate. From there, it was a short walk to Gethsemane. During Passover, we were sleeping in the caves next the olive press. It was owned by one of Jesus' relatives, on Mary's side. Since her family were Essenes, no one had asked to stay there, because Essene's celebrate Passover and the other festivals on different days and in different ways than other Israelites. They follow a solar calendar, instead of the usual lunar one all other Jews use.

Soon, I excused myself to go home to my wife. But first, I visited Caiaphas' palace. On the way, I tried to decide what to tell the High Priest.

τ

Entering Caiaphas' reception room, Annas was with him, as usual. I told them, "Jesus poses little threat. I'm wasting my time by following him." I said this double-minded, not knowing to whom my true loyalty belonged – Jesus or Caiaphas. I was homesick for my wife, but heartsick at the thought of leaving Jesus. Praying that Caiaphas would honor my request to go home, my heart also dreaded the prospect of returning to my drab duties in the Temple. Before, I was excited by the opportunities and riches my position offered. Now, the prospect of counting and managing untold coins seemed more of a curse than a reward. Before, money seemed the greatest treasure life had to offer. Now, it seemed woefully inadequate and empty. Counting cold and dirty money in the Temple, seemed a poor substitute for witnessing Jesus' ministry.

My stomach had started to hurt a few days earlier. It now ached all the time, churching from the stress of being split between two masters, serving both and neither. Having two competing loyalties is like an unpleasant circumcision where one's soul is severed in half with a dull flint knife, one-part presented to God, and the other given to Satan. The perplexing dilemma - which was which? Was Jesus right, or was it Caiaphas? In my mind, they were both right...and wrong. I was walking on the Temple's parapet, high above the pavement stones of the inner court. If I fell, the stones would smash my head like a melon. Above me hovered the Sword of Pericles, dangling by a hair. A single gust of wind would slay me, making me die from a huge headache. The choice of perishing impaled, or falling to my death on the pavement, offered little choice at all. But I feared this was the only choice left, that there was no salvation available to me, only the choice of how to die.

Caiaphas said, "What about today's riot in the Temple?

"Yes...I saw the commotion," I said nonchalantly.

"Wasn't this man, Jesus, responsible?

"Why do think so?"

"We were told it was a Galilean who started the commotion. We just assumed it was this Jesus you are following."

"Well, it may have been a Galilean. But it is Passover, and Galileans are all around. And many Galileans are Zealots." I did not know where my true loyalty lay. But it was clear who commanded my emotions. There is something about Jesus. Don't ask me what. I was not going to subject him to the chief priests' wrath for the Temple unrest, at least not now. In this matter, Jesus was more right than the chief priests. The Sadducees were more interested in profits than prayer.

"What do you have to report about this Jesus?" Annas asked.

"He's not a Zealot. He preaches no revolt."

"What about the crowds he is gathering, aren't they growing?"

"Perhaps. But you know mobs, they come and go. Many just view Jesus as good entertainment, like a fine magician...Why don't you send me back home, father-in-law? If the need arises, I can always find my way back into Jesus' confidence."

Annas leaned over and whispered into Caiaphas ear. After a few moments Caiaphas said to me, "This Jesus may or may not be of great concern. He may not have been the one swinging a whip in the riot today. But he may still have been the mastermind behind it. You are not yet in his complete confidence. This Jesus may be acting one way in public, but directing things secretly behind the scenes. This is the way Zealot leaders often act. The henchmen who carry out violent insurrections are never the real leaders. We have long suspected that certain Pharisee members of the Sanhedrin may be Zealot leaders. It is the hidden leaders that present the greatest danger. Let me ask you, Judas, which is more dangerous, the paid assassin, or the one employing him?"

"The one paying for the crime, I suppose."

"Yes Judas. Killers are everywhere. But it is the one who pulls the daggerman's strings who must be eliminated.

"Cut off a viper's tail, and he just grows another. It is the viper's head that must be severed from its body. Even after the beheading has been accomplished, a dead vipers' head can still bite and kill until sunset. True to its nature, even after death, its unconscious muscle reaction can be fatal, if one gets too near, it's lifeless bite being as deadly as when it slinked upon the ground. As the leaders of the Temple and the Sanhedrin, we must be vigilant to guard our nation from the viper's bite.

"No Judas, we cannot send you home, not yet. Continue to follow this Jesus. We will reunite you with your dear wife, as soon as the danger has clearly passed."

σ

I went home to Rachel. It was not a fond reunion. She was beside herself with disappointment, angry that I would not be with her during the pregnancy. Her morning sickness seemed unrelenting. Neither of us got much sleep that night. In spite of it all, the one joy we shared, was the coming of our baby.

In early morning before sunrise, I gave up trying to sleep. Rachel was heaving in the other room. In between gags, I gave her a kiss on the forehead.

Jesus and the others were just waking up, when I arrived back at the olive press on the Mt. of Olives. When everyone was ready, Jesus led us back to Temple. "Rabbi" I said, "after yesterday's unrest, we must be very cautious, the Sadducees are watching for you."

"Have you heard something, Judas?"

Taken aback I said, "No, I mean…um…yes. I just know the Sadducees…being one. Following yesterday's riot in the Court of the Gentiles, the authorities will be hypervigilant. It is their way."

"Do not worry, my friend Judas," replied Jesus, seemingly without a care in the world. "Can you add a single hour to your life? Don't be concerned about the minutia of this world, what you will eat or drink, or what you will wear. Satan only has the authority that is given to him by others. He is a usurper, and has little power in and of himself. But my Father has numbered every hair on our heads. The Sadducees can do nothing until the fullness of time, when the Father allows it. Do not worry about the authorities, my friend."

Nearing the Temple, we came upon the many beggars lining the entrance, crying for alms. As he went along, one-by-one, Jesus healed them. The crowds became quiet, not understanding what was taking place, or how to interpret it. All of us were confused and skeptical. I had seen Jesus' miracle with the wine, but this was even more unbelievable. We, his followers, mumbled and grumbled behind Jesus' back, as we continued towards the Temple.

"What sort of man is this?"

"Is he truly capable of such miracles?"

"If so, who is he, and what has he come to do?"

Then I saw a blind beggar. The others had all been paralytics of various kinds. I had wondered if those "healed" had been faking their disability, to make money from gullible pilgrims. But this blind beggar was cock-eyed, both orbs pointing in different directions, each covered with a whitish film. Jesus placed his thumbs over the man's eyelids and said, "Be healed."

When the man opened his eyes, the white film had disappeared, and both were looking straight ahead. Jesus said to him, "Look at me." The man looked up. "Your sins are forgiven. Go and sin no more. Your faith has healed you."

This was no trick, deception, or piece of mind-control. There was no magic to it. Jesus only touched the man, spoke two words, and he was healed.

We all saw it - family, friends and strangers alike. Everyone who surrounded the formerly blind man was hushed, struck dumb. Jesus had made a mute man speak. But now he turned those who could speak mute, shocked by what they had seen. No one knew what to say, or how to react. Then a cacophony of amazement began to build. Peter quietly mumbled in a half-believing tone, "Could this be the expected Messiah? If so, King David didn't do miracles like this. He was just a man. A King, yes, but just a frail human being. Who is this Jesus, Messiah, or something even greater? Even John the Baptizer didn't do miracles or feats of wonder."

Inside the Temple, Jesus taught in Solomon's Porch. All sorts of people had seen his miracles, and believed in him. Pharisees, Essenes, and Zealots, all had their own unique messianic hopes and dreams. Even though many shouted praises for Jesus' miraculous deeds, he would not entrust his safety to any of them. He seemed to know the crowd's approval was only partial, halting and conditional, as shifting as sea waves in winter. If Jesus did or said anything contrary to their particular party's beliefs, their support would dissipate like morning fog.

Jesus seemed able to peer within a person's heart, instinctively knowing what sort of man or woman they were. When he met each of us who had followed him, Jesus had uncanny insight into our personalities, as though he already knew us.

Some members from the various parties started to believe in Jesus, but no Sadducee did, unless you count me. Jesus had already gained a bad name among the Temple authorities. The chief priests had no use for prophets, only profits. Pharisees, Zealots, and Essenes looked for signs and wonders. But miracles meant nothing to the Hasmonean/Levitical priesthood ruling the Temple and controlling the Sanhedrin. Messiahs, rabbis, holy prophets, or angels, not one could impress a Sadducee.

That night at Gethsemane, it surprised me when a member of the Sanhedrin appeared in the garden. It was Nicodemus, a Pharisee member of the Council. He said to Jesus, "Rabbi, we know you are a teacher sent by God. No one could perform the signs you are doing, if God were not with him."

Jesus said, "No one can see God's Kingdom, unless they are born again."

Baffled Nicodemus said, "How can a person be born again, when they are old? Surely a person cannot crawl back into their mother's womb and be born a second time."

"No one can enter God's Kingdom, unless they are born of water and the Spirit." said Jesus. "The body gives birth to body, but the Spirit gives birth to Spirit. My saying, 'You must be born again,' should not surprise you. The Spirit is like the wind. It blows wherever it pleases. You hear its sound. But you can't tell where it comes from, or where it is going. It is the same way with all those who are born of the Spirit."

"How is this possible?" Nicodemus asked. "Can you explain this to me?"

"How is it that you, one of Israel's leaders, do not understand this? I speak about what I know, and tell you what I have seen. But you people do not accept my testimony. I have spoken to you about earthly things. But you do not believe. How will you ever believe, if I speak to you about heavenly things? No one has ever gone into heaven, except the One who came down from heaven—the Son of Man.

"Moses lifted up the snake on a pole in the wilderness, to heal the people and save them from their afflictions. When they looked to the snake on the pole, they were healed and saved. It will be the same way with the Son of Man, who must be lifted up. All who look up and believe in him will have never-ending life."

"God loved His creation so much, that He gave his one and only Son, so that all who have faith in him, will not die, but have never-ending life. God did not send his Son into the world to condemn the creation, but to save the creation through him. Whoever believes in him, is not condemned. But all who have no faith, stand condemned already, because they have not believed in the name of God's one and only Son.

"Light has entered the creation. But people loved darkness instead of light, because their deeds are dark and evil. Everyone who does evil, hates the light, and will not come into the light, fearing that their dark deeds will be exposed. But whoever lives by God's truth, comes into the light, so that everything they have done can be clearly seen in the sight of God."

I wrote all this down, word for word, because Jesus' words made little sense to me. They were confounding and confusing words. I did not know what to think of them, or of Jesus.

Nicodemus' reaction appeared like mine. He was obviously fond of the rabbi, like me, but seemed baffled by what Jesus had just told him.

I asked Andrew, "Do you understand what the rabbi said?" He didn't understand any better than I had. One thing for certain, Jesus' words sounded Essene. They are the only Jews who constantly talk about the forces of light and powers of darkness. It made me uneasy. As a Sadducee, I had always been taught, the Essenes were our enemies. They had rejected the Hasmoneans, and rejected the Temple's priesthood as corrupt and perverse. They didn't even share the same calendar with other Jews, calling the lunar calendar pagan, because it had been brought back from Babylon. The Essenes didn't even sacrifice in the Temple any longer. And when they celebrate the Passover, they do it without a lamb, looking forward to the day when the Temple will be cleansed, and the Passover Lamb shared.

The term "Pharisee" meant "separated ones." But many had given Essenes the derogatory nickname "contraries," because everything they did seemed contrary to all other Jews.

The thought of Jesus' spreading Essene doctrine repulsed me. But at the same time, it drew me to him. One thing was certain, Jesus was intriguing. And even though his words and manner might seem like the Essenes in certain ways, no one could pin Jesus down to a specific party or interpretation of the Law. And if he were Essene, why then did he go to the Temple and celebrate the festivals according to the lunar calendar, like all other Jews, but not like the Essenes? What party did Jesus belong to? All and none. Was he the Messiah? John said so. But Jesus referred to himself as the "Son of Man," a far loftier title. Jesus was a man of mystery. I mumbled to myself, "Will I ever figure out who and what Jesus is?" What can I report to Caiaphas about him? I didn't know. My head hurt, as I tried to figure it out.

ט

After the Passover Festival, Jesus left Jerusalem and led us beyond Jericho, out into the wilderness near the Salt Sea (Dead Sea), the same place where I first met the Baptizer and Jesus. There, on the banks of the Jordan, Jesus taught us, and those who came to be baptized by him.

John was now baptizing and teaching in the north, near Galilee at Aenon, another place where Elijah had been. Aenon was where the ravens brought food to the prophet of old.

John's disciples were upset about Jesus. Some of them asked John, "Rabbi, the man you were with - the one you witnessed about - he is baptizing. Many who had followed you, are now following him, instead."

John answered them, "A person receives only what God gives to them. You heard me say, 'I am not the Messiah, but have been sent ahead of him.' The bride belongs to the groom. The groom's best-man serves the groom, waiting and listening for the groom's voice. When the best man hears the groom's shout that his marriage has been consummated, the best man is filled with joy for the groom. This is my joy. The groom has arrived. Jesus must become greater and I, the best-man, must become less, for the bride does not belong to me.

"The One who has come from above, is above all. The one who is from the earth, me, belongs to the earth. The One who came from heaven is above all. He testifies about what he has seen and heard. Whoever accepts his testimony, affirms that God is true. The One whom God has sent, he speaks the word of God, because God has given him the Spirit without limit. The Father loves the Son, and has placed all power in his hands. Anyone who believes in the Son has never-ending life. But all who reject the Son, have no life, because God's condemnation remains upon them."

The Sanhedrin had heard that Jesus was gathering and baptizing more disciples than John. Even Pilate had become aware of Jesus, because of the large number of Judeans who were going to him at the Jordan, just as they had with John.

ς

News reached us that John had been arrested by Antipas, and was in prison not far from us, at Herod's palace in Machaerus. It was now dangerous for Jesus to remain at the Jordan. Antipas might also try to arrest him. So, we returned to Galilee once again. It being summer, it was too hot to travel the road along the Jordan. So, we took the more mountainous route, through Samaria.

We came to Sychar, near Jacob's Well. It was about noon. The others went to buy food in town. Jesus, hot and tired, remained at the well. I stayed with him. Then a Samaritan woman came to draw water. Jesus asked her, "Please give me a drink?"

Sarcastically the woman answered, "You are a Jew. Do you dare drink from my cup? It might kill you, or God may strike you dead if you drink from a Samaritan's cup." Israelites consider Samaritans apostates and mongrel half-breeds. Samaritans likewise hate Jews, and refuse to worship at the Jerusalem Temple. Jews came and destroyed the Samaritan's temple that was located at Mt. Gerizim. In turn, the Samaritans snuck into the Jerusalem Temple, even the Holy Sanctuary whose doors had been left open, desecrating it by scattering bones throughout.

Looking at the Samaritan woman with his penetrating eyes, Jesus said, "If you knew the gift of God, and who it is that is asking you for a drink, you would ask him for fresh and living water, not this stagnant water from the well. And he would have given you that living water."

The woman said, "There is no living water near here. And you have nothing to retrieve water from this deep well. Where will you get this living water you mention? Are you greater than our forefather Jacob? He drank from this well, and gave it to us. Jacob's sons, their livestock, and I also have all drunk from this well."

"All who drink this water will soon be thirsty again," said Jesus, "but all who drink the living water, that I give to them, will never be thirsty again. The water I give will be a spring, welling up in them to never-ending life."

The woman playfully said, "Sir, please give me this kind of water, so I will never again be thirsty, or have to fetch water from this well."

Smiling, Jesus said, "Go get your husband, and come back to me. Then, I will give you this living water."

Looking at the ground, the woman said sadly, "I have no husband."

"You are right to say, 'I have no husband.' You have had five husbands, and the man you now live with, is not your husband. You have answered honestly."

She said, "Are you a prophet, sir? We Samaritans worship the God of Abraham on this mountain. But you Jews, claim we must worship at the Temple in Jerusalem."

"Dear woman, listen to me, a time will soon come when no one will be worshiping, either on this mountain, or in Jerusalem. You Samaritans worship whom you do not know. Jews worship whom we do know, for salvation comes from the Jews. And yet, a time will soon come when true worshipers will worship the Father in the Spirit and in truth. These are the kind of worshipers the Father desires. God is Spirit, and his worshipers must worship in Spirit and truth."

"I know the Messiah is coming soon. When he comes, he will explain all things to us."

Jesus said, "I am the Messiah."

Just then, the other disciples returned with food. They were surprised to see Jesus speaking to a Samaritan woman. Prejudiced against her, they ignored the woman, and gave Jesus some food.

The woman left her water jar and went into town. She told the townspeople, "Come, see a man who told me my whole life. Could he be the Messiah?" Many of them came to the well to see.

Peter urged Jesus, "Rabbi, eat something."

He answered, "I have food you do not know about."

Peter asked me, "Did someone else bring him food? How about you, Judas? Did you give Jesus something to eat?"

Before I could answer, Jesus said, "What sustains me, is doing the things my Father sent me to do. Open your eyes and look at the crops in the field. They are ripe for harvest. Those who reap, earn a wage, harvesting a crop for never-ending life. One sows, and another reaps. I send you to reap what you have not sown. Others have done the hard work of planting, and you will reap the benefits of their labor. Then, both sower and reaper, will rejoice together in the harvest." Once again, I had little clue what Jesus was talking about.

When the Samaritans came from town and heard Jesus, many believed in him. They were more receptive to his message than those in Judea. They asked him to stay and tell them more. We stayed two days, and many more believed in Jesus.

Then the people said to the woman, "We no longer believe because of what you said about him. We have heard him for ourselves. This man truly is the savior of the world."

I asked Peter, "What does it mean, that Samaritans are more willing to believe in Jesus than Judeans? Should this concern us?" Peter replied with a shrug.

φ

We continued our journey. Once again we visited Cana, where Jesus had turned the water into wine. There, a Herodian official had a son in Capernaum, who was near death. When he heard that Jesus had arrived in town, he went to him. He begged Jesus, "Please rabbi, go and heal my son. He is ill and about to die."

Many of the people in Cana urged Jesus to heal the man' son, not out of compassion for the young man, or for his father, but to see whether Jesus was capable of such a thing. News of Jesus' wonders had preceded him, together with rumors that he might be God's anointed (Messiah).

Jesus looked at the crowds, noting their eagerness to test him. Shaking his head Jesus said, "Unless you people see signs and wonders, you refuse to believe."

The Herodian official said, "Please, I beg you, sir. Come to Capernaum to heal my son, before he dies."

Filled with compassion, Jesus tenderly told the official, "Go. Your son lives."

Stunned by Jesus' words, at first the father was hesitant to walk away. Staring into Jesus' face, he believed his words and left for Capernaum.

The next day, word reached us from Capernaum. The official's servant, had met the man on the road, and told him his boy had recovered. The official asked his servant, "At what time did my son get better?" He said, "The fever left him yesterday, at the time of the afternoon sacrifice," the exact time when Jesus had said, "Your son lives."

Soon, we went to Capernaum. Jesus was standing on the shore next to the sea. A crowd began to gather around him. Seeing the two fishing boats, belonging to James, John, Simon and Andrew (the two sets of brothers who were partners), Jesus got into Simon's boat and said, "Push out a little distance from shore." Then Jesus taught the people from the boat. When he finished, Jesus said to Simon, "Put out into the deep, and let down your nets."

Simon answered, "Rabbi, we worked hard all night, and caught nothing...But because you say to, I will let out the net."

A huge catch of fish was ensnared, so large the nets began to tear. Motioning to their partners in the other boat for help, the fishermen filled both boats to the point where they almost sank.

Coming ashore, Simon Peter fell down at Jesus' feet and said, "Depart from me, rabbi. I am not worthy of you. I am a sinful man."

Jesus said to Simon, "Do not fear. From now on you will be catching people."

That morning Jesus formally called the first four of his Twelve, Peter, Andrew, James and John, the four fishermen, calling them to learn the full yoke of his teaching.

Over the next few days, Jesus continued to choose the disciples to whom he would invest most of his time and effort.

He came to me. "Will you be my disciple, Judas?"

"I let people down." I said. "You don't want me."

"I know who you are, Judas. But I still call you as my disciple."

"You will regret it."

"Regret is for those who do not do what they should. I know what to do. That is what I am doing now. Will you be my disciple?"

"I will betray you, rabbi."

"Adam and Eve, betrayed the Father. But God still delivered the Hebrews from bondage in Egypt. The Hebrews betrayed the Lord by worshiping a golden calf. And yet, he honored the covenant He made with them. The Father gave them manna and quail to eat in the desert, and brought them to the Promised Land, into a land flowing with milk and honey. Yes Judas, you will betray me, just as human beings have always betrayed God. But I still call you as my disciple. Follow me. Will you do that? Will you take my yoke upon you?

"Yes rabbi. I will follow you wherever you go."

The next day, we walked down the Via Maris, passing by the tax collection booth. Levi Bar-Alphaeus (Matthew), was sitting there collecting customs.

Jesus said to him, "Follow me."

Immediately, Matthew stood up and followed him.

Choosing Matthew to be one of his disciples surprised me. This was not going to win any praise from the Pharisees, Zealots, or even the Essenes. This was an unpopular choice among almost all Israelites. Tax-collectors were hated by everyone, the only exceptions might be Sadducees and Herodians - those belonging to the existing political order.

That night, Matthew gave a large banquet, at his house in Capernaum. Many tax-collectors and sinners attended. Jesus and his disciples were also there.

As for me, I was happy to have Matthew become part of our group. I had more in common with this tax-collector than any of the other disciples. Though not a Sadducee, he belonged to the Tribe of Levi. Not only that, but we were the best educated of all Jesus' disciples. We were both good with figures, treasurers if you will. Practical men, not philosophers or dreamers, more interested in the bottom-line than theory. Matthew and I were demons for details and exact calculations. And both of us knew all the languages necessary to conduct trade, commerce, collect taxes, and keep records. Matthew and I knew Greek, Hebrew, Aramaic, and could get by in Latin, when necessary.

It was no accident that Jesus selected Matthew to be the group's secretary and scribe, picking me as the group's treasurer. Both picks seemed only logical.

When Jesus finished selecting his disciples (students), there were twelve of us in all. It was a strange group, as far as rabbis are concerned. I doubt any other rabbi, would have considered calling any one of us. Rabbis looked for the best-of-the-best, and the brightest students. None would be considered that, except me, perhaps. Jesus' disciples were not scholars of the Law and Prophets, but simple men, practical businessmen concerned with the tasks of daily life. Rabbis, particularly Pharisees, would restrict themselves to students who had graduated at the head of their class, in synagogue school. The top graduates had memorized the entire Torah. Many had also memorized the Prophets, and additional Scriptures. Pharisee disciples also memorized the traditions and interpretations of the Law given by past rabbis.

We, as Jesus' disciples, were a motley crew, having dissimilar and diverse backgrounds, belonging to varied parties. The only thing that seemed to unite us was Jesus.

What were the identities of Jesus disciples? Four fishermen made up the core. They had the Sea of Galilee memorized. But of the Scriptures, I doubt they had memorized more than the Ten-Commandments.

Eleven were Galileans. I was the lone Judean. Matthew and I were the only members of Levi's Tribe, unless one counts Jesus, who was a Galilean, but also a descendant of both the Tribe of Judah and Levi. And I was the only Sadducee. The others had all been brought up in a Pharisee understanding of the Law. Whereas Jesus' background was Essene.

The remainder of the Twelve were: Nathaniel Bar-Tholomew, Philip the Hellenist, Thomas the twin (called Didymas), James Bar-Alpheus (Matthew's brother), Judas Bar-James (known as Thaddaeus), and Simon the Zealot.

Under normal circumstance, a group like this would not be together more than ten-minutes before angry disagreements would break out, and daggers drawn. No one dared bring together Zealots, Sadducees, Pharisees, Essenes, Hellenists, Judeans, Galileans, and tax-collectors into the same group of disciples. And yet, it seemed to be working – for now. We might not have much in common, but Jesus somehow united us.

The bigger problem was this: when the leaders of the various parties looked at Jesus and his disciples, would they see something new and important, a bold statement - that Jesus was not part of any Torah school, party, or faction? Or would they view Jesus' approach as a threat to them all?

From a practical and political standpoint, I thought Jesus' approach unwise. Blazing a new trail, like he was doing, would make Jesus a target, uniting all the parties against the heterogeneous threat that the Nazarene (Branch) and his followers represented.

χ

The next day, the Torah scholars and Pharisees asked Peter, "Why does your rabbi eat with tax-collectors and sinners?" viewing that Jesus had made himself unclean by eating with unrighteous people.

Jesus relied, "Those who are healthy, have no need of a doctor. It is only the sick who need a physician. But the Scriptures say, 'I desire mercy rather than sacrifice.' I have not come to call the righteous to repentance, but sinners."

On the Sabbath, Jesus taught in the Capernaum synagogue. The people were amazed by His teaching, because he did not teach like the Pharisee's, who taught the traditions handed down to them from past rabbis, speaking like lawyers quoting opinions from bygone eras. Whereas Jesus taught with authority, offering his own interpretation of the Law.

While Jesus was speaking, a man cried out, "Let us alone! What do you have to do with us, Jesus the Branch (Nazarene)? Have you come here to destroy us? I know who you are - the Righteous One of God!"

Jesus commanded him, "Be quiet and come out of him!"

The man went into a convulsion. Crying out with a loud voice, the demon left him. The man was motionless, looking as though he were dead. Then he sat up. Looking around he said, "Where am I?" Helping him to his feet, some of his family members led him out.

The people were shaken and asked, "What kind of new doctrine is this, manifested in power and might, so that even demons obey him? By only speaking a word, Jesus casts out demons." And they discussed who Jesus might be.

ט

The next morning, Jesus got up long before sunrise, and went out to a deserted place to pray. Peter, and all of us, went searching for him. When we found him, Peter said, "Everyone is looking for you."

Jesus said, "Let's go to the nearby towns to preach there as well. This is the reason I came out." And He preached in the synagogues across Galilee, casting out many demons, and healing various diseases.

Jesus preached in the nearby town of Magdala. The Torah-stand in their synagogue is magnificent, depicting the Temple's Menorah embossed on its sides.

While teaching in their synagogue on the Sabbath, a woman interrupted Jesus, "What do you want with us, Jesus, son of the Most High?"

He asked, "What is your name."

The woman said, "Perfection - for there are seven of us." The woman had a reputation for being devout. She was from an Essene family, and had taken a vow of celibacy, as is frequently the custom among Essenes. Despite her outward religious devotion, the woman now appeared to be afflicted with demons. They raged at Jesus, begging him to leave.

When Jesus commanded, "Come out of her," she began to froth at the mouth, going into a seizure on the floor. Jesus said, "Be gone." At once, they left her. Laying on the synagogue's floor, as though dead, Jesus took her hand and said, "Arise." She stood up, peaceful, looking at Jesus with wonder in her eyes. He asked her, "What is your name, sister?"

"Mary," she said. From that hour, Mary did not leave Jesus' side, but followed him, just as we had. She helped to care for him, and for us all.

When we left the synagogue, I asked Jesus, "How is it a woman known for being religious and devout, could suddenly reveal herself to be afflicted by demons."

"Satan, evil, and demons constantly lurk near the sons and daughters of Adam and Eve. It is possible to be religious, know the Law and Prophets, appear holy, but still harbor an affliction within. In this fallen world, even devout women and men can harbor darkness inside."

"Where did the demons in Mary come from?"

Jesus said, "They did not enter her because of anything she had done. They latched onto her because of evil done by ancestors before her. These demons were handed down, generation to generation, like an evil inheritance, until they reached Mary. Like leeches, they were sucking her strength, making her weak and depressed.

"Many Galilean families have only worshipped the Lord for a generation or two, converting during Hasmonean rule. Unless the entire house is swept clean, dirt and filth may remain hidden in the corners, the rafters, the workshop, or the barn. If one's ancestors and family have not fully turned their back on idols, demons, sin, and uncleanness - drowning the demons in the cleaning waters of baptism (mikveh), Satan's minions may continue to suck the strength of successive generations. Mary is one like that. But her soul has now been swept clean."

Crowds of people now came to see Jesus from across Galilee, each for their own reason. Some came desiring healing. Most came out of eager anticipation that Jesus was God's "Anointed One

(Messiah)," who would lead Israel to war against Rome, restoring the Kingdom of Israel. But many were curious, doubting whether the miracles could possibility be true. They came to see the mighty deeds for themselves, with their own eyes, coming from as far away as Syria and Lebanon.

Jesus taught the masses beside the Sea of Galilee, and pronounced eight blessings.

"Blessed are the poor in spirit, for the God's Kingdom belongs to them.

"Blessed are those who mourn, for they will be comforted.

"Blessed are the humble, for they will inherit the earth.

"Blessed are those who hunger and thirst for holiness, for their hunger and thirst will be filled and satisfied.

"Blessed are the merciful, for they shall receive mercy.

"Blessed are those who have a pure heart, for they will see God.

"Blessed are those who work for peace, for they will be called God's children.

"You are blessed, when they insult and persecute you, telling all kinds of evil lies against you because of me. Rejoice and be glad, because your reward will be great in heaven. They persecuted the prophets before you, in the same way. God's Kingdom belongs to you.

"You are the salt of the earth. But if salt loses its flavor, how will it ever regain its saltiness? It is no longer good for anything, but to be thrown away.

You are the light of the world. A city set on a hill, like Tiberias, cannot be hidden. People do not light a lamp and place it under a basket. No, they place the light on a lampstand, so it will illuminate everyone in the house. Let your light shine so brightly before others that they clearly see the good things you do, and praise your Heavenly Father for them. "

Jesus commented on God' Law. "Do not think I have come to destroy the Law, or the Prophets' teachings. I did not come to destroy, but to fulfill the Law and Prophets. Until heaven and earth are destroyed and remade, not a letter of God's Law will be altered - not until it is fully obeyed and the Law's purpose completed.

"Therefore, anyone who breaks even the least of God's commands, and teaches others to do the same, will have the lowest position in God's Kingdom. But anyone who obeys God's commands and teaches others to do the same, will be greatly honored in God's Kingdom. I warn you, unless your holiness is greater than that of the Pharisees, and scholars who study God's Law, you will never enter God's Kingdom."

Jesus stood before the multitude, like Moses at Mt. Sinai. Just as the prophet Moses proclaimed God's Law to the Hebrews, on the slopes of the Holy Mountain, Jesus proclaimed God's word on the slopes next to the Sea of Galilee.

Jesus spoke plainly, with clarity, not preaching like any other Pharisee, Zealot, Sadducee or Essene. His interpretation of the Law was simple and severe. And he spoke with greater authority than Moses himself.

The Law Jesus presented was unbending and hard. Not only was murder a sin, but so too was hateful speech. Anyone who divorces their spouse for anything less than adultery, and marries another, is guilty of adultery. Those who sexually fantasize about a married person, are also guilty of adultery.

As I heard Jesus describe the severity of God's commands, for the first time in my life, I felt the full burden of God's impossible Law. The weight upon my back increased with each syllable Jesus spoke. With each word the burden of the black basalt millstone grew. Stooping my head and shoulders, bringing me to my knees, then prostrate - first my mind was crushed under the Law's weight, then my heart was smashed as well. I died, killed by the impossible burden of God's Law. The full weight of human sin and evil was felt by all who heard Jesus' words.

"You have heard it said, 'An eye for an eye, and a tooth for a tooth'. But I say to you, do not resist an evil person. Whoever hits you on the right cheek, turn the other to him also, so that he may strike it as well.

"If anyone sues you to take your coat, give him your cloak, also.

"Whoever forces you to go a mile, go with him two.

"Give to those who ask. And to those who want to borrow from you, do not refuse them."

I whispered to myself, "This is too much. How could this be right. If a man strikes me, and I do not strike him back, then I will constantly be hit and bloodied. How could this be right or holy?"

As Jesus spoke, he showed little similarity to the Pharisee Halakhah (interpretation) which talks endlessly about the minutia of their traditions for interpreting God's Law. He did not talk about the "clean" and "unclean," as the Pharisee and Zealot teachers do, dividing all people into one camp or the other.

Jesus' upbringing, family, and village were Essene, but he did not speak like the Essene teachers, who divide all people into the "Sons of Light" and the "Sons of Darkness" - God's friends and His enemies. One group God loves - the other He hates.

No, as Jesus spoke about the unbending severity of God's Law, he reminded me of my father, and the Sadducee teachers of my youth. They also taught a simple and severe understanding of the Torah. But what amazed me – Jesus' interpretation of the Law was even harsher and more difficult than what the Sadducees had said about the Law. And even though the Sadducees taught a severe understanding of the Torah, they judged their own deeds by a more lenient standard, reserving the Law's severity for outsiders, and those not belonging to their party.

Listening to Jesus, the multitude had dower frowns painted upon their faces. Black clouds of depressed despondency hovered over each head, as they contemplated a God so holy, that His Law was beyond human capability to obey. Crushed by the impossibility of fulfilling Gods commands, or earning God's favor, Jesus then offered the solution to the Law's severity by saying, "Love your enemies, and pray those who persecute you, that you may be sons and daughters of your Heavenly Father. For he makes the sun to shine on both the evil and the good alike, sending rain on all, both good and bad alike."

"You have heard it taught, 'Love your neighbor, but hate your enemy.' But I say to you, love your enemies. Bless those who curse you. Do good to those who hate you. And pray for those who despise and persecute you. In this way, you are children of your Heavenly Father, for he makes the sun to rise both on the evil and the good, sending rain on the just and the unjust alike. If you love only those who love you, what credit is that to you? Even tax-collectors do that. And if you only greet your brothers, how are you different than anyone else? Even tax-collectors do the same thing.

"If you only love those who love you, how is this to your credit? And if you do good only to those who are good to you, how is this to your credit? And if you lend only to those who repay their debts, how is that to your credit? Even sinners lend to sinners, expecting to be repaid with interest.

"Love your enemies. Do good. Lend without expecting it back. If you do these things, great will be your reward as God's Children. For God is kind to the unthankful, even to the evil. Therefore, be merciful, just as your Father is merciful."

"Love one another, just as I have loved you. By doing this, everyone will know you are my followers, if you love one another.

"Love is from God. Everyone who loves is a child of God, and knows God. And love overcomes a multitude of sins.

"Love the Lord, your God, with all your heart, mind, and strength. And love your neighbor as much as yourself. By doing these two things, one fulfills God's Law and the Prophets."

I began to understand what Jesus was saying. He was making us understand, that as sinful human beings, none of us were capable of fully obey God's Law. Fulfilling the Law of Moses is beyond us. Those who think they are holy and righteous, such as the Pharisees, only fool themselves. Priest and prostitute, Pharisee and philander, thief or Essene, each one is a sinner, incapable of truly doing what God requires. Jesus was telling us that mercy and love, forgiveness and compassion, these are the hallmarks of following God. The only way to be acceptable to God, is by having faith in the Lord's love and mercy, forgiveness and patience.

One of Jesus' disciples said, "Rabbi, teach us how to pray."

Jesus replied, "Pray in this manner: Our Father, who is in Heaven, holy is your name. Establish your reign on the earth, just as your will is done in Heaven. Provide for us the food we need for the day. And forgive our sins, for we have forgiven those who have sinned against us. Do not test us, but deliver us from all evil. To you belongs the Kingdom, all power and glory, forevermore. Amen.

"If you forgive others their sins, your heavenly Father will also forgive you. But if you do not forgive others, your Father will not forgive you."

It was a simple and elegant prayer, completely in keeping with what Israelites have always prayed, using as its basis the Qaddish, the prayer I have said since a child:

"O Lord, holy and exalted is Your name.

"May Your Kingdom come quickly, for the entire House of Israel, bringing peace on earth, as there is peace in heaven.

"Holy and exalted is the Lord's great name for all eternity.

"Praised, honored, exalted, extolled, glorified, adored, and lauded be the name of the Blessed One, beyond all earthly words and songs of praise, or comfort.

"May the Lord who creates peace in heaven, bring peace on earth.

"O Lord, accept my prayers and this supplication. Amen."

Ω

Jesus continued, "Whoever hears my words and does them, is like the wise person who builds his house upon the Rock. The rain fell, the wind blew, and the waves beat upon that house. But it was not destroyed, because it was built upon the Rock. But everyone who hears my words and pays no attention to them, is like the fool who built his house on the sand. The rain fell, the wind blew, and the waves beat upon that house. It collapsed completely, with nothing saved. If one builds their life on me, and my words, he has built his life upon the Rock.

Taking Jesus aside privately I asked him, "Rabbi, are you comparing yourself to the Rock of the Temple?"

"What do you know about that Rock, Judas?"

"No one has seen it, just the high priests…and then only one time each year, on the Day of Atonement. But as someone who has served in the Temple, I know about the Rock."

"And?"

"That Rock is the pinnacle of Mt. Moriah, the very place where God commanded Father Abraham to take Isaac. It was on this Rock that Abraham sacrificed the lamb that God miraculously provided to him for the sacrifice, in place of Isaac."

Jesus said, "I am that Lamb."

"What…what do you mean, rabbi?"

"Say more about the Rock, Judas?"

"It was on that Rock that the Ark of the Covenant sat, in the Holy-of-Holies. When the High Priest enters the Holy Place, on the Day of Atonement, the sacrificial blood is sprinkled on the Rock."

"Well said, Judas. What happens when an earthquake severely shakes the Temple?"

"An earthquake??...Well...there is often great damage to the Temple complex."

"But is the entire Temple damaged equally, everywhere?"

"I don't understand your question, rabbi."

"After an earthquake, is the Sanctuary damaged as much as other parts of the Temple, such as Solomon's Porch?"

"No...the sanctuary does not suffer damage. But whole sections of Solomon's Porch have collapsed, and needed to be rebuilt after an earthquake. Is that because the Lord specially protects His sanctuary?"

"Think of the parable, Judas. What happened to the house on the Rock, and the other built on the sand?"

"I'm sorry, rabbi. I still don't understand."

"God's House, the Sanctuary, is built on the Rock, Mt. Moriah. Even though the rest of the Temple is built upon huge stones that Herod quarried for the Temple courts, underneath Herod's stones is landfill, sand. So, when the earth shakes, the Sanctuary is not damaged, built upon the Rock. But other parts of the Temple complex are built on the sand. Great is the fall of those buildings, because they are not built upon the Rock."

"Is this an example for something greater, rabbi?"

"The Temple is a parable for Israel's faith. At the center is God and his Word. They cannot be moved or destroyed. But the Sadducees, Pharisees, Essenes, and Zealots have added greatly to what God built. Those parts built by God will always remain, being constructed upon the Rock. But the things added by human hands and minds, these things collapse, and terrible is their fall. Place your faith in the Rock, not the sand, Judas."

"Show me that Rock, rabbi."

"I am that Rock, Judas. But many will reject me, preferring their own human-made constructions and philosophies. I am the Rock rejected by many. I am the Temple's foundation stone."

I did not reply to Jesus, but wondered in my heart who Jesus was claiming to be. Could it be that he was claiming to be equal with God? No...only a madman would do such a thing.

But Jesus' words reminded me of the Psalms, "The stone the builders rejected, has become the capstone.

It was getting late. Jesus asked Philip, "Where can we buy bread for all these people to eat?"

He answered, "It would take more than half a year's wages to buy enough for everyone to eat just one bite."

Andrew said, "Here's a boy with five barley loaves and two small fish, but what is that among so many people?"

Jesus told us, "Have the people sit down."

We were midway between Capernaum and Magdala, next to the sea of Galilee. A carpet of green grass covered the ground. The people sat down upon it, many thousands.

Jesus took the loaves and gave thanks saying "Baruch atah A-donay, Elo-heinu Melech Ha'Olam Hamotzi lechem min haaretz (Blessed are You, Lord our God, King of the Universe, Who brings forth bread from the earth)." Breaking the loaves into pieces he said, "Take and eat," and had the disciples distribute the bread.

Jesus then blessed the fish, "Baruch atah A-donay, Elo-heinu Melech Ha'Olam shehakol nihiyah bed'varo (Blessed are You, Lord our God, King of the universe, by Whose word all things came into being)." And the fish were also distributed to the crowd.

When everyone was full, Jesus told us, "Gather all the left-over pieces. Let nothing be wasted."

We gathered twelve baskets of leftovers. It was a sign to us all, in the spirit of Moses, the Twelve baskets representing the Twelve-tribes of Israel, the tribes who were miraculously given manna from heaven. Many said, "Truly this is the expected Messiah."

The Zealots in the crowd clamored to proclaim Jesus, King of Israel, the Anointed of God (Messiah), the son of David, and inheritor of his throne. They urged Jesus to take up the mantle of Judas the Galilean, to lead Zealots and Jews in a general revolt against Roman domination, and recreate the Kingdom of God, an independent Israelite Kingdom.

Ezekhias, led a band of guerrillas against Roman rule. But eventually he was captured and executed by Herod the Great His son, Judas the Galilean became a Pharisee scholar, teaching a strict and radical version of theocracy, that God alone was king. So, Judas led a revolt against the Roman tax (census) being collected by the Roman governor, Quirinius. Judas too was executed. But the Zealot party continued on. Knowing the Zealots' intentions, Jesus quickly left, going to nearby Mt. Arbel to pray.

The next day, men came to Jesus, Pharisee scholars who had not seen his multiplication of the loaves and fish. They said to Jesus, "What sign will you do, to prove you are worthy of our allegiance? What wonder will you perform? Our forefathers were given manna in the wilderness."

Jesus said, "It was not Moses who gave you bread from heaven. It was my Father, who gives the true bread of heaven. The true bread of heaven is the bread that came down from heaven, giving life to the world."

"Give us this bread," said the Pharisees.

"I am the bread of life," said Jesus. "Anyone who comes to me will never go hungry, and whoever believes in me will never be thirsty. You have seen and heard me, but still you have no faith. Everyone the Father has called, will come to me. And anyone who comes to me, I will never send away. I have not come down from heaven to do my will, but to do the will of the One who sent me. It is His will, that I not lose any of the ones He has given to me. It is His will, to raise them up on the Last Day. It is my Father's will, to give never-ending life to all who look to the Son, and have faith in Him. I will raise them up on the Last Day."

Many grumbled because of Jesus' words, "I am the bread that came down from heaven."

"Stop your complaining," Jesus said. "No one comes to me, unless the Father calls them to me. It is written in the Prophets, 'They will all be taught by God.' All who hear the Father and listen to Him come to me. No one has seen the Father, except the one sent by God. He alone has seen the Father. Those who have faith in him, have never-ending life. I am the bread of life. Your ancestors ate the manna in the wilderness. And yet, they died." Holding out his arms, Jesus said, "Here is the bread that came down from heaven, the bread that all can eat and not die. I am the living bread that came down from heaven. All who eat this bread will live forever. This bread is my body, which I will give for the life of the world."

The Pharisees argued among themselves, "How can this man give us his body to eat?"

Jesus said, "Unless you eat the body of the Son of Man, and drink his blood, you have no life in you. Whoever eats my body and drinks my blood, has never-ending life. I will raise them up on the Last Day. My body is real food, and my blood is real drink. Anyone who eats my body, and drinks my blood, is part of me, and I am part of them. Just as the living Father sent me, and I live because of the Father. In the same way, those who feed on me will live because of me. This is the bread that came down from heaven. Your ancestors ate manna, but still died. All who eats this bread will live forever." Hearing this, they left shaking their heads.

Jesus said, "Are you offend by my teaching? What if you see the Son of Man ascend to the One he came down from? The Spirit gives life. But this physical body counts for nothing. The spiritual words I have spoken to you, are full of the Spirit and of life. But some of you have no faith."

מ

Chapter VI: Rejected

Going to Nazareth, Jesus' hometown, on the Sabbath, he went to teach in the synagogue. He was handed the scroll of the prophet Isaiah to read. Part of the passage for that day said, "The Spirit of God is upon me. He has anointed me to preach good news to the poor. He has sent me to heal the brokenhearted, to proclaim freedom to the prisoners, and to restore sight to the blind, to set the prisoners free, and to proclaim the Year of the Lord's arrival."

After reading this passage aloud to the congregation, Jesus closed the scroll, gave it back to the attendant, and sat down on the Seat of Moses to teach. The eyes of everyone in the synagogue were focused upon him. He said, "Today, as you hear these words, this prophesy has been fulfilled."

The people were amazed at the words Jesus said, asking among themselves, "Isn't this Joseph's son? Where did this man get all this? What sort of wisdom has been given to him, that miracles are performed by his hands? Isn't this the builder, the Son of Mary, the brother of James, Joses, Judas, and Simon? His sisters live in our midst."

Almost everyone in the village was related to Jesus, in some way. If they were not family, they belonged to the same clan, the Clan of David. But they were unable to see beyond their memories of Jesus as a child. As he preached, they became increasingly offended by his words.

Jesus warned them, "A prophet has honor, but not in his own hometown, with his relatives, or in his own house. During the days of Elijah, many widows lived in Israel. But when the skies were shut, and no rain fell for three-years, famine covering the entire land. Elijah was sent to no one there. Instead, he was sent to a woman in the pagan territory of Zarephath, in the region of Sidon. And in Elisha's time, there were many lepers in Israel. But none of them were healed, only Naaman the Syrian."

Insulted by Jesus' words, the people were filled with anger. They shouted "Blasphemy!" Rushing forward and grabbing Jesus, they escorted him out of the village, taking him to the edge of the rim, to the place for stoning. They intended to throw him off. And if he survived the fall, they would stone him. But Jesus appeared as though he were rubbed with olive oil, and was impossible to hold onto. Effortlessly, he broke free of the mob. Walking through the middle of the crowd, he came and joined us. And we left Jesus' hometown, never to return.

Coming to the top of the ridge, Jesus looked back at Nazareth, and shook his head. The rabbi was amazed at their lack of faith - that even his own relatives had so little faith in him. I said, "Essenes, what can you expect from such people."

He said, "Are the Pharisees, Herodians, or Zealots any better? And what of your people, Judas, the Sadducees?" It was true. The Sadducees were no better, and perhaps even worse. As for me, a Sadducee, was I Jesus' faithful disciple, or like his relatives in Nazareth, soon to become his enemy?

Jesus shook the dust from his feet, as a symbol against his hometown. Then we returned to Capernaum.

Jesus' brothers no longer accompanied him on our journeys. They remained in Nazareth, embarrassed by their brother, rejecting his teachings. Mary, Jesus mother, remained with us. Jesus' brother, James, asked her, "Do you agree with your son? If not, why do remain with him?"

Mary answered, "It is true, I don't know what to think of his teachings. But I have faith in God's promises about him. Even if I am uncertain about his teachings, my faith in God's promises about him have not changed. I must remain with my son, awaiting the fulfillment of God's promises - that he is the salvation of his people. How can I do anything else?"

ϱ

We returned to Capernaum. There, many came to Jesus with great excitement. While he was at Peter's home, the people crowded around the house. There was no room inside, as they packed the doorway.

A paralyzed man was carried to Jesus on a pallet by four of his friends. But they could not reach Jesus. So, the men carried the man up the outside stairs, and onto the roof. Directly above where Jesus sat, they tore apart the roof, making an opening. Then they lowered the paralyzed man on his pallet, using ropes.

Peter and his family were very upset about the damage that had been done to their home.

But when Jesus saw what great faith the four men had, he said to the paralyzed man, "My son, your sins are forgiven."

The Pharisees who were present asked among themselves, "Why does this man speak blasphemy? Only God can forgive sins?"

Jesus asked them, "Why do you question this in your hearts? Is it easier to say, 'Your sins are forgiven;' or to say, 'Stand, pick up your pallet and walk?' So that you know and understand that the Son of Man has the power even to forgive sins…" then he said to the paralyzed man, "Brother - stand, pick up your pallet, and go home."

The man straightened, first one leg, then the other, placing his legs beneath him. Then he tried to stand, his face bent in concentration. Wobbling to his feet, holding onto the shoulders of two people between him, he stood up. Letting go of his support, and standing by himself, his mouth transformed into a wide, toothy grin, black decay showing where white enamel once had been.

Bending over, he picked up the pallet, and walked out the door, pushing his way through the crowd.

Some of the Pharisees also left, more offended by Jesus' words than impressed by the healing, convinced that miracles cannot excuse the stoning offence of blasphemy.

Pharisees and several of John's disciples came and asked Jesus, "Why is it John's disciples and the Pharisees fast, but your disciples do not?

Jesus said, "The time of fasting has not yet arrived for them. Groomsmen do not fast during the wedding celebration? While the groom remains with them, there is no fasting, only feasting. When the groom leaves, the wedding celebration is over. That is when they will fast.

"No one mends a torn garment by repairing it with a new and unshrunk patch. If they do, when the mended garment is washed, the patch will shrink, pull away, and damage the garment with a worse tear than before.

"And no one puts newly pressed grape juice into old wineskins that have previously been stretched by the fermentation process. If they do, when the new grape juice ferments and expands, it will break the old inflexible wineskins, spilling the grape juice and ruining the wineskins. New grape juice must be placed into new and flexible wineskins, that have not yet been stretched. Then both the wine and the wineskins are persevered."

Jesus went through all the towns and villages of Galilee, teaching in the synagogues, healing all kinds of diseases, and preaching the good news of the coming of God's Kingdom.

When Jesus was teaching, a Pharisee who had not seen any of Jesus' miracles said, "Rabbi, show us a sign from heaven to prove God sent you."

Jesus said to him, "An evil and adulterous generation demands signs and proofs. But no sign will be given, except the sign of the prophet Jonah, who was also from Nazareth. Just a Jonah was three days in the belly of the fish, so too, the Son of Man will remain in the belly of the earth, and rise on the third day.

"And I tell you this, the pagan people of Nineveh will stand in judgment against this generation, and will condemn it. Nineveh, was an evil city that worshiped demons, a city guilty of every form of cruelty. But when they heard Jonah's prophesy of God's coming judgement, they repented in sackcloth and ashes, beginning with the king, and including the lowliest beggar. Look, you Pharisees, one who is far greater than Jonah stands in front of you."

While he was speaking, one of the people said, "Look, your mother and brothers are outside wanting to speak with you." His brothers intended to take him back home to Nazareth.

Jesus said, "Who are my mother, brothers, and sisters?" Stretching out his hands toward his disciples he said, "Behold, these are my mother and brothers. All who do the will of my Heavenly Father are my brothers, sisters, and mother."

σ

The next day, the local Roman centurion came to Jesus. Antipas had built a garrison on the edge of Capernaum. This man was its commander. Capernaum was near Galilee's northern border, on the Via Maris. The garrison provided security for the highway and the tax-collectors who gathered customs on the road. But the primary reason Antipas had built the garrison – this was the homeland for Zealotry, and their Pharisee supporters. The garrison was there to keep the Zealots in check, and to nip any insurrection in the bud, before it had a chance to grow and spread. Located east of town, the soldiers enjoyed more luxurious accommodations, than the local residents. The troops even have their own Roman bath house.

Jesus' fishermen disciples were born in Bethsaida, only a few miles from Gamla, birthplace of the Zealot Movement. This is what made me question the loyalties of Jesus' disciples. Peter, James, John, and Andrew, were too sympathetic to the Zealot. They rarely spoke of such things. But their families were outspoken in their political and religious passions, clearly supportive Zealot goals. Then there was Simon (not Simon Peter) who was called "the Zealot" because of his past participation in the party.

When the centurion approached, he said to Jesus, "Rabbi, my servant is lying in bed, near death, and suffering terribly."

Jesus said, "I will come and heal him."

The commander answered humbly, uncharacteristic for a Roman. He said, "Rabbi, I am not worthy to have you come under my roof. I am a gentile, and not fully a Jew. If you enter my house, according to Jewish Law, you will become ritually unclean. But if you just speak the word, I know my servant will be healed. I know this, because I am a man under the authority of my superiors. Whatever they order, this I must do. Likewise, I am a man that has authority, with soldiers under me. I say to one, 'Go' and he goes, and to another 'Come' and he comes, and to my servant 'Do this' and he does it. I know that if you simply say the word, your servants the angels, will do whatever you tell them to do."

When Jesus heard this, he was astonished and said, "I have not found faith, like this, anywhere in Israel. I tell you, Children of Israel, multitudes from the gentile nations (goy) will come and sit down with Abraham, Isaac, and Jacob, in God's Kingdom, coming from east and west. But I mourn, because many born of Israel will be thrown into the outer darkness, where there is weeping and gnashing of teeth. This will happen because of their lack of faith."

Jesus said to the centurion, "Return home. Because of your faith, what you have asked, will be done."

Before long, we received news. The centurion's servant was healed at the same time Jesus had spoken these words to the centurion.

I was stunned by Jesus actions, and worried for him. He seemingly showed none of the sectarian prejudices or divisions pervasive among the sons of Adam. Personally, I rejoiced that Jesus would give the same respect, love and mercy to a Roman, as to an Israelite. But what he did was dangerous. It would undoubtedly make him a target. Gamla was only a short distance from Capernaum. Even now, Gamla remains a hotbed of hatred against all things Roman, seething at the offenses of pagan rule. The Zealots daily pray for God's Kingdom to be established through violent revolution, also praying for the slaughter of the Romans, Sadducees, Herodians, and Hellenists. They long to purify Israel by cleansing the land of all who do not share their same narrow Pharisaical and unbending view of God's Law, and the oral traditions handed down to them.

Most Jews in Galilee are aligned with Pharisee movement. But Phariseeism is only slightly more moderate and somewhat less militaristic in its approach than the Zealots. Zealot sympathies run deep throughout Galilee. It is not unusual for residents of Galilee to harbor Zealot terrorists, when they need a place to stay. Galileans feed them when they are hungry, and hide them when pursued by Antipas' or Rome's troops. Galileans share great nationalist pride in the Zealots, who have taken on the patriotic mantle of Judas Maccabees and the Hasmoneans kings, those whose symbol of Israelite freedom is the palm branch.

As for the Roman soldiers in Capernaum - most residents grudgingly accepted their presence as a disagreeable fact of life. But when given the opportunity, locals gave the Zealots information on troop movements, helping them ambush the Roman soldiers.

Jesus' act of aiding this centurion, would be viewed by some as treasonous. Many Zealots followed Jesus, looking to him as God's anointed king (Messiah), the successor to both King David's throne, and the Hasmoneans. They expected Jesus to lead an armed revolt against Rome, and to proclaim an independent Israelite state.

But now, after helping this Roman commander, most Zealots would desert Jesus. He may even be declared a Roman collaborator, and targeted for assassination.

The centurion seemed to be a good man, a Godfearer. He had paid to construct Capernaum's lovely synagogue. But such niceties were wasted on Zealots, who believed the only good Roman, was a dead one. I wished Jesus had been more cautious, and not so rash to heal this centurion's servant.

As a Sadducee and spy for Caiaphas, I should have rejoiced at the Zealots' rejection of Jesus. But, in a real sense, I had become a true follower of Jesus. It worried me that Jesus now seemed to be alienating every Jewish party, on all sides.

I struggled to understand what Jesus was doing, or what his strategy might be. I had been sent to spy on Jesus, fearing he would lead a general revolt against Roman rule. Jesus' fame continued to grow. With every new miraculous deed, the crowds grew larger. But in a political sense, Jesus position was deteriorating. Jesus had managed to anger Zealots, Pharisees, Sadducees, Essenes, and Herodians alike. Many Essenes wouldn't even listen to him. And that was the party he had grown up in. His people, in Nazareth, even tried to stone him.

At first, I thought Jesus' teachings had much in common with the Pharisees, and many of them flocked to him. But Jesus' conflict with the Pharisees seemed to escalate with each passing day. Now they accused him of blasphemy. Some would stone him, if given a chance.

φ

Chuza sent word to Jesus from Antipas' palace in Tiberias. He had seen a communique from Machaerus. John the Baptizer had been executed.

I knew John had gone too far when he preached directly against Antipas. Antipas had viewed John as a threat for some months before his arrest. Caiaphas, Annas, and the Sadducees were concerned about him, because of the crowds he attracted and his popularity. But they also hated John for his connection to the Essenes. The Essene's were founded by Levitical priests who had left the Temple. They had rejected the Hasmonean and Sadducee priesthood as apostate, refusing to offer sacrifices in the Temple. The chief priests also feared John, because they had killed his father, Zechariah. Caiaphas himself delivered the fatal blow to Zechariah's head. If that weren't enough, Pilate too was concerned about John, because many of his followers were from Judea. And they obeyed John's words as though they were God's own.

Then John targeted Antipas for public scorn and condemnation, calling the Tetrarch to repentance for stealing his own brother's wife. Herodias divorced Antipas' brother, while Antipas divorced his wife to marry Herodias. The Tetrarch viewed John's criticism of his marriage as a political move, a sign that John would soon lead the people to revolt against his rule. But Antipas arrested John before that could happen, throwing him into the palace dungeon at Machaerus, in Perea, on the eastern side of the Jordan.

At first, Antipas worried John's arrest would create violent protests. But he was pleasantly surprised that the people's response was tepid, producing little more than grumbling.

Seeing an opportunity to execute a permanent solution to the problem named John, Antipas acted swiftly, concocting a tall-tale to explain the Baptizer's head suddenly flying off his body. When news of John's death spread, so too did a story that Antipas liked John, and did not wish his death. But the Tetrarch had made a foolish and unbreakable vow to his step-daughter, Salome, promising to give her anything she asked for. The girl's new pastime was collecting severed heads. Alas, Salome needed John's to show and impress her friends. So, the girl demanded Antipas give her the Baptizer's head, served on a silver platter.

Some might believe this ridiculous excuse for John's execution. But I knew the Herods too well. As a child, I had seen the Herods and Sadducees cook up plots and intrigues, like daily meals. Antipas' father, Herod the not-so-Great, killed several of his own sons, wives, and many babies in Bethlehem, all because of plots and threats to his rule, real or imagined. In comparison, it was a small thing for Antipas to kill a prophet or two. With John now eliminated, a target was now drawn clearly on Jesus' back.

Antipas had reigned for decades as Tetrarch, largely because he swiftly eliminated "problems" before they became too big to handle. Antipas' life ambition was to convince the Emperor to name him King of Israel, not merely Tetrarch of Galilee and Perea. But Caesar remained unimpressed by Antipas' methods. His rule was efficient in maintaining control over his tetrarchy. But he had no subtlety or finesse. His was a simple carrot and stick approach. Carrots were given to the Tetrarch's Hellenistic supporters, the Herodians, those who administered Roman rule in Antipas' tetrarchy. The remainder of his subjects were controlled by muscle, ruled by a rod of iron. But if given a chance, Galilee's "daggermen" would eagerly stab Antipas in the gut.

At least Antipas gave John a swift "Roman" death, beheading, administered quickly and with a minimum of pain. Given John's criticism of Antipas, the Baptizer might have been crucified for treason. But a quick and unheralded death was to Antipas advantage. A public execution would only stir unrest unnecessarily. Herod Antipas was his father's son, calculating, crafty, ruthless, and coldly efficient.

Worried that Antipas would not be content to only shed the Baptizer's blood, Chuza warned us that Antipas' men were looking for John's closest associates, to arrest them, making John's disciples go into hiding.

While he was alive, the Baptizer had shared center-stage with Jesus. And Antipas had focused all his attention and concern on John. Now the eyes of all, friend and foe alike, would fall on the Nazarene.

I wondered how long the authorities would wait before they arrested Jesus, or had him assassinated in his sleep.

Hearing of John's death depressed me. I didn't know what to feel. As a Sadducee, I should have rejoiced at this troublemaker's end, the man I was first sent to spy upon by Caiaphas. But I had sat at John's feet, learned his lessons, and began to understand his profound insights and message. It was through John I met Jesus, Andrew, and the other disciples. For all these reasons and more, I mourned John, involuntarily and uncontrollably. Weeping, unable to stop, I became angry at myself, for being double-minded, holding two competing and diametrically opposed opinions. Even more disturbing, I no longer knew who I was, or why I was still here with Jesus.

"It's normal to feel the way you do," a voice said. Startled, with tears in my eyes, I jerked my head backwards, looking at the man who had said them. Jesus sat down next to me. "You were born and raised a Sadducee. It's not surprising you are confused by your feelings. You are walking away from the things you were taught as a child. And yet, your father's words, and those of the high priests, still ring in your ears."

"I feel guilty," I said.

"Of course you do. The Sadducee part of you hated John, and rejoices at his death. The part of you that was John's disciple, loved him and is inconsolable at his loss."

"What am I to do, rabbi?"

"You must choose which part you will listen to and follow. If you allow John's words to continue ringing in your ears, and meditate upon them, and if you continue to listen to my words, until they are firmly planted in your heart, then you will see God's

Kingdom. But if you listen to the voices of your childhood, you will suffer the same fate the chief priests will soon face – oblivion."

τ

Several Pharisees arrived from Jerusalem, sent by their leaders serving on the Sanhedrin. They came to witness for themselves what Jesus was saying and doing, to report back to the Council. Seeing Jesus' disciples eating without performing the Pharisees' ceremonial washing, they complained to my rabbi.

Pharisee traditions, passed down from their forefathers, include elaborate ceremonial washings and purification rites. They never eat until everything is ceremonially washed and purified. And there are countless other traditions and rituals they meticulously obey. The Pharisees asked Jesus, "Why do your disciples disobey the traditions of our ancestors, eating bread with defiled hands?"

Jesus said, "And why do you obey your traditions, but disobey God's Law? God commanded, 'Honor your father and mother;' and, 'those who curse father or mother will surely die.' And yet you teach, 'If a person tells their father or mother the money that could have been used to support them in old age, instead has been pledged to the Temple offering, then the child is released from his obligation to help and care for his father and mother.' By teaching this, you are breaking God's commandment for the sake of your own human-made tradition. Hypocrites, Isaiah was right when he prophesied against you, 'These people honor me with their mouths. But their hearts are far from me. They worship me in vain, teaching human-made traditions in place of God's commands.' And you do many other things like this."

Then the Pharisees tried to entrap Jesus. They asked, "Tell us, is it lawful for a man to divorce his wife?"

"What did Moses command you?" Jesus asked.

"Moses permitted men to write a certificate of divorce to dismiss their wives, if they displeased them in any way."

"The Scriptures do not provide for this," Jesus said. "When God created the Cosmos, He made them male and female. A man leaves his father and mother, and is united with his wife. The two are no longer separate, but have become one flesh. What God has joined together, human beings must not separate.

"Anyone who divorces his wife and marries another, like Antipas, commits adultery against his true wife. And if a woman, like Herodias, divorces her husband and marries another, she also commits adultery."

Several Herodians immediately left. I am sure they went to inform Antipas that Jesus had taken up the mantle of John, restating the Baptizer's criticism of the Tetrarch and his new wife.

I whispered into Jesus ear, "Rabbi, don't you realize the Pharisees are offended by your words? They will go back to Jerusalem and give the Sanhedrin a bad report about you."

Loudly he replied to me, "Every plant not planted by my Father, will be yanked up by the roots. Leave these blind guides alone. If the blind lead the blind, both will fall into a hole."

The Pharisees said, "Are you calling us blind?"

"If you admitted your blindness, you would not be guilty of sin. But because you say to everyone who will listen, 'I have clear vision and can see clearly the path to God,' your guilt remains."

I and several other disciples asked Jesus more about ritual purity and uncleanness.

Jesus said, "Do you also have no understanding? Don't you see? Anything that enters a person from the outside, cannot make them unclean? It does not go into their heart, but enters the stomach and passes out of the body, as all food does. But the things that come out from a person, from their heart, these are the things that make a person unclean. Out of a person's heart comes evil thoughts, adultery, fornication, murder, theft, lust, wickedness, deception, slander, pride, blasphemy, and foolishness. All these evil things come from within a person's heart and make them unclean. But to eat with unwashed hands, does not make a person unclean."

Jesus went to the synagogue in Capernaum, and preached. He told the congregation, "You come to me because you ate the loaves and had your bellies filled. But do not let your stomach, appetite, and worldly lusts lead you to seek food that does not last. Seek instead, those things that last forever – those things the Son of Man will give to all those who have the Father's seal engraved upon them.

They asked, "What then must we do, to please God?"

"Have faith in the one whom God has sent."

"What sign from God will you do, to prove you are from God? Our forefathers ate manna from heaven in the wilderness. The Scriptures say, 'God gave them bread from heaven to eat.'"

Jesus said, "It was not Moses who gave you bread from heaven. It was not his sign. It is my Father who gives the true bread from heaven. Did you not recognize God's bread in the multiplication of the leaves and fish? The true manna from God is the one who came down from heaven, the one who gives life to the Cosmos."

"I am the bread of life. All who come to me, will never be hungry. Those who have faith in me, will never be thirty. But you have no faith. Everyone the Father gives me, will come to me. And those who come to me, will never be sent away. I have come down from heaven, not to do my own will, but to do will of the One who sent me. This is the will of the One who sent me - that I not lose any of those He has given to me, but lift them up again on the Last Day. This is the will of my Father, that all who see the Son of Man, and believe in him, have never-ending life. And I will lift them up on the Last Day."

The congregation grumbled saying, "Isn't this the son of Joseph the builder? We know his father and mother. They first came here to help us built our synagogue. Then how can he say, 'I have come down from heaven?'"

Jesus said, "Don't whisper among yourselves. No one can come to me, unless my Father calls them. And I will lift them up on the Last Day. It is written in the Prophets, 'They will all be taught by God.' All who hear and have learned from the Father, come to me. No one has seen the Father, only the one who is from God, this One has seen the Father. Anyone who has faith, has never-ending life. I am the bread of life, and give life to those who feed on me. Your ancestors ate manna in the wilderness, but they still died. I am the bread that came down from heaven. Anyone who eats this bread will not die. I am the living bread that came down from heaven. If anyone eats this bread, they will live in the Age to come. The bread I give, is my body. And it gives life to the Cosmos."

They argued among themselves, "How can this man give us his body to eat?"

Jesus said, "Unless you eat the body of the Son of Man, and drink his blood, you have no life in you. Whoever eats my body, and drinks my blood, has never-ending life. And I will lift him up on the Last Day. My body is true food and my blood is true drink. Those who eat my body and drink my blood remain in me, and I in them. The living Father has sent me, and I live because of the Father. Likewise, those who feast on my body, will live because of me. The bread that came down from heaven, is not like the manna your fathers ate, and yet died. Those who eat this bread will live forever."

When they heard this, many who had been following Jesus, got up and left saying, "This is an impossible teaching. Who can accept this?"

Jesus answered them, "Are you offended by my words? The Spirit gives life to the body. The body by itself is of little value. The Scriptures say, 'God took red dirt and formed the man and breathed

(Spirit) into the man…dirt to dirt, ashes to ashes.' The dead body returns to the dirt from which it came. But the words I speak to you are Spirit, and they are life. Some of you have no faith, and thus have no Spirit. I told you, no one can come to me, unless they are called by my Father. Unless the Spirit comes upon them, they are lifeless dirt."

Hearing these words, many went home and no longer followed Jesus.

Jesus turned to the Twelve, "Don't you want to leave, too?"

Peter said, "Rabbi, where would we go? You have the words of never-ending life. We have faith, and know that you are the Holy One of God."

Jesus said sadly, "I choose the twelve of you. But even one of you is a devil?"

Chuza sent word to Jesus to warn him, "Antipas is searching for you. Leave Capernaum and go somewhere else. Herod wants to kill you."

צ

Chapter VII: On the Run

Looking across the Sea, at Antipas' new capital Tiberias, Jesus said, "Tell that fox, I will continue to drive out demons and heal people, today, tomorrow, and until I reach my goal. No prophet, can die outside Jerusalem."

Knowing Antipas, his was no idol threat. I said to Jesus, "Rabbi, we must leave Galilee immediately."

He said, "We will cross to the Decapolis."

Almost in unison, the disciples said, "Decapolis? That god-forsaken place...why would we go there, rabbi?"

Peter, an expert on navigating the Sea, said, "Rabbi, this is unwise. Soon it will be dark, and it is February. Violent storms suddenly descend on the Sea from the Mediterranean. To cross the full length, in winter and at night, invites disaster."

Jesus said, "Do not fear, Peter. Just have faith."

As we set out in the boat, there was constant grumbling among the four fishermen as they said, "We are risking everything."

After several hours, we sailed past Tiberias. Antipas had inadvertently built the capital over a graveyard, making it an unclean city to devout Jews. A violent storm came upon us. It was as though an evil wind had been sent by the demons that lurked among the graves in Antipas' accursed capital. The waves began to swamp our boat. Jesus remained asleep in the stern. Peter woke him up and said, "Rabbi, help us bail out the boat, or we will all die."

Jesus said, "Why are you so afraid? Do you have no faith?" Standing up, he took hold of the boat's mast with his left hand, then he raised his right. Speaking to the wind and waves he commanded, "Be quiet!"

Everything became calm and still.

None of us said a word, dumbfounded. Jesus returned to the cushion, and laid back down.

I asked Peter, "What kind of man is this? Even the wind and the waves obey him?"

E

We arrived on the shores of the Decapolis, near Hippos, in early morning. As Jesus stepped out of the boat and onto shore, a man met him. He appeared to have come from the nearby tombs. He was naked, his hair matted into clumps, and beard full of filth. His body, well-muscled and strong, had dried blood smeared all over it, from small cuts that covered each of his appendages and chest. Like pagan priests who try to please their deities by punishing their bodies, the man had apparently cut himself attempting to appease the "gods" that tormented him. Inches from Jesus' face, he screamed with a loud deep voice, spittle flying into Jesus face, "What do you want with me, Jesus, Son of the Most High God? I beg you, in God's name, do not torture me."

"What is your name?" Jesus asked.

"My name is Legion," said the multifaceted and inhuman voice, "because there are many of us." They begged Jesus not to send them out of this pagan region, the Decapolis, the home of many Greco-Roman temples and every form of Hellenistic vice and evil.

A large herd of pigs was feeding on the hillside nearby. The demons begged Jesus, "Send us into the pigs, so we may enter into them."

Jesus gave them permission. The demons left the man and entered the pigs. Then the herd ran towards the cliff overlooking the Sea. The entire herd jumped off into the Sea of Galilee, and were drowned.

The pig-keepers ran to Hippos, telling everyone what Jesus had done. They told the residents that Jesus had, "driven out the gods from the man called Legion, and destroyed thousands of holy pigs." The swine had been raised as sacrificial animals for the pagan temples of the Decapolis, to be offered to Zeus, Artemis, Bacchus, and the other deities.

When the people arrived, and looked over the cliff, they were appalled at the financial loss, and worried their gods would be angry at them. They went to Jesus. The man who had the legion of demons was seated next to him, clothed, and in his right mind. Terrified at what their gods would do to them for these sacrileges, the people begged Jesus, "You are a Jew, accursed by our gods. Leave us, depart from our shores, before you bring the wrath of our gods down on us."

Jesus climbed back into the boat with his disciples. The man who had been delivered from the demons begged to go with us.

Jesus refused saying, "Go to your home, to your friends and family. Tell them all the wonderful things the God of Moses has done for you, and how the one true God has had mercy on you."

He left and did as Jesus said. Later, we heard many stories about him, how he had gone through the cities of the Decapolis, telling about the wonderful thing Jesus had done for him. This produced a fervent desire among the people of the Decapolis, to hear and see Jesus for themselves, because of this man's testimony.

Due to the danger of returning to Capernaum or Galilee, we decided to sail along the eastern seashore to the hometown of Peter, James, John and Andrew - Bethsaida, a few miles east of Capernaum. We would leave the boat there, and journey on to Lebanon - to Tyre and Sidon.

When we reached Bethsaida, someone recognized Jesus, a Pharisee who began to criticize our rabbi. When the man left, Jesus spoke to us as we walked along the road, "What can I compare these people to? They are like children. John came not feasting or drinking - and they said, 'He has a demon.'

"When the Son of Man came, both feasting and drinking, they said, 'Look, a glutton and a drunkard, a friend of tax-collectors and all kinds of evil people.'"

Then Jesus began to condemn the towns where most of his miracles had been done, because the people did not heed his words, or turn from their sins. He said, "Condemnation is yours, Chorazin! And woe to you, Bethsaida, for if the wonders performed in your midst were done in Tyre and Sidon, they would have turned from their sin long ago, in sackcloth and ashes. I tell you, Tyre and Sidon will receive a more lenient sentence on Judgment Day, than you. And what of you, Capernaum? You were exalted, and received many miracles from heaven. But you will be thrown down into the Abyss. If the miracles performed in your midst, had been done in Sodom, they would have repented - and the city of Sodom would still exist today. I tell you, Sodom will be judged less severely on Judgment Day than you, Capernaum."

Then Jesus said, "I thank you, Father, that you have hidden Your plans from the intelligent and wise, but have revealed them to simple children," motioning to us.

"Everything has been revealed to me by my Father. No one knows the Son, only the Father. And no one knows the Father, only the Son - and those whom the Son chooses to reveal Him to. Come to me, all of you who are weary or overburdened, and I will give you rest. Take my yoke upon your shoulders and learn from me. I am gentle and humble. You will find rest in me. My yoke is easy to carry, and it is has little weight.

After several days of walking, we arrived in the region of Tyre and Sidon. We went to stay at a house, not wanting anyone to know Jesus was there. But word had preceded his arrival, such was his fame. Even in this pagan place, there was no anonymity. Not being safe, we didn't stay long. Soon, we returned the way we had come, traveling back to the Decapolis.

The man called "Legion" because of the many demons that had afflicted him, had spread news of Jesus not only in Hippos, but across the entire region of the Decapolis. Because of the man's testimony, Jesus now received an eager welcome from many people. They were excited to see what miracles he would do, and hear what he would teach.

When we arrived in the area, one of the residents recognized Jesus. Soon a small crowd gathered, and a deaf man was brought to him. The man also had a severe speech impediment. They begged Jesus to lay hands on him, that he might be healed.

After leading the deaf man away from the crowd, Jesus placed his fingers into the man's ears. Then he spat on his finger and touched the man's tongue.

Looking up into the sky, Jesus sighed deeply and said, "Ephphatha" (Aramaic for "Be opened").

Hesitantly the man said, "I…can speak…clearly…and hear!"

Wanting to remain as anonymous in the region as possible, Jesus ordered the man not to tell anyone about this miracle. But immediately, he went back to the crowd and shouted, "It is a miracle. I can both hear and speak. This man, Jesus, does everything well, even making deaf men hear, and the mute speak."

We camped in the desolate countryside of the Decapolis, far from any town. But when news spread among the gentile population that Jesus had come, large crowds soon came to Jesus, seeking healing and wanting to hear his words.

For three days, Jesus healed the sick and taught the crowd. Beginning with God's creation of the Cosmos, continuing with the story of Abraham and God's plan for salvation, he instructed them in the Law and Prophets, and the ways of God.

When he finished, Jesus called the twelve of us together and said, "I am concerned for the people. They have remained with us for three-days, and have had nothing to eat. If I send them home with no food, they may collapse on the way. Many have come a long distance."

We answered, "Rabbi, in this deserted place, where can we buy bread to feed such a large crowd?"

"How many loaves do you have with you?

"Seven, and a few dried fish from Magdala."

"Give them to me." Then he commanded the people to sit down on the ground. Taking the seven loaves and the fish, he blessed them with the thanksgiving prayer. He broke the loaves and fish and handed everything to us to distribute among the crowds.

Everyone ate until they were full, more than four-thousand people. Then we gathered the leftover pieces, filling seven baskets.

Bringing the baskets of left-overs to Jesus he asked, "Do you understand the significance of collecting seven baskets of leftovers?"

None of us said anything, confused by what the rabbi was asking.

"And the multiplication of the loaves on the other side of the Sea, how many baskets of leftovers were collected?"

"Twelve," I said.

"What was the significance of the Twelve baskets of leftovers?"

"...was it symbolic of the Twelve tribes of Israel?" Peter said hesitantly.

"Yes. If there were twelve baskets of leftovers collected when the Children of Israel were fed, what is the significance of the seven baskets of leftovers collected here in the Decapolis?"

"...standing for the gentiles?" I asked.

Jesus said, "The Law of Moses lists the seven heathen peoples God drove out of the Promised Land - 'the Hittites, Girgashites, Amorites, Canaanites, Perizzite, Hivites and Jevusites, seven nations larger and stronger than you.' So, what do the seven baskets symbolize?" None of us answered.

"It means," said Jesus. "that even though the pagan nations are more numerous and appear mighty, God's word is more powerful than they are. The nations will bow before the victory of God's salvation."

After sending the people home, we climbed into the boat and went across to Magdala.

As we neared shore Jesus said, "Be careful. Beware of the yeast of the Pharisees and Sadducees.

It was then we realized, we had forgotten to bring the leftover bread with us. Peter whispered, "The rabbi is angry that we forgot the bread."

"Why are you whispering among yourselves about forgetting bread? Do you still have so little understanding? Don't you remember the five loaves that fed five-thousand, and how many leftovers were collected? Don't you remember the seven loaves that fed four-thousand, and how many baskets of leftovers were collected? I am not talking about bread. You must beware of the yeast of the Pharisees and of the Sadducees, which is hypocrisy. As you know, Passover preparations include a careful search to cleanse the house of any remaining yeast. Yeast is symbolic of sin, and quickly spreads. A tiny amount in one piece of dough will quickly spread to the entire batch. No piece of the dough is safe from the spread of yeast, just as sin spreads quickly in a person's life, leaving no part safe from its infection. Likewise, if yeast invades the body, and it spreads throughout, it will bring death to the body.

The yeast of the Pharisees and Sadducees is their hypocrisy. They are like actors on a stage. Outwardly, the mask they wear appears holy and righteous. But behind the mask, they lack faith or true understanding of God. Instead, they are full of sin and evil."

Reaching shore at dusk, we immediately went to Mary's house, and spent the night there. We were careful not to let anyone know

Jesus was here, Magdala being so near to Antipas' capital (4 miles from Tiberias). After spending the night in Mary's house, early the next morning, we sailed across to Bethsaida.

Passing through town, someone recognized Jesus and brought a blind man to him, begging that he heal him. Jesus led the man outside of town. He spit in the man's eyes and asked, "What do you see?"

Opening his eyes, the man looked at Jesus, then at people passing by on the road. He said, "I see people. But they look like walking trees."

Then Jesus put his hands on the man's eyes. Removing them, Jesus asked, "Now what do you see?"

He stared at Jesus, tears coming to his eyes. Then he looked at all of us. Turning he looked at the countryside. Both crying and smiling at the same time he said, "It is so beautiful…The fields are so beautiful. I can see the beauty of all God's creation."

Jesus told him, "Don't go back into town, or tell anyone about this. Go to your home with joy. Quietly praise God, for all He has done for you."

As we left, continuing down the road to the next town, I asked Jesus, "Why did you need to heal the blind man twice?"

"He had two different diseases, requiring two different kinds of healing," said Jesus. "His eyes needed to be restored. But his mind also needed healing. And there is a third kind of blindness, even more severe than this man's, that of having a heart that is blind to God and deaf to His voice."

Jesus led us north. We entered Herod Philip's Tetrarchy. Philip is Antipas' brother. The next day we came to Philip's capital, Caesarea Philippi. Jesus led us toward the Grotto of Pan. When it became clear where Jesus was taking us, Peter asked, "Rabbi, why are we going to this evil place?"

"You will see."

As we neared the Grotto, many evil things were taking place, in the woods and among the bushes. I could hear sounds of sensual ecstasy. Every form of sexual misdeed forbidden by Moses' Law was taking place around us, among the hedges and bushes, the "Panic sex" Greeks and Romans deemed pleasing worship for the deity. Pan is the horned god, half-human and half goat - in the Hebrew mind, Satan incarnate. Pan is "the Beast" who calls to our baser instincts, tempting us to toss aside all spiritual restraints and give in to the lusts of the flesh. Reveling in corporeal and material pleasures of the here and now, all vows of marriage or concepts of familial loyalty as shattered, as each person focuses on the temporal self, the autonomous One, the "god within," who longs to be master, lord, and god of his or her own life. Nothing illustrates the stark contrast between the Jewish and Greco-Roman worldviews of life and religion than the stark contrast between the Hebrew God, YHVH, versus the animalistic, Pan.

When we came to a spot where we could clearly see Pan's Grotto, Jesus stopped. In front of us stood Pan's shrine, next to the Temple to the Emperor, and the Temple of Zeus. Part of Pan's Grotto was a cave, regarded as an entrance to the Underworld, referred to as the Gates of Hades.

Jesus asked us, "Who do people say the Son of Man is?"

Andrew said, "Some say John the Baptizer come to life again."

I said, "Some say you are Elijah returned."

James said, "Others believe you are Jeremiah, or one of the other prophets come back to life."

"But who do you say I am?" asked Jesus.

Peter answered, "You are God's anointed king, the Messiah, the Son of the living God."

"Simon Bar-Jonah, you are blessed, because flesh and blood did not reveal this to you, but my Heavenly Father. You are Rock (Peter/Cephas). Upon this Rock, I will build my Church. And the Gates of Hades cannot stand against it."

Jesus commanded us not to tell anyone that he was the Messiah. Then he told us that he must go to Jerusalem, suffer greatly under the chief priests and Sanhedrin, and be killed - but rise from the dead on the third day.

Peter said to him, "God forbid! This will never happen to you."

Jesus said to Peter, "Leave me, Satan. You put a stumbling block in front of me. Your thoughts are not focused on the things of God, but on human concerns.

"If anyone wants to follow me, they must forget self and take up their cross. Anyone who tries to preserve their life will lose it. But anyone who loses their life, because of me, will find it. What does a person profit if they acquire the whole cosmos, but at the cost of their own soul? What can a person pay to buy back their soul? Anyone who is ashamed of me and my words, in this faithless and sinful generation, I will also be ashamed of, when the Son of Man comes in the Father's glory, accompanied by his holy angels.

"All who acknowledge me before other people, I will acknowledge to my Father in heaven. But whoever denies me before others, I will deny to my Father in heaven.

"I have not come to bring peace to the world, but a sword. Because of me, 'a man will turn against his father, a daughter against her mother, and a daughter-in-law against her mother-in-law. Your enemies will be members of your own family.'

"Some of you are Zealots, others were raised a Sadducee or a Hellenist, some were raised in the way of the Pharisees - then there are the Essenes. If you take up your cross and follow my teachings, your kinsmen will reject you, just as my kinsmen have rejected me.

"The one who loves father or mother more than me, is not worthy of me. And the one who loves son or daughter more than me, is not worthy of me. Anyone who does not take up their cross and follow me, is not worthy of me.

I asked Andrew, "What is this cross, Jesus is telling us to carry. Does it symbolize something?"

Andrew shrugged his shoulders, "Surely he is not talking about real crucifixion."

We journeyed farther north, to Mt. Hermon. Arriving at the top, a cloud descended upon Jesus and us. It reminded me of Moses climbing to the top of Mt. Sinai. The Scriptures say, "When Moses climbed up the mountain, a cloud covered it, and God's glory remained. The cloud covered the mountain for six days. On the seventh day, God called to Moses from within the cloud." I also thought of the prophet Elijah, who climbed that same mountain, then called Horeb, and spoke to God while enveloped in the cloud, wind and fire.

Jesus appeared transformed, in the midst of the cloud. His face glowed like the sun, just as Moses' face had after speaking to God. Jesus' clothes appeared whiter than white. Two other men appeared and spoke with him. Judging from their conversation, they appeared to be Moses and Elijah.

A bright cloud then covered them and obstructed our view. A whispering voice was heard from within the cloud saying, "This is my beloved Son. In Him I am very pleased. Listen to him."

When we heard the voice, we fell on our faces, trembling with fear, afraid to look. It seemed to be the voice of God.

After a few moments, Jesus said, "Stand up. Do not fear."

When we lifted our faces from the ground and looked up, the cloud had lifted, and no one was standing there, only Jesus.

Climbing down the mountain, he commanded us, "Don't tell anyone about this, until the Son of Man has risen from the dead."

I said to Peter, "What does this 'risen from the dead' mean, that the rabbi keeps talking about? Is it some new kind of teaching?"

K

Leaving Philip's tetrarchy, we came again to Galilee, not wanting anyone to know we were there. Jesus' focus was on teaching the twelve of us. He said, "The Son of Man is going to be delivered into the hands of evil men. They will kill him. When dead and buried, on the third day he will rise." None of us understand what he was talking about, and did not want to ask him about it. I was becoming disenchanted, and wondered about Jesus' mental state. He seemed to make less and less sense, and was sewing dissention everywhere he went. I began to reevaluate what I thought about Jesus. His miracles were undeniable. I couldn't explain them. But Caiaphas, and yes even Antipas, had good reason to fear what Jesus might do. Not only was he unpredictable, but a general revolt could easily be started by him, not necessarily led by him, or even intentionally started by him, begun simply by his unmeasured and controversial teachings. Jesus was a cipher. Most disturbing to me - I felt no closer to knowing his plans or motivations than when we had first met. The other disciples seemed confused too, getting into disagreements with one another over his words and teachings.

Jesus asked, "What were you arguing about on the road?"

Everyone kept quiet, because some were arguing which was Jesus favorite disciple, and which one was Jesus' right-hand man. They were even arguing about who would be prime minister, when Jesus became king, and proclaimed the restored Kingdom of Israel.

Peter, James, and John discussed which of the three would be Jesus' first choice. Matthew had told them Jesus would make him the royal chief steward, since he knew taxes, finance, and several languages.

I avoided the argument. A restored Kingdom of Israel had no appeal to me. What do these foolish fishermen think – that the Romans are going to pack up and sail home to Rome? If the Israelites won the war, by some miracle of God, at what price would victory come? Who would be left alive? Would Jerusalem remain standing, or be a pile of rubble? Would the Temple remain, or be a heap of toppled stones? And the economy - how could people make a living? Do they suppose Rome would still trade with us, and Roman bankers continue to give Israelites loans? Revolutionaries and Zealots rarely consider the true costs of their actions. When they do, it's usually too late - when the bill has already come due.

Sitting down, Jesus called the Twelve to his side and said, "Anyone who wants to be first, must become last, and the servant of all. In the same way, the Son of Man did not come to be served, but to serve, and to give his life as a ransom for many in bondage."

That evening, tax-collectors and other sinners gathered around Jesus, to hear his teaching. When the Pharisees came and saw this, they grumbled, "This man is a friend of evil people, and eats with them."

Hearing the Pharisees' criticism, Jesus said to them, "There was an old man with two sons. The younger son said to his father, 'Give me my share of your estate.' So, the father divided his property between his two sons.

"The younger son then sold his assets, gathered all his belongings, left his family, clan, tribe and Israel, and traveled to a pagan city."

"Looking down on the city from the final hill, the younger son saw all the grandeur and temptations the pagan world has to offer. Below him was the stately beauty of Greece and Rome - impressive temples, beautiful harlots calling to prospective patrons from their porches. An aqueduct provided running water, with an inviting Roman bath in the center of town. Emerging from the bathhouse were prosperous citizens wearing fine togas, their bodies freshly steamed and cleaned, rubbed with olive oil to preserve their skin from the hot noonday sun. A bustling forum offered delectable delicacies that Jews are forbidden to eat. A massive theatre provided daily entertainment to the masses, as did a hippodrome for sporting events. The younger son compared these sights and sounds to his boring Israelite hometown, built of modest black basalt, having roofs made of mud and sticks.

"The younger son joined the pagan lifestyle of his new city. Turning his back on God, Israel, and his family, the younger son squandered all his money on pagan revelry, temple prostitutes, eating swine that had been offered in pagan rituals, and feasting on all sorts of unclean foods. He indulged himself in every form of Hellenistic pleasure, Roman baths, theatre, games, blood sports, and philosophy discussions in the gymnasium.

After the younger son spent all his money, a severe famine came upon the region. He was without food and began to starve. So, he went to work for one of the citizens of that city-state, who sent him into his fields to tend his herd of "sacred pigs." The younger son was so hungry, he longed to eat with the pigs and eat what the swine ate.

"Driven by his hunger, he remembered his homeland and family. The son said to himself, 'My father's servants have more than enough food to eat. But here I am starving to death. I will return to my father and say to him: 'Father, I have sinned against God, and against you. I am not worthy to be called your son. Make me one of your servants.' So, he returned to home.

"In the distance, the father saw his son. Filled with compassion, he ran to him, threw his arms around his son, and kissed him.

"The son said, 'Father, forgive me. I have sinned against God and against you. I am no longer worthy to be called your son.'

"But the father commanded his servants, 'Quick, bring my best robe and put it on him. Put my signet ring on his finger, testifying to all that he has my full authority, as my son. And put sandals on his feet. Bring the fattened calf prepared for the Temple Festival in Jerusalem. Kill it, and let's have a feast to celebrate. This son of mine was dead. But, once again, he is alive. He was lost, but is now found.' So, the entire household began to celebrate.

"The older son was in the fields. When he neared the house, he heard music and dancing. He called to one of the servants and asked what was going on. 'Your brother has returned,' the servant replied, 'and your father has killed the fattened calf, because his son has returned safe and sound.'

"The older brother was angry and refused to go in. So, his father went to him. He pleaded with the older son to join the celebration. But he said, 'Look, all these many years I've slaved for you, and never disobeyed your wishes. But you have never given me so much as a goat to celebrate with my friends. When this son of yours, who has wasted all your money on prostitutes, when he comes home, you slaughter the fattened calf for him!'

"'My son,' the father said, 'you are always with me, and everything I have is yours. We had to celebrate, because your brother was dead, but now has risen from death to life. He was lost, but now is found.'

Then Jesus said, "And so I ask you, Pharisees, why do you refuse to join the celebration?" Jesus then motioned towards the sinners surrounding him, "These brothers and sisters of yours were lost, but now are found."

At this, the Pharisees left, offended by Jesus' comparison. Jesus' parable was all too relevant. Jewish families across Judea and Galilee had wayward sons such as the one Jesus spoke about. Almost every Israelite family had a prodigal or two, led astray by the allures of Hellenistic culture. Many such sons now live in the cities of the Decapolis, Antioch, Alexandria, or even Rome. Not all have entirely turned their back on everything Jewish. Some have. Others live "mixed" lives, retaining elements of Judaism, but also fully participating in pagan life and culture.

Then there are the Jewish sons who have joined the Legions of Rome. Several hundred years ago, it was Jewish mercenaries who helped found the great capital of the Seleucid Empire, Antioch. In the same way, some Jewish sons join Rome's legions, turning their backs on every aspect of Jewish life and culture. For it is impossible to obey Jewish dietary laws, or fulfill the regulations of ritual purity, while under Caesar's command. But the benefits of serving Caesar are numerous and alluring, including full citizenship in Rome.

To receive these great advantages requires a 25-year enlistment. When an Israelite son joins Rome's legions, he turns his back on family, faith, tribe, and nation, until his enlistment is concluded. If one is not killed in battle during those decades, the prodigal is unlikely to return to his Jewish roots, lost for all time and eternity.

Then, Joanna arrived. She brought word from Chuza about Antipas' intentions. She warned Jesus to leave Galilee. Antipas still sought to arrest and kill him. She also told us Chuza was facing increasing opposition in Antipas' court. Some of the Herodian bureaucrats complained that Chuza was squandering money on unworthy causes, was too generous in distributing public funds, and too lenient on tax-collectors who gathered Antipas' taxes.

Jesus told another parable, "There was a very powerful and rich man. He heard that his chief financial minister was spreading money too generously among the people."

We knew who Jesus was talking about. This was a thinly veiled story about Antipas and his chief financial minister, Chuza, who had been helping Jesus, and those of us who followed him.

Jesus continued, "So this powerful man asked his chief minister, 'What is this I hear about you? Give an account of your management, because you can no longer be my financial manager.'

"The manager said to himself, 'What shall I do? My master is taking my job away. I'm not strong enough to dig, and too ashamed to beg. I know what I'll do, so that when I lose my job, people will welcome me into their homes.'

"So the manager called in all who owed his master taxes. He asked the first, 'How much do you owe my master?'

He replied, "'Nine hundred gallons of olive oil.'

"The manager told him, 'Take your bill, sit down, and make it four hundred and fifty.'

"He asked the second, 'How much do you owe?'

"'A thousand bushels of wheat,' he replied.

"'Take your bill and make it eight hundred.'

"When the powerful man heard how shrewd his manager had been, the master laughed. The servant was as crafty as his master."

Jesus said, "Powerful people in this world are shrewder in dealing with their own kind, than are people of the light. Use worldly wealth to gain friends for yourselves, so that when it is gone, you will be welcomed into eternal dwellings.

"No one can serve two masters, both God and Mammon (wealth gained in a dishonest way). Either you will hate the one and love the other, or you will be devoted to the one and despise the other. Choose this day whom you will serve."

Jesus continued, "There was a powerful and rich man who dressed in purple, fine linen, and lived in luxury every day."

This story too, was about Antipas. It is illegal for anyone to wear purple, except for those in power. In Rome, Caesar alone can wear an all purple robe. Caiaphas revels in wearing his robe with a purple fringe. The cost of purple cloth is the same as gold. One pound of purple cloth costs one pound of gold. It requires 100,000 shells to make enough dye to color just the fringe of a robe.

Jesus said, "At the rich man's gate lay a beggar named Lazarus. He was covered in sores and longed to eat anything that might fall from the rich man's table. Even the dogs came and licked his sores.

"The beggar died. God's angels carried him to Abraham's side.

"The powerful man also died, and was buried. In Hades, he was in torment. Looking up, he saw Abraham far away. Lazarus was by his side. The powerful man called, 'Father Abraham, have pity on me. Send Lazarus to dip the tip of his finger in water and drip the drop onto my tongue to cool it. I am in agony in this fire.'

"Abraham replied, 'Son, in your life you received good things, while Lazarus received only bad. But now, he is comforted here in Paradise, but you are in agony. Besides, a great gulf and chasm has been placed between us, so that those who want to come from here to you cannot, nor can anyone cross from you to us.'

"The man answered, 'Then I beg you, father. Send Lazarus to my family. I have five brothers. Let him warn them, so they do not follow me to this place of torment.'

"Abraham said, 'They have Moses and the Prophets to guide them.'

"'No, father Abraham,' said the man, 'they will not listen. But if someone rises from the dead and goes to them, then they will listen and repent.'

"Abraham said, 'If they will not listen to Moses and the Prophets, they will not listen, even to one who rises from the dead.'"

ח

Chapter VIII: O Judah, I Weep for You!

It was nearly time for the Feast of Tabernacles (Sukkot). We left Capernaum for Jerusalem, traveling down the Sea's eastern shore, going through Bethsaida and the Decapolis, avoiding Tiberias, the center of Antipas' authority.

When we arrived in Jerusalem, I went home to Rachel. She told me, "Judas, your father suddenly became sick, while you've been gone…he died."

Shocked, I was silent for a moment, then said, "How?"

"I don't know. One day he collapsed in the Temple. Within a few hours, he died. You should have been here."

It was hard enough to hear of his death. But her last words struck me to the heart. She was right. I should have been here…and yet, I felt strangely relieved. Was I a bad son? Perhaps I was. I grieved that my father was dead. But for the first time in my life, I felt strangely free, for never again would I disappoint my father. Whether I remained in the Temple treasury or not, whether I remained a Sadducee or rejected it for another party, I would no longer feel compulsion or criticism from my father.

"When are you going to return to your job in the Treasury?" Rachel asked. I no longer had a Sadducee father judging my decisions. But I still had a Sadducee wife, the daughter of Caiaphas, who would continue to judge me.

I said, "When you tell me my father has died, do you think it wise to nag me about returning to the Temple?"

"Nagging, is it? I haven't seen my husband for months, and gave birth while he is roaming around Galilee with an itinerate vagabond. I'm saddled with taking care of a newborn, managing our household, and taking care of every aspect of our family, including burying your father. You have a strange definition of nagging. To be nagged, you would have to be present once and awhile. Most people think I'm a widow, since there is no husband anywhere to be found."

Wearily I said, "Do we have to argue about this now?"

"Well, if I wait, you will rejoin your precious rabbi before I have a chance to say anything. Tell me, are you even staying the night, or are you going back to your second wife, your precious teacher?"

She had me there. I had planned to return to Jesus before sunset. I said, "Your father, Caiaphas, gave me this mission. What else should I do?"

"Yes, and I warned about not letting my father run you. You should have stood up to him, at the beginning, and refused to go. You should still do that, now. Go to him tomorrow - tell him you are done following this Galilean rabble."

I spent the night with Rachel. Even though our time together was tense, it reminded me what I was sacrificing to follow Jesus. One thing was certain - the situation couldn't continue. Something had to change.

Ξ

Early in the morning, I went to Caiaphas' palace. He said, "So, our Galilean Messiah has come to the feast, has he?"

"Yes."

"It's time to deal with him, Judas."

"Deal with him how?"

"That is a question we have not agreed upon. Some, like Antipas, want to execute him as quickly as possible. Pilate, has not been as concerned about this strange teacher, since most of the trouble he has caused is in Antipas' domain. The Pharisees are divided about him, and his teachings. As for us, the Sadducees, our only concern is maintaining peace and order in the Temple, among the crowds, and in the city. The thing all of us agree upon - this Jesus should be taken into custody and placed in my dungeon, until we can decide what to do with him."

I said, "This is unwise, father. It will cause more trouble and unrest than it solves. Jesus preaches no revolt. He has insulted the Pharisees and Zealots, and even helped a Roman centurion in Capernaum. He provides a moderating influence over the rebellious rabble. Arresting him will cause unrest and may even cause riots."

Caiaphas replied, "Antipas says that if the mobs did not riot when the Baptizer was arrested and executed, they will not rise up if this Galilean is arrested."

"Do you want to take that chance?"

"It has been decided, Judas. As soon as the Temple Guard can take hold of him, they will bring him before the Sanhedrin. Can you lead them to this Jesus?"

"No. I was at home with Rachel for the night. I would first have to find the rabbi myself."

"Why are you so hesitant to arrest this man, Judas? I thought you were eager to return to your home, child, and wife. Why aren't you rejoicing at the arrest of this false prophet."

"I am eager to return home. But I don't want to make a mistake, making the time I spent with him pointless. You sent me to Jesus to determine his intentions and allegiances. He is not a rebel leader. He is not guilty of the things you feared about him."

"That may be, but he has made clear his hatred for the Sadducees. And you yourself said he is an Essene, one of our mortal enemies."

"I did not say he IS an Essene. He was raised as an Essene. There is a difference."

"The difference escapes me," said Caiaphas.

I excused myself and went to the Temple to find Jesus. Torn by my competing desires and conflicting loyalties, I considered warning Jesus that the Temple Guard was looking for him.

Jesus was teaching in Solomon's Porch. The Judeans gathered there were amazed by his words and asked, "How did this man become so knowledgeable? He never studied in the Temple, under a respected rabbi."

Jesus told them, "My teaching is not my own. It is from the One who sent me. I do not speak on my own authority. Those who speak for themselves, seek their own glory and praise. But the man who is sent, speaking words given to him, seeks praise and glory for the One who sent him. He is faithful, and there is no evil in him."

At the Feast of Tabernacles, the Great Water Procession was celebrated. This had always been one of my favorite Temple traditions. The priests go down the nine-hundred steps, from the Temple to the Pool of Siloam. There, they collect water from the Gihon Spring. Taking the special ceremonial golden ewer, the priests draw water and ascend back up to the Temple, in a great and joyous parade through the Temple's Water Gate. The trumpet (shofar) sounds, and the procession enters the gates of God's Holy House. The priests then carry the water to the altar. After circling it seven times, they pour the water, greatly rejoicing and celebrating, remembering the water that flowed from the rock in the wilderness, when Moses struck it.

Jesus said in a loud voice, in front of the crowd, "To all who are thirsty, let them come to me and drink. Whoever believes in me, as Scripture tells us, rivers of living water will flow from within them."

Once again, Jesus was drawing an unmistakable connection between Moses and himself - Moses the Lawgiver, and Jesus the one who completes the Law. He was also equating himself to the rock from which the water flowed in the wilderness. Throughout the Law and the Prophets, YHVH refers to himself as the Rock.

I thought of the prophet Jeremiah who spoke in God's voice, "My people are guilty of two sins: they have forsaken me, the spring of living water; and they have dug their own cisterns, broken cisterns that are not able to hold water."

And I remembered the prophet Zechariah, "A day of the Lord is coming, Jerusalem. I will gather all the nations to Jerusalem to fight against it. Then the Lord will go out and fight against those nations. On that day, his feet will stand on the Mt. of Olives. The Lord my God will come, and all God's saints with him. On that day, there will be neither sunlight nor cold, or frosty darkness. On that day, living water will flow out from Jerusalem, half of it east to the Salt Sea and half of it west to the Mediterranean - in summer and in winter. On that day, the Lord will be king over the whole earth."

Hearing Jesus' words, some of the people said, "Surely this man is the prophet who is to come."

Others said, "He is the Anointed One (Messiah)."

Still others asked, "How can the Messiah come from Galilee? The Scriptures tell us the anointed king will come from David's line and descendants, from David's town, Bethlehem, where King David was from." So, the people were divided over Jesus.

Also present were many pilgrims from across the Roman Empire and beyond, mostly Hellenized Jews, many who knew neither Hebrew nor Aramaic, but only spoke Greek. Confused by Jesus and the events surrounding him, they had little interest in a new Israelite Messiah (king), or in a reestablished Kingdom of Israel. Their lives were lived in the Greco-Roman world. These controversies were of little importance to them.

Σ

The Temple Guard arrived. Knowing the captain, Malchus, I took him aside and asked, "What do you think of Jesus the Branch (Nazarene)?"

"He is certainly intriguing, not the typical Zealot half-wit, who is thirsty for Roman blood."

I quizzed him further, "Do you think it wise for the Sanhedrin to arrest him now, and in this place?"

"Perhaps not, but that is Caiaphas' order."

"And what of your own safety? Do you think the Sanhedrin has clearly considered that?"

"What do you mean, Judas?"

"The Temple Guard is not very large. What are your few men in comparison to this huge crowd? What if the mob decides to oppose you, to save Jesus from arrest?" I pointed at Peter. "Do you see that man there? Look at his belt. What do you see?"

Malchus turned his head, looking intensely at Peter. "A Roman short sword? Why is he carrying that in the Temple?"

"That, Malchus, is Jesus' closest disciple, his right-hand man. Do you see how strong he is? He's a fisherman by trade, a real brawler." Then I pointed to Simon, sometimes called the Zealot. "Do you see that man?" Malchus jerked his head to stare at Simon. "He is a Zealot daggerman. Malchus, look at the rest of crowd. There are thousands of Galileans present. How many do you think are Zealots with daggers under their tunics, ready to stab in the gut anyone they consider a Roman collaborator?"

"I hadn't thought about that," said Malchus.

"But I have, my friend. Let me help you. Jesus will be staying outside the city, tonight, and will be leaving the region in the morning. Why sacrifice your life, and that of your men, for a problem that is leaving town on his own two legs? Go back to Caiaphas and tell him it was not possible to arrest the Galilean prophet. You know the High Priest is my father-in-law. I will back you up in this, on one condition…"

Eagerly Malchus asked, "And what condition is that?

"You owe me, my friend. If I need help in the future, you owe me."

"Agreed," said Malchus. He and the Guard withdrew.

Jesus and the disciples left the Temple in late afternoon. I then went to Caiaphas' chambers in the Temple. Malchus soon arrived to meet with Annas and Caiaphas.

Caiaphas asked, "Where is the Galilean troublemaker you were sent to arrest, Malchus?"

He replied, "No one ever spoke the way this man does."

"Don't tell me this madman has deceived you too?"

A Pharisee leader of the Sanhedrin was also present and said, "No one in the Sanhedrin approves of him. The Pharisee scholars reject his teaching. Only the unlearned rabble, those who know nothing about the Law, the accursed and unwashed mob, they are the only ones who listen to this man."

Malchus said, "We are not deceived by this man. But have you seen the miracles he does in front of the crowds? Have you heard what he says to the mob, and how they eagerly accept every word he speaks? There was no way to make our way through the crowds, and take the man into custody. Even if we had reached him, how do you think his adoring masses would have reacted to his arrest? His followers were armed."

A Pharisee member of the Sanhedrin, Nicodemus, spoke, "Are we so forgetful of the Law, that we now judge a man guilty, before we hear his defense for what he has done?"

Annas replied to him, "Are you from Galilee, too? Look into it, Nicodemus. No prophet comes from Galilee."

Being a Sadducee, perhaps Annas was not well versed in the prophets. But even I recalled that the prophet Jonah was from Galilee. If that were not enough, Jonah's hometown was located virtually on the same ground as Nazareth.

Caiaphas commanded everyone to leave his presence, except Annas, Malchus, and me. Caiaphas said to Malchus, "You were wise, today. Clearly this man must not be arrested in the Temple, while surrounded by his followers. This will only create a violent response. We will wait until the Galilean can be quietly arrested at night, or in a deserted place, when he is not surrounded by crowds. Judas, it is your duty to lead Malchus to the man, when he is asleep or alone."

I said, "Jesus is staying outside the City tonight, and is leaving the region in the morning."

"Very well," said Caiaphas. "we will bide our time until he returns to Jerusalem. But when he returns, Judas, you lead the Temple Guard to the Galilean." I nodded, yes.

Π

Jesus and the Twelve left the region of Jerusalem. But the places he could safely go were fewer by the day. Whenever someone recognized Jesus, throngs would gather around him. Danger to Jesus from the authorities was now pervasive. It was not safe anywhere in Galilee, because Antipas and the Herodians were on constant watch for him there. Most Pharisee leaders hated him, and had declared him a blasphemer. The region around Jerusalem was not safe, because the Sadducees wanted his arrest. Even Pilate had alerted his forces to watch for Jesus, in Judea and Samaria. The safest places in Judea were in small Essene communities, located in the sparsely populated hill country, or in the Judean wilderness, which is where we remained for a time.

Then we went to Bethany, only a few miles from Jerusalem. It was an Essene town. Jesus had friends there – Lazarus and his two sisters, Mary and Martha. All three lived celibate lives dedicated to God. Celibacy was accursed by Sadducees, Pharisees and most other Jews, who thought God's command to "be fruitful and multiply," was of primary importance. But celibacy was widely practiced among the Essenes, viewing it as a superior way to serve God with all one's heart. It was one of the Essene practices John the Baptizer and Jesus both honored.

Lazarus and his two sisters eagerly welcomed us into their home. Mary, sat at Jesus' feet, enthralled by his every word. But Martha was harried and overwhelmed by cooking and serving a houseful of guests.

Martha went to Jesus and said, "Rabbi, don't you care that my sister has left me to do all the work alone? Tell her come help me."

Jesus stood up, and tenderly placed his hand on Martha's cheek to comfort her. Smiling and looking into her eyes he said, "Martha, Martha, you are worried about many things. But at this moment, only one thing is important. Mary has chosen that one good thing. And it will not be taken away from her."

T

The Feast of Dedication drew near. The Sanhedrin would be particularly antsy, at this time of year. The Feast of Dedication concerns Israel's deliverance from its cruel Greek ruler, Antiochus Epiphanes, and the creation of an independent Israelite Kingdom, God's Kingdom, some two-hundred years earlier. This has always been a feast when Zealots cause unrest and trouble. Every year, rebels wave palm branches through the streets of Jerusalem and in the Temple courts, because the palm branch was the symbol of a restored and independent Israelite kingdom. By waving them at the feast, Israelites showed they remained unbowed and undefeated, even in the face of Roman rule.

It was not safe for Jesus in Jerusalem. But he went to the festival, nonetheless. While in the city, I stayed away from Caiaphas and the Sanhedrin. They were sure to demand I lead Malchus and the Temple Guard to the rabbi, to arrest him. While in the Temple, crowds surrounded Jesus. So, the authorities could do little to arrest him. At night, he stayed outside the city, sleeping at Bethany, or at the olive press (Gethsemane), on the Mt. of Olives.

While Jesus was teaching in the Temple, Pharisee rabbis brought a woman to him. She had been caught in the act of adultery. They hoped to trap Jesus in his words, or to have an accusation to bring against him to the Sanhedrin.

They made the woman stand in front of the crowd as they asked Jesus, "Rabbi, this woman was caught in the act of adultery. The Law of Moses tells us to stone such women. What do you think? Should we stone her?"

Jesus bent down and wrote with his finger in the dirt. He scribbled the commandment, "You shall not commit adultery." Under that he wrote, "I will not punish your daughters when they turn to prostitution, or your daughters-in-law when they commit adultery, because the men consort with harlots and sacrifice with pagan temple prostitutes. A people with no understanding will come to ruin."

The Pharisees questioned Jesus again, "Well rabbi, what is your response?"

Jesus stood up and said, "Whichever man among you has no sin, let him be the first to throw a stone on her." Then he knelt down again, and wrote on the ground, "I desire mercy and not sacrifice."

The oldest men had the most sins in need of forgiveness. So, the eldest left first, dropping the stone he held in his hand. One-by-one they all began to scatter, until only a few teenagers remained. Seeing they were alone, they too dropped their stones and walked away. When everyone had left, Jesus stood up and asked the woman, "Where are your accusers? Has no one condemned you?"

"No, not one," she said.

"Then neither do I condemn you, daughter. Go and sin no more."

I said to Jesus, "Rabbi, the Pharisees and Sadducees will now accuse you of opposing Moses' Law?"

"What does the Law say about adultery, Judas?"

"It says a woman caught in adultery must be stoned."

"You are mistaken, Judas. The Law of Moses says, 'If a man commits adultery with another man's wife - both the adulterer and the adulteress must be put to death.' A woman does not commit adultery by herself. This woman was discovered in the act of adultery. Where is the man who was defiling her? By bringing only the woman for judgement, her accusers were breaking Moses' Law.

ϒ

Walking to the Temple the next day, we saw a man who had been blind from birth. We asked Jesus, "Rabbi, whose sin caused this man's blindness, his or his parent's?"

"Neither," said Jesus, "this happened to demonstrate God's glory and mercy through him. As long as there is daylight, we must do the work of the One who sent me. Night will come soon enough. Then no one can work. While I am in the world, I am the light of the world."

Jesus spit into his hand and made some mud with his saliva. Then he put the mud on the man's eyes. "Go," he told the blind man, "wash in the Pool of Siloam."

I asked Jesus, "Why have you sent him so far, rabbi? How will a blind man walk from the Temple, down the nine-hundred steps to the Pool of Siloam to wash? Wouldn't it have been better to send him to the Pool at Bethesda? It is much closer."

Jesus said, "Many believe Bethesda's waters bring healing to whichever person first enters the water, after it has been stirred by the water-spirits. Do you remember the paralyzed man sitting by Bethesda? I did not tell him, nor would I tell anyone, to wash in those demon-filled waters for healing.

I sent this blind man to Siloam to test his faith. A man must have much faith to stumble one's way down the nine-hundred steps to Siloam. If his faith is strong enough to complete the journey, he will be healed."

The blind man went, washed in the Pool of Siloam, and came back able to see.

Φ

We went into the Temple, to Solomon's Porch. Many rabbis belonging to the Pharisee party were teaching their disciples there. When Jesus appeared, a multitude gathered around him. A mood of excitement filled the crowd. But when the people turned from the Pharisees to hear Jesus, the rabbis became angry.

One of the Pharisees asked sarcastically, "How long will you keep us guessing? Tell us clearly, if you are the Messiah."

Jesus said, "I have told you, but you have no faith. The deeds I do, in my Father's name, are my witnesses. You do not believe, because you are not one of my sheep. I am the Shepherd of Israel. My sheep listen to my voice. I know them, and they follow me. I give them never-ending life, and they will never die. No one will remove them from my hand. My Father, who has given them to me, is greater than everyone. No one can steal them from my Father's hand. I and the Father are one and the same."

The Pharisee shouted, "Blasphemy! Wouldn't we be justified to stone you right now?" The other Pharisee rabbis agreed with him and began to chant, "Stone this blasphemer."

A scuffle began. The Pharisees, and their disciples, rushed forward to grab Jesus, to drag him to the stoning place, located outside the city's western gate. An abandoned stone quarry near the hill where the Romans crucified those judged guilty of treason, such as Zealots. Massive amounts of rock had been removed from the quarry for Herod's building projects, producing a cliff sixty-feet above the bottom. Those deemed worthy of stoning were thrown down from the cliff into the pit below. If the condemned person survived the fall, the mob would then take large rocks, laying nearby, and heave them on the person below, deliver the fatal blows.

Jesus' disciples, and his others supporters, surrounded him in a protective ring. Jesus shouted to the mob of Pharisees, "I have done many good deeds and miracles, in the name of my Father. For which of these good deeds do you want to stone me?"

The Pharisee who began the ruckus shouted back, "We are not stoning you for good deeds, but for blasphemy. You are merely a man, like all of us. But you are claiming to be God."

Jesus shouted to him and the crowd, "Listen and learn, you hypocrites. The Psalm say, 'You are gods. You are all sons of the Most High.' If the Father calls those to whom He gave the word of God, 'gods', and the Scriptures cannot be ignored, then what about the One that God has set apart, God's Son - the Son of Man, having sent him into the world? How can you accuse me of blasphemy? Don't believe in me, unless I do God's work. But if I am doing the Father's work, then even though you have no faith in me, you should believe in the deeds that I have done. You must come to know and understand that the Father is in me, and I am in the Father."

This just enraged the Pharisees more. They shouted, "Blasphemer! Stone the blasphemer." Once again they tried to grab Jesus. But we shook free of the mob and quickly left, not only the Temple, but Jerusalem too.

Events were racing out of control. Rather than smoothing things over and calming troubled waters, every word Jesus spoke fed the growing storm of unrest that swirled around him.

Ravenous wolves now surrounded Jesus, not just the Roman or Herodian breeds. His opponents, now numerous, sought to grab and bite him any way they could.

The Pharisees were divided. A few counted themselves as Jesus' supporters. But the majority, especially the most revered rabbis, were adamantly opposed to him, offended by his sharp criticisms, and bitter he called them hypocrites.

Zealots were also divided. Most viewed Jesus as too mild and forgiving. But some still hoped he would proclaim a new Kingdom of Israel, announce himself Messiah, and call for a general muster of the populous to expel the pagan Romans.

Hellenistic Jews found Jesus too legalistic and conservative for their tastes.

The only groups that gave Jesus unwavering support, were the poor and common people, outcasts, sinners, tax-collectors, Samaritans, and some of the Essenes. But many of the Essenes had also rejected him, because he no longer followed the solar calendar, choosing to celebrate the feasts according to the lunar calendar that Pharisees and Sadducees use.

X

The Twelve followed Jesus down the Jericho road to the Jordan, to the place where John had preached, I first met John, and where Jesus was baptized. There we remained. The crowds began to come to him there, just as they had come to hear the Baptizer. The focus of Jesus' ministry had changed. Before, most of his followers were Galileans. But now, his audience was increasingly Judean. Those who came to Jesus at the Jordan said, "Everything John said about this man is true." And many had faith in him.

We wintered in the warmth of the Jordan Valley, a good place to make a quick escape, if necessary. If Antipas learned of Jesus location in Perea, on the eastern banks of the Jordan, we could cross the river into Judea, Pilate's domain. While on the western bank, if Pilate or the Sanhedrin sent soldiers to arrest Jesus, we could cross to Antipas' realm, and then go to the Decapolis, which was only a short distance farther north. Even so, we never slept more than one night in the same place.

This was the Essene heartland, close to the Salt Sea (Dead Sea). The largest of the Essene monastic centers, Qumran, was nearby. Many Essenes had believed in the Baptizer. Now, many of them also believed in Jesus.

I returned home to Rachael several times that winter, and spent time with you, my young son. But just as Jesus had stirred unrest everywhere he went, conflict also followed me home. Rachel was increasingly angry, demanding I end my pilgrimage with "this strange Galilean," as she called him. She gave little credence to her father's concerns about Jesus, nor did she understand my eagerness to continue a mission that seemed to her a waste of time, a pointless endeavor. Each time I came home, her anger grew. Her rage was not just directed at me, but at her father, and Jesus too.

Besides, there was no fooling her. She had sensed, long before, there was more to my following Jesus than merely fulfilling a mission given by Caiaphas. She could tell by the way I talked about the rabbi, that he had largely won me over, that in some sense, I truly viewed him as my rabbi.

A few weeks after the incident at the Feast of Dedication, Rachel and I had a new argument. Well…not a new argument - the same one we had whenever I returned home. She said, "How can you love this strange rabbi more than your son and me?"

"My little lamb, you know I love you more than the world."

"No you don't, Judas. If you did, you would be home with us, not wandering all over Israel to every flea-bitten village your rabbi leads you too."

"You don't understand, my love."

"Then explain it to me."

"I…I can't."

"Why not? If it's so important, you should be able to explain it to me."

"There's something about him."

"What?"

"I don't know…he's unlike anyone I've ever known."

"If he's so special, why don't you divorce me and marry him?"

Grabbing Rachel by the shoulders and looking deep into her beautiful brown eyes I said, "I would…but Jesus is celibate."

"Very funny. But I think you are mistaking yourself for Aristophanes," she replied.

We both laughed. I hugged her and said, "You know how much I love you, and our son. But trust me. I know what I'm doing (I didn't)."

"Alright, husband," she replied, "like Odysseus' faithful wife, Penelope, I will support your Trojan Horse endeavor…a little longer. Mind you, only a little longer. I will give you until the Passover. During that time, you must defeat Troy, slay the Cyclopes, and make your way back home. But Judas, I warn you, when the Passover begins, if you are not back home to stay, then I am going to welcome into my home all suitors who are interested in a like new and slightly used wife. Do you understand me, Judas?"

"Yes, my little lamb, I promise to be back home…by Passover, if not sooner."

Ψ

Later, when Passover neared, Jesus led us from the Jordan, without telling us where we were going. As we walked west, the Twelve became concerned. Thomas asked, "Rabbi, where are we going?"

Jesus said, "We are going up to Jerusalem." Then he stopped and said, "The Son of Man will be betrayed to the High Priest and Sanhedrin. They will condemn him to death, and bring him to the Romans, who will mock and whip him, spit upon him, and kill him. On the third day, he will rise again." Then, once again, Jesus turned and started walking. All of us were dumbfounded. Not knowing what to say, we said nothing.

I whispered to Thomas, "Does the rabbi have a close confident among the Sanhedrin who has told him these things?" He shrugged his shoulders in unknowing ignorance.

I said to myself, "Jesus must have a spy of his own. How else could he know the High Priest's intentions and plans, or those of the Sanhedrin." For a long time, I had wondered if Jesus knew my true identity - that I was a wolf in sheepskin...or a sheep in wolf's fur...or a combined abomination, a chimera who betrays both sides, a traitor who offends all. Yes...that might be who I am, a scorpion, an unclean insect that stings and hurts anyone who draws near. I wished Jesus could tell me my true identity, for I ached to know, and to discover my eternal destiny...whether it was to spend eternity in heaven or hell...that is, if Sadducees believed in paradise or hades...which they don't. Was I a demon of the dark domain, or an angel of light...but Sadducees don't believe in those things either. The almighty denarii, shekels, and sesterces - earthly pleasure, power, and might - unrighteous Mammon, these are the immutable tenets of Sadducee faith, heaven in the here and now, not in the hereafter. And yet...even though I was far remove from all the treasures that are so near and dear to the Sadducee heart, I still could not turn my back upon the Tribe of Levi to which I was born and belonged. My wife who is the daughter of Caiaphas, and my infant son who will be a Sadducee priest and Levite - what of them? I could not turn by back on my family. But could I turn my back on my Galilean rabbi, Jesus the Branch of David?

Walking down the road, filled with shame, the stench of betrayal oozed from my pores. I could not lift my head, sure that anyone who looked into my eyes, would see my sin, obvious and on full display, as though my pupils had "traitor" written across them. I was convinced that anyone who looked at my face, would see my true identity - Caiaphas' spy.

Ω

When we walked through Jericho, passing down the street, Jesus looked up into a tree and saw a man above him, sitting on a branch. Jesus said, "What is your name, brother?"

"Zacchaeus."

"Zacchaeus, why are you in a tree?"

"Rabbi, as you can see, my legs are very short. I could not see you over the crowd. So, I climbed this tree."

"Hurry, come down from there, Zacchaeus. Such perseverance must be rewarded. I will be a guest in your home tonight."

The man climbed down, and we followed Zacchaeus to his house. Going inside I heard some of the Pharisees complain, "Why has the rabbi gone to stay with this evil man. Jesus must have little discernment, if he doesn't know the chief tax-collector for the area is an evil man, made wealthy by cheating his fellow Judeans out of as much money as he can squeeze, extorting every dime from anyone he gets his hands on."

At dinner, Jesus spoke to Zacchaeus for a long time. Deeply moved, the chief tax-collector regretted his wicked lifestyle. Filled with love for God, he stood up and said, "Look rabbi, I will give half of all I own to the poor. And to anyone I have extorted, I will pay them back, four-times as much as I took from them."

Jesus said, "Zacchaeus, today this house has been spared from God's coming wrath. This prodigal son of Abraham has returned to the fold, and to his flock. This is why the Son of Man, the Shepherd of Israel, came into the world. He has come to seek and to save the lost lambs of Israel."

I mumbled to Matthew, who himself had been a tax-collector under Antipas, "Isn't it enough that the rabbi has Antipas chasing him and wanting him dead. Does he also have to subvert Pontius Pilate's chief tax-collector too? Romans do not take such offenses kindly, without exacting revenge."

Matthew replied, "Would you rather Zacchaeus remain lost to God and our nation?"

I grumpily said, "It's not that. I wish the rabbi would consider the political ramifications of his actions. There is such a thing as practicality and pragmatism."

Matthew shrugged, "When Jesus reestablishes the Kingdom of Israel, all the tax-collectors will be working for him anyway."

I said to myself, "My God! Am I the only one who sees things clearly? Am I surrounded by fools?"

Mary and Martha sent word to Jesus at Jericho. Lazarus was seriously ill and might die. They asked him to come at once. Jesus said, "This illness will not result in death, but bring glory to God. The Son of Man will be glorified in this."

Jesus loved Martha, Mary, and Lazarus. They had much in common. When they were together, they could talk the night away. So, it surprised us when we remained in Jericho. After several days, Jesus said, "Let us go to Bethany."

We said to Him, "Rabbi, the Judeans tried to stone you last time you went near Jerusalem. Are you going there again?"

Jesus said, "There is twelve hours of light in a day. If anyone walks in the daylight, he does not trip and fall, because the light shows him the path. But if one walks in the night, he stumbles and falls, because there is no light for his path." Then he said, "Our friend Lazarus sleeps. I must go and wake him up."

Peter said, "Rabbi, if Lazarus is only sleeping, he will get up on his own. There is no need to go wake him."

Jesus said, "Lazarus is dead. For your sake, I am glad I was not there, so that you will see and believe. Let's go to him."

In resignation, Thomas said to the rest of us, "Let's go with him. If the rabbi is going to his death, we should die with him."

When we arrived at Bethany, Lazarus had already been in the tomb for days. It being only a short walk from Jerusalem, many friends and relatives had come from the city to comfort Martha and Mary.

When Martha was told, "Jesus is approaching," she went to meet Him, while Mary continued to mourn inside the house.

Martha said to Jesus, "Rabbi, if only you had been here, my brother would not have died. Even now, I know anything that you ask of God, He will do for you."

Jesus said to her, "Your brother will rise to life."

Martha said, "Yes rabbi, I know and have faith that God will raise him up at the resurrection, on the Last Day. This is our comfort."

Anyone who believes in me, even though they die, will live. And whoever lives and believes in me, will never die. Do you believe this, Martha?"

"Yes rabbi, I believe that you are God's Anointed One, the Son of Man, the one we have been waiting for."

"Where is Mary? Bring her here."

Martha went into the house and told Mary, "The rabbi has come, and is asking for you." She ran out to meet Jesus. When she came to him, Mary fell at his feet weeping and said, "Rabbi, if only you had been here, my brother would not have died."

When Jesus saw how deeply she was mourning, and saw the grief of the others, he let out a guttural moan of deep pain, suddenly overtaken with uncontrollable sorrow, he wept. Then Jesus cried out, "Where have you placed him?"

"Come and see." Mary and Martha said. All three, weeping together, walked towards the family tomb.

When their friends and relatives from Jerusalem saw Jesus' grief and his uncontrollable weeping, they said, "Do you see how much he loved Lazarus?"

One of the people who had seen Jesus do miracles in the Temple accused him, "This man opened blind eyes, healed the sick, and cured those who were paralyzed. Why didn't he come and stop his friend from dying?"

As they neared the tomb, once again Jesus moaned. The tomb was a cave, with a large stone rolled across its entrance. Jesus said, "Roll away the stone."

Martha said, "Rabbi, there will be a terrible stench. Lazarus has been dead four days."

Jesus said, "Didn't I tell you, if you have faith, you will see God's glory?" They rolled the rock from the tomb. Standing at the entrance, Jesus looked up and said, "Father, thank-you that you hear me. I know you always hear me. But I say this for the sake of everyone around me, so they will see, hear, and know, that You sent me." Then he cried with a loud voice, "Lazarus, come out!"

Everyone was still, silent, shocked at Jesus' words. The silence seemed deafening, lasting for what felt like hours. Then a subtle sound was heard from inside the tomb, a shuffling. Soon a white figure appeared at the tomb's entrance. It was Lazarus - his arms and legs bound by the shroud and wrappings, his face still covered by the burial cloth. Jesus said, "Take off the wrappings and set him free." Mary and Martha kissed Jesus, and hurried to their brother, amazed that the one who had been dead, was now alive once more.

When the mourners from Jerusalem saw this, many believed that Jesus was the Messiah, God's anointed king.

That night, I returned home to spend it with my family. The next morning, I went to the meeting of the Sanhedrin, to see if word had reached them about Jesus and what had happened at Bethany. I expected the Sadducees to be unimpressed by any miracle Jesus might do. Being thoroughly materialistic, scientific, and logical, they had a cold pragmatism, and assumed all things could be reduced to facts and figures, dollars and cents, profit and loss. But I expected the Pharisees to be swayed by the raising of a dead man, even if they had only a grudging awe or respect for Jesus.

Some Pharisees who had witnessed Lazarus' raising, gave their testimony about what they had seen. Every one of them rejected Jesus and his miracle. Each explained it away.

Some said "It's a hoax. This man Lazarus was never dead."

Others said, "Lazarus' family made a mistake when they placed him in the tomb. He was so sick and near death, he only appeared dead. But when time passed in the tomb - four-days, Lazarus woke up." It was just a coincidence that Lazarus awoke at the precise moment Jesus called him out of the tomb.

Still others speculated that someone else's dead body had been placed in the tomb, while the living Lazarus hid waiting to be called forth…or that the real Lazarus died and someone else sprung out of the tomb. Their explanations became ever more outlandish.

Only two Pharisees defended Jesus. Every other member of the Sanhedrin, both Sadducee and Pharisee, rejected the miracle. Their sole concern was how to stop Jesus, destroy his fame, discount his deeds, and make sure he caused them no further trouble.

One of the members of the Sanhedrin wrung his hands and fretted, "What shall we do? This man does many feats of magic, false though they are. If we let Him alone, to continue doing his deeds of wonders, like this one, he will win most people to his cause. If a general revolt arises in the Temple, the Romans will remove Caiaphas from office, and take away the Sanhedrin's power, replacing us all. And you remember how Antiochus Epiphanes placed a statue of Zeus in the Holy-of-Holies. These Romans would do the same, if given enough reason."

Caiaphas stood up and said, "Why are you so dense? You know nothing at all. Why are we struggling with so much worry and concern, all because of one man, a Galilean at that? It is better that one man die for the sake of the people, than for the nation to perish."

I thought about our party. Like all Sadducees before me, I am an honest to God agnostic. Agnostic means "without knowledge," and no one knows less about God than a Sadducee. What we know about God wouldn't fill a thimble. Sadducees like it that way. The less we know, and the less God is involved in our world - the more we are free to live our lives, and run the world the way we see fit, without meddling interference from the Prime Mover of the Universe.

The Sadducee God is an unknowable, unfathomable, and a cold deity. After speaking the cosmos into existence, the Almighty handed Moses five short lists of instructions, the Torah. Then he exited the earthly stage, leaving his favored creatures to direct the play in the way they see fit. Sadducees are interested in the here and now, not the hereafter, content to enjoy paradise in this life, instead of the next.

Being God's chosen people, among the chosen people, the Almighty has blessed us Sadducees with great riches and power, a circular reasoning wherein our material blessings prove we are righteous, otherwise God would not have blessed us so much. Likewise, the plebian dregs of Israel are sinners and unrighteous fools, proved by the fact they are poor and downtrodden. If they were truly righteous, God would have rewarded them with as many material blessings as he did us. But since he has cast his purple robe of majesty on us, not them, we are clearly the righteous ones, no matter how many heinous sins we may commit.

Freed from seeking knowledge about God, we Sadducees can pursue more enjoyable pastimes. Besides the gluttonous accumulation of money and power, we Sadducees are free to baptize our bodies, minds, and senses, in every amusement the Greco-Roman world offers, whether it be theatre, sport, philosophy, or sensual pleasures (within certain limits to avoid outright transgression of the sexual restrictions in the Levitical

Code…or failing that, to at least be discrete in one's carnal abominations).

No one is more blessed than a Sadducee, blessed by a God he does not know - free to enjoy a pagan world that offers many more thrills than dower Pharisee legalism, or Essene celibate austerity - both of which obsess over getting to heaven, and laboring to learn more about God.

Sadducees have paradise on earth. As for the common Israelites, the ones who eke out a living in the barren Judean hills while a Roman boot stomps on their head - or the Galilean fisherman who barely reaches shore before Antipas' tax-collectors demand payment for each fish caught - there is no paradise on earth for pawns such as these. It is not surprising then, that the Israelite masses DO care about the hereafter, heaven and hades, angels and demons, and all the things a Sadducee regards as the superstitious illusions of weak willed people in need of a spiritual crutch.

A

I returned to Jesus and the Twelve, who were still at Lazarus' house. I told Jesus what happened in Jerusalem, but not that I had attended the Sanhedrin's meeting. I said, "Rabbi, word has spread in Jerusalem. The High Priest intends to arrest and execute you."

"I know, Judas. I know."

He obviously was not surprised by my words. Once again, I wondered if he had a spy among the Sanhedrin, perhaps one of the two Pharisees who had spoken in his favor.

We left Bethany the next morning. It was too close to Jerusalem for safety. But the others were blissfully ignorant that as long as I accompanied them, danger was traveling in their midst. We went north for a few days, back into the hill-country near the wilderness, to Ephraim and its vicinity, where many Essenes live.

Then the Feast of Passover neared. We joined the throngs that were walking to Jerusalem.

Then, six days before the Passover (four days before the Essene Passover), we arrived back at Bethany. We had supper there. Martha served, while Lazarus sat at the table with us. Mary then took a pound of very expensive oil of spikenard, something only the rich can afford. She anointed Jesus feet with it, gently rubbing it in. Then she wiped his feet with her hair. The whole house was filled with the smell.

It angered me. I whispered to myself, "Is Jesus as corruptible as the rest?" Always before, he willingly led the life of a poor man, taking the side of the downtrodden and oppressed, living simply. But now…was he buying into all the accolades from the masses, and the Zealot demands for him to declare the Kingdom of Israel, proclaiming himself as the Messiah, the God anointed king. My concerns were heightened when I heard Peter, James and John continue their argument about which one would be prime minister in Jesus' newly reformulated Kingdom of God.

Angry, I asked Jesus, "Why wasn't this expensive oil sold for three hundred denarii and given to the poor?" At that moment, I didn't care about the poor. I was overcome with fear and anger. No matter who Jesus was, no matter whether a prophet, or someone greater, it would be disastrous if he were to proclaim a new Israelite Kingdom, or declare himself king. On this point, Caiaphas and the Sanhedrin were right. To do so, would bring disaster and ruin upon the nation.

Jesus said to me, "Leave her alone, Judas. Mary has kept this for the day of my burial. The poor will always be with you. But I will be with you for only a short time more."

His words only angered me more. Not only was this costly oil wasted, but Jesus paid no mind to my concern, dismissing me with an offhand remark.

Word spread by morning, that Jesus had returned to Lazarus' house. Crowds gathered, not only to see Jesus, but Lazarus too. Many came from Jerusalem, only a couple of miles away. I wondered if Caiaphas would send Malchus and the Temple Guard to arrest Jesus. But it was unlikely. The crowds were too large, even at Bethany. And venturing into an Essene community with Sadducee Temple Guards would be a risky move.

My worries continued to increase. As tens-of-thousands began to arrive in Jerusalem, to prepare for the Passover, many of the pilgrims gathered around Jesus, making it seem a general revolt was real possibility. I increasingly feared Jesus might declare himself king at the Feast, God's Anointed ruler.

During the months I followed Jesus, my loyalty had slowly shifted from Caiaphas to Jesus. But now - it seemed Caiaphas' concerns about the Galilean prophet were valid. Perhaps the High Priest was wiser than I had realized. And perhaps, Jesus was not as "other-worldly" as I had previously believed.

פ

Chapter IX: Riot

Setting out from Lazarus' house, James and John came to Jesus and said, "Rabbi, we want you to do something for us."

"What is it you want?"

"Promise us, when you are enthroned, that the two of us will sit on your two sides - one on your right, as prime minister, and the other on the left, as your chief financial steward."

"You don't know what you are asking. Are the two of you capable of sitting at my table, drinking from the same cup I drink from, and washing in the same mikveh that I bath in?"

"Yes rabbi, we are able to do that."

Jesus said to them, "Yes, you will drink from the same cup I drink. And you will be washed in the same mikveh that I am washed in. But I cannot promise that you will sit on my right and left. Those chairs are reserved for the ones specially prepared to occupy them."

John said to James, "Who, besides us, is better prepared?" Then they walked away from Jesus, visibly upset that he did not honor their request.

Everything I heard and saw that day made me angrier and more concerned. When the other disciples heard John and James ask to be made the most powerful ministers in Jesus' kingdom, they ridiculed the two of them. Jesus' disciples were no longer unified, but were quickly dividing into factions.

Jesus called the Twelve around him, "As you know, gentile rulers, like the Romans, act as tyrants over the people, demanding to be served by all, requiring shouts of "Hail Caesar," and forcing the people to worship the Emperor at his pagan temples. But it will not be this way among us. Any of you who aspires to leadership, must be a servant. And any of you who wishes to be first in authority, must be the slave of all. Even the Son of Man did not come to be served, but to serve. He came to sacrifice his life as an atonement for many."

On the one hand, I admired what Jesus said. Never was there a truer statement of what a Jewish king was supposed to be, a servant of all, God's representative to the people. But at the same time, this discussion seemed to confirm that Jesus was going to declare formation of the Kingdom of God. If not, why was he speaking about leadership. The Twelve were not leaders of anything, unless you count the lizards and scorpions sunbathing on the Jericho Road.

What should I do? Stand by, while he brings disaster on the Temple, Jerusalem, Israel, and my family? Perhaps Caiaphas was right. It may be better that one man die, than for the nation perish.

δ

When we drew near Jerusalem, at Bethphage Jesus said to Peter and James, "Go into the village. At the first house, you will find a donkey. Untie it and bring it to me. If the owner of the house asks, 'Why are you taking the colt?' say, 'The Messiah needs it.' And immediately he will send it with you."

Everything happened just as Jesus had said. They brought the donkey to him. We threw our cloaks on its back, and he mounted the animal. I was upset. All this time, I thought Jesus presented little threat to the Sanhedrin, or to Roman rule. But this was an unmistakable sign. Jesus was revealing himself to be a very real threat to the established political and religious order. Riding into Jerusalem on a donkey, was an obvious political statement - that he was claiming David's throne. It was on a donkey that Israel's kings rode, especially when entering Jerusalem in festal procession.

As Jesus made his way to Jerusalem, the crowd cut palm branches, spreading them on the road in front of him.

Thousands upon thousands of pilgrims were camped on the hills surrounding Jerusalem, having already arrived for Passover. Those coming from far nations had no idea who Jesus was, or the reason for this parade. They asked, "Who is this man on the donkey? Why is there such a commotion in his honor?"

They were told, "This is the prophet from Galilee, the new Messiah, come to deliver his people from pagan rule."

Many of the pilgrims were shocked, unaware of Jesus and his ministry. Being Hellenized Jews, perfectly satisfied with their lives in the Roman provinces, many recoiled, and drew back from the procession, having no wish to be part of a revolt.

I was horrified, when Galilean and Judean pilgrims began to wave the palm branches, while praising Jesus. The palm branch was the primary symbol of the Hasmonean Kingdom, the flag and banner of an independent Jewish state. Palm branches had even been engraved upon Hasmonean coins, as the symbol of God's Kingdom.

The Hasmoneans not only ruled Israel as kings, but also served as priests in the Temple. This was the heritage of the chief priests and Sadducees - my heritage. Caiaphas, the Sadducees, and the Sanhedrin regarded themselves not only as the religious leaders of Israel, but also the rightful rulers of the nation. As long as Rome is in control, Sadducees will comply and cooperate with them. But should the day ever come when the Romans no longer exert their power over the Land of Israel, the chief priests and Sadducees intend to present themselves as the rightful kings and princes of the realm, the rightful successors to the Hasmonean kings.

This is why Herod the Great had such testy relations with the Sadducees. They viewed Herod as a usurper of their throne. This is also why Herod favored the Essenes, giving them many benefits and favors, allowing them to establish their monastery on Mt. Zion in Jerusalem. Herod and the Essenes hated the Sadducees, and vice versa. Now that Jesus, a man raised as an Essene, was entering the City of David as a king, there was no way the Sadducees would refrain from brutal action. The Romans too, will see this as an unmistakable threat, a treasonous act that endangers Roman rule and order.

I said to Peter, "Do you see what they are doing? Look at what is happening? The Sanhedrin and Romans will see this parade, the procession of a new king entering the ancient Israelite capital, and view this as an act of treason."

Peter grabbed a palm branch. Beginning to wave it, Peter said, "Yes Judas, isn't it glorious? Think of how many decades Jews have waited for a new Messiah, to sit on King David's throne. And Just imagine, you, the others, and I, will be part of Jesus' royal court. We may only be Galilean fishermen, but we will rule a restored Promised Land with Jesus."

"But Peter" I protested, "the Sanhedrin and Romans will not allow this. Don't you see this will only result in catastrophe and death? Don't you remember Judas the Galilean? The Zealots took Galilee's capital, Sepphoris. But when the Roman legions came to take back the city, it was utterly destroyed. The rebels were killed in a most brutal way. Surviving residents of the city were sent into slavery. Is that what you want for Jesus, yourself, and Jerusalem?"

"Judas, where is your faith?" said Peter. "You saw Jesus raise Lazarus. He made the wind and waves obey him. Countless sick people have been healed by Jesus. God is with us, Judas - just as he was with the Hebrews when Pharaoh came against them with his chariots. God, the ruler of sea, wind, and wave, drowned the Egyptian chariots in the Red Sea. The Romans don't stand a chance."

The crowd began to sing a Psalm, "Save us (Hosanna) Son of David! Blessed is the one who comes in the name of the Lord!

Blessed is the kingdom of David that comes through the name of the Lord! Save us Lord!"

When Jesus came into Jerusalem, the whole city was in a commotion and many asked, "Who is this man?"

They were told, "This is Jesus, the Branch of David (Nazarene), the prophet from Galilee."

Jesus entered the Temple. Just as he had done two years before, Jesus began to cleanse the Temple, driving out the money-exchangers, and those selling sacrificial animals. This time, I did not take part. But many who had surrounded him on the "Hosanna procession" enthusiastically joined in, driving out the merchants and money-changers. Many of the people taking part were Essenes. From the beginning of the Essene party, they have called for a cleansing of the Temple, and the replacement of its priesthood.

The unrest had the appearance of a general riot. The Temple Guard stood on the periphery. The size of the crowd was so large and the rioting so widespread, there was nothing they could do. Then, I saw the Roman cohorts Pilate had brought with him from Caesarea, to maintain order during the festival. The legionnaires began to flow out of their quarters in the Antonia Fortress, located on the northwest corner of the Temple. They were lining-up in formation, preparing for action. Given Pilate's violent nature and his history of extreme actions against the Judean people, I knew a general slaughter might result. I said to Jesus, "Rabbi, the Romans are coming." Immediately, he raised his arms and called to the mob. I was surprised, because the rioters obeyed him, and became quiet.

Jesus said to the crowd in a loud voice, "Enough! God is a God of order, not of chaos. Our point has been made."

At once, he withdrew from the Temple, before the Romans could act. We left Jerusalem as well, returning to Bethany for the night.

β

The next day was Lamb Selection Day, when the Passover Lamb is chosen by each household. Being the treasurer for the Twelve, I had the common purse. While walking with him to the Temple I asked Jesus, "Rabbi, do you want me to go buy a lamb? Or are we going to celebrate the Passover meal with another household?"

He said, "We will eat the Passover meal by ourselves. But we do not need a lamb."

I said, "Rabbi, how will we celebrate the Passover without buying a lamb?"

"Judas, when God commanded Father Abraham to bring his son here for the sacrifice, to Mt. Moriah, did Abraham bring a lamb with him?"

"No rabbi. He only brought his son, Isaac."

"Where did the lamb come from that was sacrificed on Mt. Moriah, on the spot where the Temple's Holy-of-Holies is located?"

"God miraculously provided the lamb."

"It will be the same for us. My Father has brought his son to Mt. Moriah, and the Passover Lamb will be miraculously provided."

Jesus' answer disturbed me. It is the Essenes who celebrate Passover without a lamb, viewing the Sadducee priesthood to be polluted. Was Jesus going to make us celebrate Passover in the Essene manner? Everything Jesus now did disturbed me. He did not seem to be the person I thought he was.

I wondered if Jesus knew what he was doing. The whole city was descending into chaos. Even though I loved my rabbi, it was Caiaphas' words I heard ringing in my ear, "An uprising against Rome must be prevented at all costs. If there is a major revolt, the Romans will destroy our Temple, our city, and threaten the very existence of our nation."

It was true. As a Sadducee, I knew the true state of things better than these fishermen from Galilee. Pilate did not have so much as a legion under his command, having no more than three-thousand troops to enforce Roman rule in all of Judea. The Romans were masters of efficiency in administrating their provinces. They did not waste precious denarii by stationing legions across the countryside. They didn't need to. Everyone knew what Rome was like. If they were slapped, the Romans answered with a kick to the groan. A punch would earn a stab to the gut, in return. And anyone foolish enough to swing a sword against the Empire, would be tortured and made to suffer, before the merciful release of death came.

Rome's policy was simple - play nice with us, and we will play nice with you. Dare to oppose us - and we will make you curse your mother, for giving you life.

Rome's army consisted of twenty-five legions, each having some five-thousand troops, a total of only 125,000 men. Even though their numbers might seem modest, each legionnaire was granted citizenship in Rome, no matter where they had been born. This bought fierce loyalty. Thoroughly trained, highly disciplined, battle hardened by their twenty-five-year term of enlistment, and equipped with every weapon needed to wage devastating war - one legionnaire was worth ten rebels.

If Judea became pregnant with revolt, giving birth to general insurrection, Pilate and his troops would be quickly dispatched to a new castra (Roman encampment) in dark Sheol. It would not be difficult for the Zealots to accomplish this much, because Pilate had few troops at his disposal. Following the elimination of the Prefect and his cohorts, the self-righteous Zealots would then eradicate all "vermin" Jews who had collaborated with Rome, beginning with the Sadducees. No one was more closely aligned with, or more essential to, Roman rule than the Sadducees, including my family.

But this would only be the beginning of the conflagration. The Zealot's misadventure would unleash Rome's mighty dogs of war.

Tease it, pull its tail, and jab Rome with a stick, and you will be fatally bitten, torn limb from limb. With a bloodcurdling cry of "Havoc!" the invading legions would initiate a general slaughter, laying waste to the Land of Israel, visiting the plagues of Tartarus upon us all. The first to arrive would be the X Legio Fretensis (Tenth Legion of the Strait), stationed in Damascus. Soon, other elite troops would land on Israel's shores, turning the Promised Land into an object lesson for all who dare oppose Rome.

At that moment, I made a fateful decision. As much as I hated myself for doing it, Jesus had to be stopped. I will do what Caiaphas had instructed me. I will lead Malchus and the Temple Guard to Jesus, that he might be arrested. For I had concluded: the needs of the nation, outweigh the needs of just one man.

When we returned to the Temple, Sadducee priests and members of the Sanhedrin came and asked Jesus, "By whose authority do you come into God's House and cause such unrest? And if you claim to have rightful authority, who gave it to you?"

Jesus said, "I will answer your question, if you will answer mine. Tell me, John the Baptizer's authority – did it come from God, or was it merely of human origin?"

The leaders discussed it among themselves and said, "If we say, 'From God,' he will ask, 'Then why didn't you have faith in him?' But if we say, 'it was merely of human origin' this mob may stone us, for they believe John was a prophet of God." They answered Jesus, "We don't know."

Jesus said, "Since you will not answer my question, then neither will I tell you by what authority I do these things."

ζ

Later in the day, some Pharisee teachers and Herodians came to Jesus, to catch him in his words. They said, "Rabbi, we know you are a man of integrity. You are unswayed by others, because you pay no attention to a person's station or office, but teach the way of God in accordance with what you view to be the truth. As you well know, for many years it has been debated whether Jews should pay Caesar's imperial tax. Judas the Galilean revolted against Rome, refusing to pay the tax. The Zealots today, teach that no Jew should pay the tax. But others, like the Sadducees, say we should pay it. What do you say? Should we pay the tax or not?

I was amazed by how crafty their question was. Jesus appeared to have no way out. Either answer would be ruinous. If he said Caesar's tax should be paid, most of the crowd would turn on him, because they did not support the tax. Telling the people to pay the tax would destroy any claim Jesus might have of being the Messiah, because the crowds believed no anointed king of Israel would tell the Jewish people to pay a pagan Roman tax.

On the other hand, if Jesus told people not to pay the tax to Rome, this would be a seditious statement, that could result in a charge of treason. And Jesus could be brought to Pilate and crucified for such a statement.

Jesus said "Why are you trying to trap me? Bring me a denarius and let me look at it." They handed him an imperial coin. He asked them, "Whose idolatrous image is this?"

"Caesar's," they replied.

"And what does the idolatrous inscription on the coin say?"

"Caesar, Son of God"

Jesus said to them, "Give to Caesar what belongs to Caesar; and give to God what belongs to God."

I was amazed at the skill and wisdom of Jesus' answer.

η

Noting how wise Jesus' answer had been, one of the rabbis tested his knowledge of the Torah by asking him, "Of all God's commands, which is the most important?"

Jesus answered, "The most important commandment is, 'Hear, O Israel, the Lord our God, the Lord is one. Love the Lord your God with all your heart, with all your soul, with all your mind and with all your strength (Deut. 6:5).' The second most important is, 'Love your neighbor as yourself (Lev.19:18).' There are no commandments more important than these."

"Well said," replied the other rabbi. "You are correct in saying that God is one, and that there is no other, only Him. To love Him with all your heart, with all your understanding, with all your strength, and to love your neighbor as yourself, these are more important than all burnt offerings and sacrifices (1 Samuel 15:22, Psalm 40:6)."

When Jesus heard how wisely the rabbi had answered, he said to him, "You are near to God's Kingdom."

But the man wanted to show the crowd his spiritual wisdom and learning. He asked Jesus, "And who is my neighbor?"

Jesus said, "A Judean was traveling down from Jerusalem to Jericho, when he was attacked by Zealots. They robbed him, stripped him of his cloths, beat him, and left him bleeding on the road, half dead. A Sadducee priest was traveling down the same road. When he saw the injured man, he passed by on the far side, fearful the Zealots would attack him also, if he stopped to help. Soon, a Levite, who also served in the Temple, saw the injured man - and passed him by on the other side, unwilling to risk himself for the man, even though he was a fellow Israelite. Then, a Samaritan came upon the injured man. Samaritans and Jews hate one another, as you well know. And yet, when the Samaritan saw the injured man, he was filled with compassion for him. He anointed the man's injuries with salve, and bandaged his wounds. Then he put the man on his donkey, took him to the inn near the Ascent of the Red Rocks (Ma'ale Adummim), and took care of him. The next day, the Samaritan took two denarii out of this purse and gave them to the innkeeper saying, 'Take care of him. When I return, I will reimburse you for anything more you spend on him.'

"Which of these three do you think was a neighbor to the man who was attacked by Zealots?"

The rabbi said, "The one who had mercy on the man."

Jesus said, "Go and act in the same way."

I wondered what Jesus thought he was doing. Before, he seemed to be rallying the crowds, readying them to rise-up in revolt under his leadership. Now, he was telling stories about Zealots, that surely offended them, and those who were sympathetic to their cause.

I

Jesus then asked, "Why do the rabbis call the Messiah, David's son? Don't they realize that David prophesied through the Holy Spirit, 'The Lord said to my Lord: "Sit at my right hand until I put your enemies under your feet."' If David himself calls the Messiah 'Lord,' then how can he be David's son?

"Rejoice in the word of God given to King David, 'The Lord will extend your mighty shepherd's staff from Zion, saying, "You are a priest forever, according to the clean and unpolluted priestly order of Melchizedek." The Lord is your right hand. He will crush kings on the day of his wrath. He will judge the peoples, piling up the dead, crushing the rulers of the whole world."'

Jesus told another parable in the presence of the Pharisee rabbis. "Two men went up to the Temple to pray. One a Pharisee, and the other a tax-collector. The Pharisee stood at the entrance to the inner court of the Temple, looking intently at the Sanctuary, God's House. There he prayed, 'Lord, I thank you that I am not like other people - robbers, sinners, adulterers - or even like that tax-collector over there. I fast two days each week (Monday and Thursday) and give God a tithe (10%) of everything I earn.'

"But the tax-collector remained in a far corner of the Temple. Looking down, he beat his chest and said, 'Lord, have mercy on me, for I am a terrible sinner.'

"I tell you, it was the tax-collector who went home forgiven by God and reconciled to him, not the Pharisee. All who praise and promote themselves, will be brought down and humbled. And all who humble themselves, before God, will be lifted up."

It appeared as though Jesus was purposely offending people, just as he had done in Galilee. What was he doing?

Jesus told another parable. "God's Kingdom is illustrated by a king who arranged a marriage for his son. He sent his servants to call all the invited guests to come to the wedding. But the guests refused.

"A second time, the king sent out servants saying, 'Tell the guests the banquet has been prepared, the cattle have been slaughtered and cooked, and everything is ready for you to come to the wedding celebration.'

"But the guests were not interested, and went about their own business - one to his fields, another to his shop. Some of the guests took the king's servants, beat them, and killed them.

"When the king was told what the people had done to his servants, he was filled with wrath. He sent his armies and destroyed those murderers, and burned their city.

"The King said to his servants, 'The wedding is ready, but those who were invited were unworthy. Go out to the roads, and whomever you find, bring them to the wedding.

"The servants went out and gathered as many as they could find, both bad and good. And the wedding was filled with guests.

"When the king came in and saw the guests, there was a man who had refused to wear the wedding robe that had been given to him by the king's servants. He did this to protest the marriage.

"The king said to him, 'Friend, why did you come to the wedding, if you were going to refuse a wedding robe?' The man did not answer.

"The king told his servants, 'Tie this man's hands and feet and carry him away. Then throw him out of the city gates and into the darkness, where there is much weeping and gnashing of teeth.'"

I wondered why Jesus was telling a parable about Herod. Herod the Great came to Jerusalem and asked the city to accept him as king, but they refused. After marrying the Hasmonean princess, Mariamne, he laid siege to Jerusalem, and many who refused to accept Herod's marriage or kingship were killed. I wondered what Jesus was illustrating by telling this parable?

Jesus told another parable to the people, the crowds who hoped God's kingdom would soon be established in Israel. He said, "A prince went to a distant country, to the Capital, that he might be appointed king, and then return home to rule."

Shaking my head, I mumbled to myself, "This sounds like the story of Achelaus, Herod's successor in Judea."

Jesus continued, "The prince called ten of his servants and gave each of them ten minas. 'Invest the money,' the prince told his servants, 'until I return as ruler.'

"But the prince's subjects hated him so much, they sent a delegation after him, to tell the Emperor, 'We don't want this man as our king.'"

I said to myself, "Yes, the parable is definitely about Achelaus."

Jesus went on, "The Emperor confirmed the prince as ruler, and then the prince returned home. He sent for the servants he had given the money to, that they might report their profits.

"The first came and said, 'Lord, your mina has earned ten more.'

"'Well done,' said the ruler, 'you are a good and faithful servant. Because you have been trustworthy in this small matter, here are ten cities for you to manage.'

"The second came and said, 'Lord, your mina has earned five more.'

"The ruler said to him, 'Here are five cities for you to manage.'

"Another servant came and said, 'Lord, here is your mina. I kept it hidden in a cloth. I was afraid of you, because you are a cruel man. You take out where you have not put in, and harvest where you did not plant.'

"The ruler replied, 'You evil servant, I will judge you by your own words. You knew, did you, that I am a cruel man, taking out where I have not put in, and harvesting where I have not planted? Why then didn't you deposit the money with a banker, so that when I came back, I could at least have my money back with interest? Take the mina away from this man, and give it to the one who has ten.'

"The servants said, 'But master, he already has ten.'

"The ruler replied, 'I tell you, everyone who has, will be given still more. But those who have nothing, even what little they have will be taken away from them. As for those enemies of mine who did not want me to rule them - bring them here in my presence, and kill them.'"

This was truly a strange parable. Indeed, Archelaus was a hard man. Before going to Caesar in Rome, seeking to be made king, he killed some three-thousand in the Temple, and canceled the Passover Festival that year. I wondered if Jesus was warning the people about the consequences of revolt against Rome, or the rulers. The rabbi kept me guessing. Even after being one of his closest confidents for all these months, I could not figure out what his ultimate intentions, plans, or strategies might be.

Jesus told another parable. "There was a landowner who planted a vineyard. He placed a protective hedge around it, constructed a winepress, built a guard tower, and leased it to tenants. Then he left for a distant country.

"When harvest came, the landowner sent servants to the tenants, to collect the landowner's share of the fruit, as the lease payment.

"But the tenants took the landowner's servants, flogged one, stoned another, and one they killed.

"The landowner sent more servants. But the tenants treated them the same way as the first group of servants.

"Finally, the landowner sent his son, saying, 'The tenants will respect my son.'

"But when the tenants saw the son, they said to themselves, 'This is the landowner's heir. Let's kill him, and take his inheritance.'

"So the tenants took the son, threw him out of the vineyard, and killed him.

"When the landlord returns to his vineyard, what will he do to those tenants?"

They answered Jesus, "He will utterly destroy those evil men, and give the vineyard to new tenants, who will willingly pay the lease payment – giving the fruit to the owner when it is harvested."

Jesus said, "Have you read in the Scriptures, 'Even though the stone was rejected by the builders, this same stone will become the capstone. This is the Lord's doing, and it is an amazing thing to witness?' Therefore, I tell you, God's Kingdom will be taken from you evil tenants, and it will be presented to a people willing to give the fruit to the owner, when it is harvested.

"Whoever falls on this stone will be broken into pieces. But on anyone the stone falls, it will grind them to powder."

When the Sadducee and Pharisee members of the Sanhedrin heard this parable, they knew Jesus was speaking of them. They seethed with hatred against him, red in the face, perspiring, having clenched teeth and fists. But there was nothing they could do in the daylight, with the crowds surrounding Jesus, because many still regarded him as a prophet, hoping he would soon proclaim God's Kingdom, the restored Kingdom of Israel.

I said to Jesus, "Rabbi, don't you see how full of rage the leaders are? They will stop at nothing to kill you."

"Did you hear my parable, Judas? The tenants killed the son. Do you think these tenants, the priests and Sanhedrin, will do less to me?"

"Then what is the point, rabbi, if the birth of the Kingdom is murdered in its crib, and its Messiah killed before his reign can begin? What is the point of all this?"

"Do you still have so little understanding, Judas? My Kingdom is not like the reign of past kings. I came to do what no man or woman could do for themselves. God loved his creation so much, that he gave his only son, so that everyone who has faith in him will not perish, but have never-ending life."

Jesus then shouted to the crowd, "Sorrow, grief and mourning is your fate, Sadducees and Pharisees, you actors (hypocrites)! You shut the door to God's Kingdom, so no one may enter. You refuse to enter. And will not allow anyone else to go in, either.

"Sorrow, grief and mourning is your fate, Sadducees and Pharisees, actors! You steal widows' houses, and perform like actors in the theatre, reciting long prayers in public. Therefore, you will receive the harshest judgement.

"Sorrow, grief and mourning is your fate, Pharisees, actors! You cross the land and sea to make a single convert. But you make him two times-more an offspring of hell (Gehenna) than you are.

"Sorrow, grief and mourning is your fate, Sadducees and Pharisee, blind guides. You say, 'Whoever swears an oath on the Temple, is not bound by it. But whoever swears on the gold in the Temple, this is a binding oath!

"You blind fools. Which is greater - the gold, or the Temple that sanctifies the gold?

"And you say, 'Whoever swears by the Temple's altar, is not bound by such an oath. But whoever makes an oath by the sacrifice placed on the altar is bound by that oath.

"You blind fools. Which is greater - the gift, or the altar that sanctifies the gift?

"Sorrow, grief, and mourning is your fate, Pharisees, actors! You give a tenth, of all your riches to God, but you have broken the more important laws – about faith, hope, mercy, and love. You should have obeyed these commands, as well as doing the others.

"Blind guides - you choke on a gnat, but eagerly swallow a camel.

"Sorrow, grief and mourning is your destiny, Pharisees, actors! You perform elaborate cleansing rituals to clean the outside of the cup and bowl. But inside, you are full of robbery and gluttony.

You blind Pharisees. First clean out what is inside the cup and bowl, so that the outside may be clean, also.

"Sorrow, grief and mourning is your destiny, Sadducees and Pharisees, actors! You are white-washed tombs, freshly painted white and clean on the outside, but inside there is nothing but dead bones and every kind of filth and uncleanness.

In the same way, you appear righteous to others. But inside, you are full of hypocrisy, sin, and uncleanness.

"Sorrow, grief and mourning is your destiny, Pharisees, actors! You build shrines to the prophets, and decorate the tombs of the saints saying, 'If we had lived in the days of our ancestors, we would not have rejected or killed the prophets, or had their blood on our hands.'

"But you testify against yourselves. You are descendants of the people who persecuted and killed the prophets. And you commit the same sins your ancestors did before you, filling up your cups of sin and evil to the brim.

"Snakes, children of vipers, how will you ever escape being sent to the Pit, the Abyss?

"Behold, I will send more prophets, saints, and rabbis to you. Some of them you will kill, and others you will crucify. Some you will whip in your synagogues, persecuting them from city to city.

"Therefore, you are covered in all the blood of the prophets and saints shed upon the earth, all righteous blood, from the blood Abel to Zechariah - whom you murdered between the Temple and the altar.

"I warn you, you will be held accountable for all these things."

I wondered if Jesus had a death wish. It seemed that way. Yes, "the prophets of old were persecuted and killed." Even the Baptizer, and his father Zechariah, were killed. On many occasions, Jesus had told us he would be killed. Maybe he believes this is what's predestined to take place – ordained by God.

Leaving the city, as we walked up the Mt. of Olives, Peter looked back and remarked, "Look rabbi, at how magnificent the Temple is, with its the massive stones. How beautiful, eternal, and unmovable the Temple truly is!"

"Do you see all these huge and magnificent buildings on the Temple Mount?" replied Jesus. "Before long - not one stone will be left standing upon another. Each and every one will be demolished - and thrown down below."

I remembered the prophet Daniel who wrote, "the Christ (Messiah) will be put to death. The soldiers of a king will come and destroy the city, and the Temple. The end will come like a flood, devastating everything. War will last until the end, and the abomination of desolation will continue, just as it was written."

Λ

The next day, while teaching in the Temple, Jesus said, "I am the light of the world. Anyone who follows me, will never walk in darkness, but will have the light of life."

The Pharisees said, "Here you are, acting as your own witness again. Your testimony is false."

Jesus said, "Even if I testify about myself, my testimony is true. I know where I came from, and where I am going. You have no clue where I came from, or where I am going. You judge things by manmade traditions and human reasoning. I judge no one. But if I do judge, my judgment is true, because I do not judge alone. I stand with the Father, who sent me. The Law of Moses says the truth is to be established by the testimony of two witnesses. I am one witness. The second witness is my Father, who sent me."

They asked, "Where is your father?"

"You do not know me, or my Father. If you knew me, you would also know my Father."

Then Jesus said, "I am going away. The time will come when you search for me, longing to see me. But you will die in your sins. Where I go, you cannot come."

The rabbis joked among themselves, "Is he going to kill himself? Is that why he says, 'Where I go, you cannot come?'"

Jesus continued, "You are from below - but I am from above. You are of this world. - but I am not of this world. You will die in your sins, if you do not believe that 'I am.' If you do not have faith that 'I am He', you will die in your sins."

"Who do you claim to be?" they asked.

"The One I have told you about. 'I am' from the beginning. I have much to condemn you for. But He who sent me is trustworthy and true. What I have heard from Him, I tell to the world.

"When you lift up the Son of Man, then you will know that 'I am,' and that I do nothing on my own, but speak only what the Father has told me. The One who sent me is with me. He has not left me alone. I always do what He tells me."

Speaking to Nicodemus and Joseph of Arimathea, the two members of the Sanhedrin who had faith in him, Jesus said, "If you continue to obey my teachings, then you indeed are my disciples. You will know the truth - and the truth will set you free."

But the Sadducees, and some of the Pharisee leaders asked, "We are Abraham's children, and have never been a slave to anyone. Why do you tell us, 'You will be set free?'"

"I tell you the truth, anyone who practices sin, is a slave of sin. Slaves are not a permanent part of the family. But the Son is part of the family forever. If the Son sets you free, then you are free, indeed. I know you are Abraham's children. And yet, you are trying to kill me, because my words find no home in your hearts.

"I speak of the things I have seen my Father do. And you also do the things you have seen your father do."

They replied, "Abraham is our father."

"If you were Abraham's children, you would do the same things Abraham did. But you want to kill me, one who told you the truth about God. That is not what Abraham would do. No, you do the things your father did."

They said to Jesus, "We are not bastards, born out of wedlock, like you. We have one Father, who is God."

"If God were your Father, you would love me. For I am begotten by, and come from God. I have not come by my own authority. It is He who sent me. Why can't you understand my teachings? It is because my words do not find a home in you. You are children of your father, the devil. And your father's desires are what drive you. He has been a murderer from the beginning, and does not tolerate the truth, because there is no truth in him. When he speaks a lie, he speaks from his heart, because he is a liar and the father of lies. Because I tell you the truth, you will not believe me. Which of you can accuse me of sin? If I speak the truth, why won't you believe me? Those who come from God, listen to what God says. You refuse to listen, because you are not from God."

Then they said to him, "Aren't we right, when we say are a Samaritan and demon possessed?"

"I do not have a demon. I honor my Father. But you dishonor me. I seek no honor of my own. There is only One who deserves honor, the One who judges all things. I tell you the truth, if a person obeys my teachings, they will never die."

"Now we know you are demon possessed. Abraham is dead, and so are the prophets. But you say, 'If a person obeys my teachings, they will never die.' Are you more important than our father Abraham, who is dead, or the prophets, who are also dead? Who is it you claim to be?"

"If I were to honor myself, that honor would amount to nothing. It is my Father who honors me, the One you call God. You do not know Him. But I know Him. If I said, 'I do not know Him,' then I would be a liar, like you. But I do know Him, and obey His commands. Father Abraham would have rejoiced to see my arrival. He prophesied about me and rejoiced."

Then the Sadducees said to him, "You are not yet fifty-years-old, and yet you claim to have seen Abraham?"

"I tell you the truth, before Abraham was, 'I am.'"

They picked up rocks to stone him shouting "Blasphemy!" But Jesus walked through the middle of the crowd, and we left the Temple.

Π

It was now only two days before Passover. I went to the meeting of the Sanhedrin, or perhaps I should say the "executive committee" or "rump council" that consists only of the chief priests who had served as High Priest. They discussed the details of secretly arresting Jesus, and putting him on trial. Caiaphas said, "The Galilean must be arrested before the Passover begins, when the crowds are not so large. If we arrest him during the feast, the crowds may riot." I gave them assurances, that I could lead Malchus and the Temple Guard to the place where Jesus would be sleeping, to avoid a violent insurrection.

I also said, "If I do this, there are two things I require of you. The rabbi has done nothing deserving death. He is a good man, a righteous man, a holy teacher, and a patriot. He may even be a prophet. I will turn Jesus over to you, because he does not understand the dangerous game he is playing. But Jesus does not intend to revolt against the authorities, no matter how questionable his methods may appear. You are right. If he continues, a general insurrection may result. The Romans will punish us, and our nation, for the misdeeds of those who use Jesus as an excuse to revolt. But secondly, if I give you Jesus, I want you to promise his disciples will be left alone - that Jesus will be the only one imprisoned. There is no need to overreact…Do I have your promise?

Caiaphas replied, "My son Judas, we are honored to have such a measured and reasonable man, who is able to help and advise the Sanhedrin. Let me ask you, will the Galilean's follower be so weak-kneed as to let him be taken - and then simply go home with their tails tucked between their legs. Will they let his mantle fall to the ground unclaimed? Or will they do as Jesus did, who took up the Baptizer's mantle, once he was eliminated?"

"Father," I said, "Jesus' followers are not like John or Jesus, nothing at all like them. They are fishermen and simple Galileans. Not one is capable of piloting anything larger than a fishing boat, let alone an insurrection or movement. When Jesus is removed from their midst, the threat will dissipate. Being from Galilee, they will slink home, out of our hair, never to bother the Sanhedrin again."

"You are a very keen observer, my son. Very well, we will only arrest this rabbi. As for promising that nothing will happen to Jesus…this I cannot do. The Sanhedrin is a court of law. I cannot order the Sanhedrin to do what I say. Likewise, no one can say what the rabbi will do between now and his arrest, or what he may do during his trial…or what Pilate will demand of us. What I will promise is this - I will do my best to honor your feelings and request. But you must trust me, and my decisions concerning this matter. Will you do that, my son Judas?"

"Yes father, thank-you for your promise and assurances. I know you will do what is best."

ι

Jesus said to Peter and John, "Enter into the city, through the Essene Gate. You will see a man carrying a water jar, follow him. When he enters a building, go inside and say to the manager, 'The rabbi asks, can he eat the Passover here, with his disciples?' The manager will show you a large upper-room in the Essene guest house, furnished and ready. Make preparations to share the Passover meal there tonight."

Jesus had gone too far. It now appeared we might celebrate the Passover meal, not on the usual night, but according to the Essene calendar. If that were not enough, the meal was going to be shared in the Essene Quarter, in the monastery's guest house. Two days earlier, on Lamb Selection Day, Jesus had told me not to buy a Passover Lamb. So, it appeared we were going to celebrate Passover like the Essenes, in every way. They are the only Jews who do not sacrifice in the Temple, or share a lamb for the Passover. I was surprised none of the other disciples voiced an objection. None of them were Essenes, either. They had all been brought up in the traditions of the Pharisees and Zealots. But for me, this was the last straw, reaffirming my decision to hand Jesus over to the Sanhedrin.

Jesus' family, with Peter and John, went into the city. They made preparations, just as Jesus had told them.

When evening neared, Jesus and all the Twelve arrived at the guest house. Then the Hag ha-Herut began (Feast of Freedom), freedom being the primary focus of the meal. While we reclined at the table and ate, Jesus said, "One of you is going to hand me over to the authorities, one who is eating this meal with me."

The others became upset, asking one another who it might be. Some suspected it might be one of Jesus brothers.

"It is one of the Twelve, who is dipping their bread into the bowl with me," said Jesus. "The Son of Man must go, just as it is prophesied in the Scripture. But how tragic it will be for the man who hands the Son of Man over to his enemies. It would be better if that man had never been born." Jesus looked at me while he said these words. I wanted to confess what I had done…and what I was about to do…and ask the rabbis' forgiveness. But I was not the one who had created this impossible situation. Someone had to do something - someone with a cooler and more logical head than Jesus, or his dullard fishermen disciples. They would thank me later, when it becomes clear I was right.

The Passover meal was nearing its end. Jesus took bread, blessed it, broke it, and gave it to his disciples saying, "Take and eat it. This is my body." Then he took the cup, blessed it, and handed to the disciples saying, "This is my blood, spilled for the new covenant, poured out for the sins of many." And we all drank from the cup.

The Twelve began to argue among themselves, yet again, disagreeing about who was the most important, and whom Jesus would appoint to the highest positions in his Kingdom.

Jesus said, "You will all flee from me tonight. It has been prophesied, 'I will kill the shepherd, and the sheep will be scattered (Zech. 13:7).'"

But Peter bragged, "Even if all the others run away, I never will."

Jesus whispered to him, "Today, this night, before the rooster crows - three times you will deny you even know me."

Peter loudly swore an oath saying, "Even if I have to die with you, I will never deny you." And all the other disciples swore the same oath.

After the meal, everyone left to sleep at Gethsemane for the night (the cave with the olive press on the Mt. of Olives). But I slipped away, to find Malchus and the Temple Guard.

As it turned out, the Temple Guard were not the only ones who accompanied me. Caiaphas was concerned the Guard was not large or powerful enough, if there was resistance. He asked Pilate for a cohort of Roman soldiers, as backup. Pilate was eager to help.

The two forces met up in the Temple, in the Court of the Gentiles, the legionnaires coming from the Antonia Fortress, on the Temple's northwest corner.

I said to Malchus, "In this darkness, it will be hard for you to tell which man is the rabbi. I will go kiss him as an obvious sign, showing you which man is Jesus. As soon I kiss Jesus, take him into custody. But make sure your men use constraint. His disciples are simple fishermen. They are of little danger."

"Little danger? said Malchus. "Before, you pointed to their swords and told me what dangerous men they were..."

"Never mind that now," I said to Malchus. "When we arrest Jesus, they will scatter, like lambs attacked by a pack of wolves."

We left Jerusalem through the Eastern Gate, the Golden Gate. Having torches, we walked the short distance across the Kidron Valley to the Mt. of Olives, and Gethsemane. I worried that our approach was too obvious, if anyone was awake or standing watch.

As we neared, I was surprised by Jesus. He was standing directly in front of us. Coming near, I could see some of the disciples dozing nearby. Going directly to Jesus I said, "Rabbi," and kissed him. The Temple Guard took Jesus into custody. At that moment, Peter woke up in a start. Before we knew what was happening, Peter had drawn his sword. Rushing towards Malchus with a scream, he swung his sword overhead, bringing it down with murderous rage, using all his might. The blade struck the Captain of the Guard on his helmet. If he had not been wearing one, his skull would have been cut in two, smashed like a squash. But when the sword hit the helmet, it was deflected to the side, and cut off his ear.

Malchus screamed in pain shouting, "To arms."

Fearing a bloodbath, I jumped between Malchus and Peter saying, "Peace, my friends, peace."

Peter stopped. His act was that of a man suddenly wakened from a nightmare, not a voluntary act of resistance. That was Peter alright - act first, think second - impetuous as always.

Malchus said, "You Galilean bastards, born of half-blood harlots. I'll kill you sons-a-bitches."

Not yet bound, Jesus violently grabbed Malchus head, placing his hand over the place where his ear had been. He said, "Enough." Then Jesus let go of Malchus' head.

Malchus said, "It's stopped."

"What's stopped?" I asked.

"The pain."

"Here, let me look at your ear," I said. But Malchus had his hand over his ear, so I still couldn't see it. I said, "Let me look, Malchus." Slowly bringing down his hand, I held up the torch. There was some blood on his face. But the ear was now fully formed, perfect, having no injury that I could discern.

Jesus said, "Am I leading a rebellion against Rome, that you come to me with swords and clubs to capture me? I have been teaching in the Temple every day. But you did not arrest me then."

John, the youngest disciple, had been asleep in the cave. He came out, wearing nothing but a linen tunic. When he saw all the soldiers, he turned and ran. One of the guards tried to grab him. But all he got was a piece of his tunic. John continued to run, leaving his garment behind, in the hand of the guard. John ran away naked.

When that happened, one the other disciples also ran away. A couple of guards tried to stop him. But I said, "Let them go. We have done what we came to do." Then all the other disciples fled, also.

Jesus stared at me with a sad look, and said, "Do you know what you are doing, Judas?"

I didn't answer, but whispered to myself, "I hope so."

ϰ

On the way into Jerusalem, Jesus did not say a word, and neither did I. As ordered, Malchus, and the Temple Guard, took Jesus to Caiaphas' palace. Jesus' disciples had fled. But as we entered the city, where there was more light, I noticed Peter was following at a distance. He entered Caiaphas' courtyard behind us. I watched to see what he would do.

One of Caiaphas' female servants saw Peter warming himself by the fire. She kept staring at him. She asked Peter, "Weren't you with Jesus the Branch (Nazarene)?"

"What...you talking to me? I don't know what you're talking about." Then Peter crossed to the other side of the courtyard and stood by the gate.

The servant watched him and said to the others standing by the fire warming themselves, including some of the guards, "That man," pointing at Peter, "the one over there by the gate. He was one of the Galilean's disciples."

Peter yelled, "Damn you woman - I don't even know the man."

The guards came to Peter and said, "It's true. You are one of the Nazarene's disciples. You were with him tonight, when he was arrested. It's obvious from your accent that you are a Galilean."

Peter called curses down on the guards, then swore an oath, "I swear on the Temple and the Torah, I don't know this man you're talking about." Weeping, he ran out of the gate, afraid he too would be arrested.

When a rooster crowed, I remembered Jesus' words to Peter, "Before the rooster crows in the morning, you will deny and disown me three times."

Jesus' preliminary hearing began, a mere formality. Annas questioned him about his activities, his doctrine, and his contacts, focusing on his connections to the Zealots and the Essenes.

Jesus would not cooperate saying, "I taught openly wherever I went, teaching in the synagogues, in the Temple, and everywhere that Jews meet. I have said nothing in secret to anyone, whether Zealot, Essene, Pharisee or Sadducee. Why are you questioning me? If you want to know my teachings, ask those who have heard me. They know what I teach."

Annas motioned to Malchus. He slapped Jesus hard with his open hand saying, "You don't speak to a high priest in that tone of voice. Where is your respect?"

"If I speak lies, then prove that my testimony is false," said Jesus. "But if I speak the truth, why do you strike me?"

Annas said, "Jesus Bar-Joseph, you are charged with blasphemy, and seeking to stir revolt against the rightful authorities of the Temple, and of the Emperor. How do you plead."

Jesus remained silent and would not answer.

"Since you refuse to offer a defense of your actions, I find there is sufficient evidence to place you on trial for these changes," said Annas.

Jesus, and the rest of us, then went to the Council chambers. Soon, all the Sadducee members of the Council had arrived. But the Pharisee members had not been notified of the trial. For this reason, it was not technically legal. But I understood Caiaphas' reasoning. Given the massive crowds at Passover, including many Zealots, Essenes, and Pharisees - if Jesus' trial were held with the required notice, and during the daytime, the result may be an insurrection, the very thing Jesus' arrest was intended to prevent.

Annas called for the witnesses to give their testimony against Jesus. He was acting as prosecutor, while Caiaphas presided as Judge. The testimony offered was conflicting and tenuous at best. A witness came forward, "This man said, 'I will destroy the Temple, and then rebuild it in three days.'" Once again, not very damning testimony, rather nonsensical, considering the size and strength of the Temple.

Then Caiaphas stood up and questioned Jesus himself, "Do you hear what the witnesses are saying against you? They say you hate the Temple, and wish its destruction - and that you have no respect for our faith or traditions?"

Jesus remained silent.

"Alright, Jesus the Branch (Nazarene), what of the charge of blasphemy? You are under oath before the living God. As God's High Priest, I command you – tell us plainly if you are the Messiah, the Son of Man."

Jesus spoke, "'I am.' And you will see the Son of Man, sitting at the right hand of the Mighty One, on the clouds."

Shocked by Jesus' words, Caiaphas tore his clothes as a sign of grief and mourning for what he regarded as blasphemy. Then the High Priest said, "We have no need of further evidence. You have all heard this man's blasphemy from his own lips. He claims to be the Son of Man, equal to God. What is your verdict?"

Each member of the Sanhedrin stood, one at a time, and said, "He has condemned himself. According to God's Law, this man must die."

When the first one said this, I whispered into Caiaphas' ear, "You promised that Jesus would only be imprisoned. You must commute his sentence."

Caiaphas shrugged his shoulders and said, "I cannot help it if the man has condemned himself. There is no way I can commute his sentence after a statement like the one he just made."

"But father, the Romans do not allow us to execute a man, even if the Law of Moses requires it," I said.

"You are right, Judas. If the sentence is confirmed by the full Sanhedrin tomorrow, it is in Pilate's hands. Who knows, perhaps he will have mercy on this Galilean."

After each Sadducee had voiced their verdict, one-by-one, they came to spit in Jesus' face. Malchus then blindfolded him and struck Jesus with his fist saying, "Prophesy, Son of Man. Give us more of your wise words." The other guards also began to beat him.

I cried out, "Stop! His sentence has not yet been confirmed by the full assembly. It is not legal for you to beat him in this way."

Malchus looked to Caiaphas who said, "Take him to the pit."

When the blindfold was removed from Jesus' face, he looked me in the eye and said, "Do you know what you are doing, Judas?"

I said to myself, "No, I don't think I do."

ק

Chapter X: The Playwright

After Jesus had been removed from the room, Caiaphas said, "Come Judas. If you are going to be involved in ruling the Temple, and sitting on the Sanhedrin…"

Annas completed Caiaphas' sentence, "you must know how these things are done. Follow us."

Leaving the Council chambers, we walked out of the Temple, and over the bridge, making the short journey to Pilate's Praetorium. It had been the royal palace for the Hasmonean kings. But now, it was used by Pilate as his administrative center, when he visited Jerusalem.

Pilate had no use for anything Jewish, especially Israelite Temple rituals. But being the Roman Prefect of Judea, maintaining order was of prime importance. If revolt were to arise, the few Roman cohorts stationed in Judea would not be enough to crush a full-scale rebellion. In such a case, Pilate would have to send for the troops from Syria. The reinforcements would likely arrive after Pilate and his meager garrison of troops were slaughtered. This led Pilate to act proactively, preventing any insurrection before it could occur, or putting unrest down swiftly and ruthlessly before a revolt could build – plunging a dagger into the gut of every looming threat, crushing revolt before it could sprout or grow.

The three of us entered the gates of the Hasmonean Palace. Crossing the threshold into the building, I said, "Aren't we ceremonially unclean now, this being a pagan building?" I was shocked that Annas and Caiaphas, or any Temple priest, would enter a pagan home with such little hesitation.

Annas said, "You are very young, Judas. Many of our people are too unbending. As you grow older, you will learn that compromises must be made with the pagan world."

I nodded yes, but knew this was wrong. Passing by the huge official audience hall where Herod the Great, and now Prefect Pilate, held court and conducted official meetings, I said, "Didn't we just pass the audience hall?"

Annas said, "Sensitive matters are conducted privately and quietly, where prying ears cannot hear. This is part of what you must learn as a leader of Israel. As my grandson, by marriage, you must be groomed for the tasks ahead. This is one of them. The slightest rumor can set Judea or Galilee aflame. Much of what we do, must be done in secret, keeping the ignorant masses in the dark. In front of the mob, we do and say what is necessary. But we speak the truth only in whispers, behind closed and locked doors. You should feel truly privileged, young Judas. Secrets will be revealed to you this night that only a select few are privy to. Like your father-in-law, grandfather-in-law, and uncle-in-law before you - one day you may become High Priest, and see the ultimate secret, the Temple's Holy-of-Holies, where only the High Priest can stand before the Lord. To be High Priest is to be a man of secrets." Once again I nodded, but knew in my heart Annas was wrong.

Guards led us to Pilate's private office. To my surprise, Pilate greeted us warmly, "Come in my friends. Have a glass of wine."

Annas whispered in my ear, "Whether you want wine or not, you must accept it. This reassures him we are friends of Rome, and not his enemies. Otherwise it will offend the Prefect."

Ornate goblets of wine were handed to each of us. We all drank. Pilate downed the contents of his glass, demanding a refill from the steward. I took a sip of the wine and choked, never having drunk unmixed wine before. Jews always drink it diluted by a large amount of water, making the wine less strong, while the alcohol cleanses any impurities in the water.

"Tell me, my friends," Pilate said, "who is this handsome young man you have brought into my presence?"

The way Pilate said this made my skin crawl. His words had a lecherous tone, his eyes staring with a penetrating and lustful gaze.

Caiaphas said, "This is my son-in-law, whom I told you about."

"The one who wormed his way into the rebel's confidence? Excellent." Raising his newly refilled glass, Pilate said, "I salute you…what did you say your son-in-law's name was?"

"Judas, your honor, Judas Bar-Simon."

"Judas Bar-Simon, we salute you for your cunning and resourcefulness. You are sure to go far." Pilate gulped down the second glass of wine.

Pilate asked, "Were you successful?"

Caiaphas said, "Completely."

"Without violence?"

"Almost without incident. Only one follower drew his sword. But he wasn't much of a swordsman. Aiming to crack open a head, he missed."

"That surprises me. I anticipated more resistance," said Pilate.

Caiaphas responded, "Oh, it is not unusual. These Zealots are brave, when they outnumber their victims. But when taken by surprise or confronted by a superior force, their courage flees, and they run away, chasing after it. That is what happened tonight. When we arrested this "king" all his companions fled.

"I'm very pleased, my friends. Once again you have shown yourselves to be competent leaders of your nation, deserving another year in the High Priest's office…and what of the trial before the Sanhedrin? Did it go as planned?"

"There were a few minor glitzes, from putting together a hurried prosecution…difficulties in getting witness testimonies to agree. But, in the end, all that was irrelevant. Our "Messiah" confessed with his own lips."

"Truly? He confessed to a rebellion, to being a rebel king?"

"Your honor, I do not want to bore you will our people's customs and laws. But desiring to become an Israelite King, a Christ (Messiah), is not a punishable offense in our Law. To convict him of a crime deserving death, this man needed to be found guilty of blasphemy against our God. To our astonishment, that is just what he did before the Sanhedrin. He claimed to be God."

Becoming sick, I rushed to a pot at the side of the room and vomited.

Pilate said, "Our young visitor does not hold his wine very well. I doubt he finished one glass."

By turning Jesus over to the Sanhedrin, I thought it would do three things: save Jesus from Pilate or Antipas killing him; prevent a violent insurrection that the Romans would violently crush in a bloodbath; and make it possible for me to return home to my family. But now, it appeared Caiaphas had lied to me and played me for a dupe. He never intended to spare Jesus' life. I heard an accusing voice inside my head say, "Who are you fooling, Judas? You knew Caiaphas wanted Jesus dead. He had said so. Caiaphas knew you were looking for an excuse to soothe your betrayal. So, he promised Jesus would be spared. But you knew the truth all along."

Tasting and swallowing the truth soured my stomach. More sickening, I was now Pilate's friend, a friend of Rome. These were realities I could not swallow and keep down.

"And the verdict?" Pilate asked Caiaphas.

"Death."

"What's next."

"Our Law requires the verdict be confirmed by the entire Sanhedrin, the next day, in the daylight. Given tonight's events, it is merely a formality. Then we will bring this Jesus to you. By Roman edict, we are not permitted to carry out capital punishment."

Pilate said, "Annas and Caiaphas, when you bring this Messiah to me tomorrow, let us be fine actors (hypocrites) and finish well our play - a tragedy. Tomorrow, this Israelite hero's fatal flaw will be revealed to the audience - the ignorant Judean masses. Being good actors, we will put on our masks, and play our parts on the stage of life. When the audiences' emotions of love and hate, mercy and rage, are stimulated, played with, and manipulated to the full, then the final tragic act will be performed, when the hero meets his ignoble and sad end. This will bring catharsis to the audience, relieving tension, and making violent insurrection less likely during the Passover Festival."

"No one is as crafty and coldly efficient, as you, your honor," Caiaphas said admiringly.

Pilate continued, "Tomorrow, this is what I want you to do, my friend Caiaphas. You will bring the criminal in through the gates of the Praetorium, to the courtyard. You will refuse to enter my 'pagan' home, as is your usual public practice, showing your unbending devotion to Israel's God, and your people's traditions. I will not come out, immediately. My tribune will come out and demand your entrance. You will steadfastly refuse. After a short delay, I will concede the point, making it look to your countrymen as though you are a strong leader of your people, able to make the Roman Prefect back-down, giving you increasing respect and honor in your nation, being a good and holy High Priest.

"When I come out to the courtyard, you will present the charges against this Messiah. Keep in mind that Rome has no such charge as blasphemy, and cares little if this man claims to be your god, or even the incarnation of Pan. The charge you must bring to me is treason, that he makes himself out to be the king of Israel, that he is leading an insurrection against Rome.

"After you have laid out the charges, I will be hesitant and unconvinced. You will protest and demand his execution. Then, I will take the man and question him myself, acting as though I wish to set him free. You will continue to press me, demanding his execution.

"I have three Zealot insurrectionists held in chains, minor rebels caught robbing and killing on the road to Jericho. I will bring the leader out to stand with this Christ. After whipping up the crowd into a frenzy, I will ask them which of the two, the crowd wants released. This will make me appear merciful to the crowd.

"Your job, Caiaphas, is to pack the crowd with as many Sadducees and Temple servants as you can gather. Have them cry out to release the Zealot. His name is Abbas...or something like that. Releasing a minor Zealot bandit, presents little danger to public order. It is those who incite the crowds, like the Baptizer, or this Christ, they are the ones we must chastise severely and make an example of.

"Caiaphas, you will continue demanding the Christ's execution. I will continue to act as though I wish to set him free. Make the crowd of Sadducees and Temple servants back you up. Have them demand this Christ's crucifixion. At last, I will relent, and bow to what the crowd demands."

Seeing the water-basin, Pilate giggled, "I just thought of a nice touch to add more drama to our play. The water basin will be sitting near the Judgement Seat. When I bow to the crowd's demands, and pronounce the death sentence on this man, I will tell the crowd it is all their doing, that I have nothing to do with it. Then, in front of the crowd, I will wash my hands of this man's blood.

"You see, my friend Caiaphas, we are both helped by this drama. It makes me appear merciful and reasonable to the Judean masses. And it shows you can move the Prefect, when you have a mind to, able to effectively plead Judean demands before Rome's representative.

"Then, I will execute the coup de grace. I will have my troops thoroughly chastise this Christ, and make him wish he had never been born. Then he will carry his cross naked through the streets of Jerusalem, in front of all the crowds gathered for the Passover

Festival, his honor dangling limp and shrived for all to jeer," Pilate cackling in delight at the thought.

"My troops will lead this 'king' outside the city gate. At the entrance to the city, they will crucify him with the other two insurrectionists, for all the stiff-necked Zealots and rebels to see. It will illustrate my carrot and stick approach. This Abbas-fellow will be the symbol of my mercy. The three malefactors on their crosses will illustrate the cruel treatment meted out to all who oppose Rome or the High Priest.

"Get some sleep, my friends. Tomorrow's little play will take most the day. I know it will be a busy day for you, sacrificing all the Passover Lambs in the Temple, as well as attending this trial.

Pilate said joyously to his steward, "Fill our guests' glasses. Let us toast to tomorrow." Pilate downed the whole glass, yet again.

Walking back to the Temple, we passed near Jerusalem's theatre. Once more I felt sick. Annas and Caiaphas continued to discuss all that would take place the next morning, and what preparations needed to be made for the coming Passover.

Arriving at the Council chambers, I said bitterly, "You promised Jesus would not be killed."

Caiaphas said, "Judas, what is that to us? We brought you along with us to Pilate, to toughen you for being a member of the Sanhedrin, and so you would better understand what it means to be High Priest. You must be pragmatic, a man who knows the reality of life under Roman rule. You must have a strong stomach, to compromise when needed. Leadership is never easy. And you will have blood on your hands, whether you like it or not."

"Blood on our hands…innocent blood?" I asked.

"Innocent…who do you have in mind? Point to the person you think is innocent, Judas. You are more naïve than I thought."

"And what of justice?" I asked.

"Before justice comes survival. My son, if our nation is destroyed by the Romans, where is the justice in that? The only choice we have in life is whose blood will be spilled - ours or someone else's. Everyone has blood on their hands. As priests, we are used to blood. You must become used to it also, Judas.

"No, I don't believe that."

"You must, my son."

The thought of being a "son of Caiaphas," made me sick, nauseous yet again. Then the terrible truth hit me. Yes, I was a true son of Caiaphas. Every day that had passed, I became Caiaphas' son more completely - just as Caiaphas had become a son of Annas, before me. Both Caiaphas and I became adopted sons, sons-in-law, molded and formed into the image of our fathers-in-law. I had been hand-picked to become High Priest, just as Caiaphas had been hand-picked by Annas before me, both of us groomed to succeed to the priestly throne. A father strives to make his son like him. And I was becoming more like my adoptive father with each passing day. By betraying Jesus, I had demonstrated that I was Caiaphas' disciple and son. And with each lesson I learned from my father-in-law, this made me more a son and disciple of hell.

Caiaphas continued, "My son, you must love the blood. As priests, we shed the blood of lambs, goats, and cattle. We spill their blood to atone for the sins of the people. We sprinkle it here and there, on the altar, and on the Children of Israel. As High Priest, on the Day of Atonement, Annas and I have each entered the Holy-of-Holies. On the holiest day of the year, we have parted the curtain and entered the most forbidden place in all the world, entering the presence of the Lord. Passing through the veil and into the cloud of God's presence, there we have sprinkled blood onto the stone summit of Mt. Moriah, the Rock, where the Ark of the Covenant once lay, the place where the Almighty led our Father Abraham to take his son, Isaac. God ordered Abraham to sacrifice his only son on that Rock. Abraham went obediently to Mt. Moriah. When he arrived, the Lord miraculously provided a lamb to be offered in Isaac's place. Abraham spilled the lamb's blood, and sprinkled it on the Rock of Mt. Moriah. The Children of Abraham have now sprinkled blood for more than a millennium, on that same Rock, located in the Temple's Holy-of-Holies."

I shouted, "I am sick of hearing about blood, both of animals and men." Thinking of the blood-red wine at Pilate's Praetorium, I also remembered drinking the Passover wine when Jesus said, "This is my blood." I tried to close my ears to Caiaphas' words, having had my fill of both wine and blood.

Caiaphas said, "As priests, we love the spilling of blood. It is a reminder given to us by God. By the spilling of blood, our sins are forgiven and atoned for. Just as it is right that a lamb should die to atone for a man's sin, it is better that this one man's blood be spilled, this Jesus, to save our nation. You must toughen yourself to the awful truth." Then he handed me a purse.

"What is this?" I asked.

"Your salary. I usually give it to Rachel. But you have truly earned your wages tonight, Judas."

I said, "Take back your money. It's blood money. I want no part of it."

"Do you think giving it back will change anything?"

I opened the purse. Looking at the silver, once again I remembered the words of Zechariah the prophet, "'If you think it best, give me my pay. But if not, you can keep it.' So, they paid me thirty pieces of silver. And the Lord said to me, 'Throw it to the potter,' the princely price they paid for me. So, I took the thirty pieces and threw them to the potter, in the House of the Lord."

The realization hit me. I had prostituted myself cheaply. Jesus, his mother, and the Baptizer were celibates, faithful to their vows. But I was a harlot, seduced by unworthy lovers, who paid a pittance for my services. Caiaphas has seduced me. But it was not enough for me to be his whore. He also sold me to Pilate, making me a camp follower for the Roman oppressors. Israel, God's bride, has always had a problem with adultery, running after other gods in place of her husband. I was like Gomer, the prophet Hosea's wife, a harlot before their marriage, and a harlot after.

Sickened by my adulteries, I threw the money at Caiaphas' feet saying, "I don't want your blood-money." Then I went into the Temple to think, but was unable to pray.

Sitting there, in Solomon's Porch, where Jesus had frequently taught, I was tormented by the foolish choices I had made. I remained there through the night. In early morning, sleep finally came to me, and also a dream. In it I was with Caiaphas. Both of us were dressed in priestly robes. He was dressed in the garments of the High Priest, complete with breastplate. I was covered in the seamless white tunic, worn by all Temple priests as the foundation of their attire, as commanded by God when he gave his instructions to Moses. I had the priestly turban upon my head. And we both had ceremonial sacrificial knives in our hands. It was the eve of Passover, its beginning only hours away at sunset. The Passover Lambs had been led through Jerusalem's northeastern gate, the Sheep Gate. Caiaphas took one perfect lamb. Then we walked it into the center of the Temple. There, on the altar, Caiaphas picked up a chalice, and taking his priestly knife, he opened the lamb's vein. Holding the chalice below the flow of blood, Caiaphas filled it to the brim. Then, while the lamb stood there bleeding, Caiaphas gave the chalice to me and said, "Drink."

In horror, I shouted at him, "No, as High Priest, you know no Jew may drink blood, for it contains the essence of life."

"But you must drink, Judas," Caiaphas said to me.

"No. I will never drink the blood of the lamb."

"As you wish," Caiaphas said. Then he threw the blood on the altar. It dripped down the altar's horns. Putting down the chalice he said, "Let us do our duty." We both readied our priestly knives, finishing the lamb's sacrifice, its body without spot of blemish. We killed it and butchered its body, that all might partake of its meat.

From deep within the Temple's sanctuary, I heard a rumbling deep voice, like that of an earthquake. The voice said, "It is accomplished."

Startled, I ran toward the sanctuary's doors. They had been flung wide open. Looking inside God's House, I saw the Holy Curtain that hides the Holy-of-Holies. Beginning at the top, forty-cubits above (a cubit is 18 inches), it began to tear in two, from top to bottom. Then, emerging from behind the curtain, from within the Holy-of-Holies, a pillar of cloud rushed out, blowing out all seven lamps of the Holy Menorah as it passed, then leaving through the sanctuary's wide-open doors. When the cloud entered the Temple's inner courtyard, it ascended above, expanding until the entire sky turned black. It had been a bright and sunny Passover eve. But when the cloud ascended into the sky and spread, the light was extinguished, like the plague of darkness in Egypt, when Pharaoh refused to let God's people go. Then I heard a voice from heaven say, "Moses stretched out his arms towards the sky, and darkness covered Egypt for three days."

Returning to the altar where Caiaphas was, I looked at the lamb that had been sacrificed. But it was no longer a lily-white lamb. In its place, lay Jesus, who was dressed in his seamless white tunic. I screamed, "No!"

At that moment, I woke up. Standing and trying to shake the cobwebs from my brain, I left Solomon's Porch and went to the Sanhedrin's chamber. Lurking on the side, in half shadow, I stood to watch the proceedings.

In spite of being half-hidden, Caiaphas saw me and said, "Glad to see a night's sleep has brought you to your senses, Judas." But my only concern was to know what they would do to my rabbi.

Members of the Sanhedrin straggled in, some grumbling about the early hour.

Then Jesus was brought in, bound. It was clear he had been beaten during the night. His right eye was swollen shut, the left eye showing red in the white, his upper lip swollen, and much of the face black and blue. But he was alive. I was afraid that when they threw Jesus into Caiaphas' pit (dungeon), that he might not survive the night, conveniently hanged or otherwise come to an unfortunate accident before daybreak. But there he was, my rabbi. I could not help but think of the Psalm we sing in the Temple, "He brought me up out of the horrible pit, out of miry mud, and set my feet upon the rock, guarding my every step." Jesus' survival was living proof that no pit is so deep, that God is not deeper still.

Caiaphas spoke, "Yesterday, Jesus the Branch (Nazarene) was convicted of blasphemy - claiming to be the Son of Man, making himself equal with God. This man was judged deserving of death. A capital case must me reaffirmed on the second day by the entire Council. What say you, leaders of God's people?"

Nicodemus, one of the two Pharisees who believed in Jesus stood and said, "Why, what proof was presented against this man?"

Shutting down any discussion Caiaphas said, "This is merely a hearing to affirm the trial's sentence. We do not revisit the trial's evidence here. These proceedings are limited to a yes or no vote, not a debate...But in a spirit of generosity towards our esteemed Pharisee member, Nicodemus, I can tell you the accused confirmed the blasphemy with his own lips." Turning to the other chief priests making up the executive committee of the Sanhedrin he said, "Isn't that right, my friends?"

They shook their heads in agreement and uttered, "That's right," and "He certainly did."

Nicodemus looked at Jesus, clearly wanting to save him. But the Sanhedrin's rules left him few tools to push for Jesus' release.

Caiaphas said, "Time to vote. Do each of you, as members of the Sanhedrin, affirm this man's sentence?"

One by one, the vote was taken, Nicodemus and Joseph of Arimathea voted "No," and a few other Pharisee members abstained. But all the Sadducees voted as a block, affirming the sentence.

Caiaphas said, "The sentence is affirmed. Roman edict has denied us the power to execute criminals without the consent of the Prefect. Therefore, we are adjourned to gather before Pilate. All Sanhedrin members voting for conviction, should come with us to the Prefect's Praetorium."

A procession left the Sanhedrin's chamber. Pilate's administrative center was only a short distance from the Temple. Caiaphas had arranged for all non-essential Temple staff to join the delegation, several hundred strong.

The Temple Guard led Jesus by a large rope. It was tied around his waist, looking like the "cable-tow," which is tied around the High Priest before he enters the Holy-of-Holies, on the Day of Atonement. In this way, if God strikes the High Priest dead, the other priests can retrieve his body, without violating God's Most Holy Place.

The Guard had also placed a blindfold over Jesus' eyes. So, as they led him along the street, he stumbled on the uneven stone pavement. Caiaphas, Annas, I, the Sanhedrin, and the rest of the Temple mob, followed behind.

The guards taunted Jesus on the way, saying, "Hey magician, do us a rope trick. Make it rise like a cobra out of our hands."

"You made blind eyes see, Jesus. Now, your seeing eyes have been made blind."

And, "Moses set the Hebrews free from bondage, let's see you break free of your bonds."

The procession led Jesus into the courtyard of Pilate's Praetorium. Passover being near, Antipas was also in Jerusalem. When attending the Temple's Festivals, Antipas stayed at the more expansive and opulent palace, the one his father, Herod the Great, had built on the western side of the city.

Pilate's overbearing pride and sense of self-importance was shown by his frequent bitter complaint, "Why should the tiny tetrarch of pathetic Perea and grimy Galilee, occupy more stately quarters than the Roman Prefect of Judea?" But it was Antipas' father who had built the palace. And the office of Prefect was little more than a glorified military commander, Roman or not. Being a member of the Equestrian class, Pilate's pride and haughtiness knew no bounds.

The Sanhedrin, Sadducees, and other Temple staff, filled Pilate's courtyard beyond capacity, the overflow standing beyond the gates, clogging the street outside. This made it impossible for the crowds to pass, as they prepared for the Passover that would begin at sunset.

Caiaphas informed Pilate's tribune, "We are here to see the Prefect."

"What is your business."

"We have a capital case for him to affirm."

After going inside, the tribune came back and said, "The Prefect will grant you audience. Follow me."

Caiaphas replied, "We cannot defile ourselves by entering a goy dwelling."

"Goy," snorted the tribune, "what is a goy?"

"A pagan, my boy, like yourself. Now run along and ask the Prefect to come speak with us."

Fire flashing in the tribune's eyes, hand on his sword, appearing ready to cut Caiaphas' throat with the slightest provocation, the tribune stared at Caiaphas while standing nose to nose with him, "Better a pagan than an atheist Jew, a Jew who hates the gods, practicing all sorts of vile Jewish ceremonies." Then the tribune turned and went back inside to speak with Pilate.

After a fifteen-minute delay, Pilate emerged from the palace. He asked, "What is the accusation you bring against this man?

Caiaphas said, "Prefect, there is no accusation for you to hear. We have already tried this man according to the Law of Moses. He has been found guilty, and judged worthy of death. If he were not a criminal, we would not have brought him to you, especially on the eve of Passover."

Pilate answered, "Take him then, and punish him according to your own law.

"Prefect, it is not lawful for us to put a man to death."

"Death? Wouldn't a strenuous scourging do just as well?"

"No Pilate. This man must die."

"Why? What has he done?" asked Pilate.

"He claims to be the King of the Jews," said Caiaphas.

Without saying a word, Pilate entered the Praetorium. He then ordered the guards to bring Jesus to him, alone and without his accusers. I could hear Pilate loudly ask Jesus, "So, are you the King of the Judeans?"

Jesus answered, "Do you ask this yourself, or have you been told this about me?"

"Am I a Jew? Your own people and the priests of your Temple have brought you to me. Why is that? What is your crime?"

"My Kingdom is not of this world. If it were, my servants would fight, and I would not have been delivered to the Temple authorities. But my Kingdom is not of this time and place."

"You are a king, then?

"You say that I am a king. That is the charge you bring against me. I was born and came into the world, to testify to the truth. Everyone who loves truth, listens to my voice."

"What is truth?" Pilate sneered sarcastically.

Pilate came back out and said, "I find no guilt in this man - none at all."

Caiaphas said, "We witnessed this man leading the nation astray, forbidding payment of taxes to Caesar, claiming to be the king - the anointed king chosen by Israel's God."

Pilate had his guards bring Jesus back out in front of the crowd. He asked Jesus, "Are you the King of Israel?

Jesus said, "You say that I am."

Again, Pilate said to the chief priests and the people, "I find no fault in this man. He's just a pathetic fool, like all your supposed 'Messiahs.'"

Caiaphas and the Sadducees fiercely objected, "This man is stirring up the people, in Judea, Samaria, Perea, Galilee and beyond. He began his mischief in Galilee. Now he is inciting unrest in Jerusalem and the Temple."

Pilate said, "Galilee? Isn't that where the Zealot leader, Judas, was from?"

Caiaphas said, "My point exactly, Prefect." Caiaphas, Annas and the Sadducee members of the Sanhedrin spewed further accusations against Jesus, accusing him of every imaginable crime. But Jesus stood silently, not saying a word in his defense.

Pilate asked Jesus, "Don't you hear how many crimes they accuse you of? Have you no defense at all?"

Pilate asked Caiaphas, "You say this man is a Galilean?"

"Yes, from a small town, near the old capital of Sepphoris."

"Well, that is good luck," said Pilate. "Galilee's Tetrarch, Antipas, is here for the Passover. I will send this man to him. Maybe Antipas can coax the truth out of him." Pilate wrote a short note, in Greek, and gave it to the guards to present to the Tetrarch.

The Roman soldiers took Jesus to Herod's Palace, a short walk farther west. The chief priests, Sadducees, Temple servants, and I, followed close behind. We fought through the jammed streets filled with pilgrims, who were making final preparations for the Passover. The journey took twice the usual time.

Bringing Jesus into Antipas' audience hall, the commander of the cohort handed Pilate's letter to the Tetrarch. Breaking the seal, Antipas read it and chuckled.

The letter said,

My dear illustrious Tetrarch-

We have had our differences in the past, but thought this would be a refreshing amusement for your day. I send to you, Jesus - the Branch of King David. He is a resident of Galilee. Perhaps you have heard of him.

This Jesus is accused of making himself out to be the new King of Israel, a subject upon which I believe you have some knowledge and experience. If I am not mistaken, you have ambitions to occupy the same office as this man, like your father before you, King Herod.

Question him as you like, abuse him to your heart's content. If you desire, judge and execute him, as the Temple authorities request.

If not, send him back to me, and I will treat him in a manner befitting his high and royal status.

It is my hope you will see this as a peace offering, a practical joke among friends.

Your newfound friend,
Pilate

Antipas laughed loudly, happy to finally meet the trouble-maker of Galilee. For many months, Antipas had tried to lay hold of Jesus, because of the unrest he brought wherever he went.

But when word spread that Antipas had beheaded the Baptizer, Jesus no longer lingered in Galilee, spending increasing time in Herod Philip's domain, the Decapolis, Tyre, Sidon, Samaria, and Judea, making it impossible for Antipas to arrest him.

Jesus frequently returned to Galilee. But whenever word reached Antipas that Jesus was within his domain, the miracle-worker and his disciples had already moved on to the next town, never staying anyplace more than one night.

When he first heard of Jesus, Antipas' superstitious nature got the better of him. He thought Jesus might be the Baptizer reincarnated or resurrected, returned to haunt Antipas for the cruel treatment he had given John. But the Baptizer did not do feats of magic, even though he had a huge following that regarded him as a prophet.

Jesus was obviously a different man. He was known less for his sharp tongue and condemning harangues of sinners, than for the many miracles he performed, far greater in scope and kind than any magician or charlatan.

Antipas was happy to finally meet Jesus. He hoped to witness for himself whether the miracles were as great as had been reported.

Jesus was led in front of Antipas' court. Chuza, Antipas' Minister of Finance, was standing next to the Tetrarch. Chuza's wife, Joanna, stood behind him and to the side. I tried to be as invisible as possible, standing among the delegation of Sadducees. Looking down, I tried not to catch anyone's eye, especially Joanna's. But when I glanced up to look at Jesus, her eyes locked onto mine, anger seething within her. Immediately, I averted my eyes.

The Tetrarch questioned Jesus about the stories he had been told. But Jesus would not answer him. He would not even look at Antipas, but only stared at the floor. Clearly, he was not going to give respect or any regard to the man who had imprisoned and beheaded his cousin, John.

Members of the Sanhedrin began to make accusations to Antipas against Jesus. But the Tetrarch was preoccupied by the rabbi's silence. Standing in front of Jesus, Antipas took his scepter. Placing it beneath his chin, lifting it up, he forced Jesus to look him in the eye. Antipas said, "If you refuse to answer my innocent questions, perhaps I should order my men to cut out your tongue.

I doubt the masses will be amused by a wonder-worker who can't speak or heal himself."

Jesus remained silent. Chuza leaned towards Antipas and said, "Your Majesty, clearly this man is no threat to you or your reign. Wouldn't it be expedient to free him? His execution or imprisonment will stir more anger than letting him go."

Joanna then stormed out of the room, weeping. Passing directly in front of me, when she passed, she spat in my face, the spittle hitting me on the forehead. Before I could wipe it away, it oozed down into my eyes. Annas handed me a handkerchief and whispered, "One of your conquests, eh Judas? A man must have his diversions. It speaks well of you to seduce such a highly placed muse. Don't worry, I won't tell your wife. We Sadducees protect our own."

Antipas began to mock Jesus, "Clearly the stories and rumors about you are just that, fables having little truth. At least the Baptizer was a man. He was not afraid of me or anyone. Even while in jail, he condemned me for my sin, unafraid of any king or earthly authority." Then Antipas acted out a swinging motion, as though he were bringing down a heavy sword on John's neck, "When I had John's head cut off, he didn't whimper. Like a king pardoning a faithless subject, before the fatal swing was swung, the Baptizer forgave me and the soldiers who executed him. Even though John was the one awaiting execution, like the priest he was, the Baptizer pronounced absolution over us, forgiving us of our sin. As for you, Branch, either you are too scared to speak, ready to soil yourself, or you are just too dumb and ignorant to grasp the dire nature of your situation…

"Since you are too 'kingly' to answer my questions, we will dress you in a manner befitting your station, O King of Israel." Antipas removed the purple robe from his shoulders, and placed it on Jesus. Then, Antipas bowed down before Jesus and worshiped him saying, "Hail, King of Israel! The tetrarchs and prefects are defeated and dead. Long live the new King of the Jews."

The whole crowd laughed at Antipas' antics, as they repeated after him, "Hail, King of the Jews."

Then the Tetrarch sent Jesus back to Pilate. The Roman guards, Jesus, the chief priests, Sadducees, myself, and the crowd, trudged back on the same jammed streets we had passed before, returning to Pilate's Praetorium.

Yet again, Pilate came out into the courtyard. He said to Caiaphas, "You brought this man to me, saying he was leading the people to revolt. Behold, I have examined him, and find no guilt in him, concerning the crimes you list. Herod Antipas, the Tetrarch of Galilee, has not found him guilty, either. Antipas did not hesitate to execute the rebel, John the Baptizer. If he thought this Galilean guilty, he would have executed the man himself - not returned him to me. I judge this Jesus as having done nothing worthy of execution. But to please you, and to set a stern example, I will have the man beaten, before his release."

The Roman soldiers wove together a crown of thorns, and put it on Jesus' head. Wearing Antipas' purple robe, they handed Jesus a reed scepter, as he stood erect before the cohort.

Saying, "Hail, King of the Jews," they slapped him with their open hands. Then they beat him with their fists, until his face was unrecognizable.

When they had finished, Pilate went out to the crowd again, saying, "Look, I present this man to you, that you may know I find no guilt in him." Jesus was pushed towards the crowd, wearing the crown of thorns, and the purple robe. Pilate said to the crowd, "Behold the man!"

When the chief priests and Temple authorities saw Jesus dressed in mock royal attire, they chanted in unison, "Crucify him, crucify him."

Pilate answered the crowd, "You take him, and crucify this man. I find no guilt in him."

The mob of Sadducees and Temple attendants replied to Pilate, "We have a Law. By God's Law this man must die. He claimed to be the Son of Man, equal with God Almighty."

Pilate asked Jesus, "Where are you from? Tell me, who are you." But Jesus remained silent.

Pilate said to him, "You refuse to answer me? Don't you know I have the power to crucify you, or to have you released?"

Jesus replied, "You have no authority over me at all, only the power that has been give you from above. Those who delivered me into your hands are guilty of the bigger sin." Hearing Jesus' words, I cringed, feeling as though a sword had been thrust into my gut.

Pilate said to the crowd once more, "Truly, I believe this man should be released."

The mob cried out, "If you let this man go, you are not a friend of Caesar's. Whosoever makes himself out to be a king, opposes Caesar."

"I see your point, my friends," Pilate shouted to the crowd. "Even though he is a pathetic example of man, laughable, a giant only in his own warped mind, unable even to offer a defense, still, any man who calls himself a king, is a traitor to Rome and to your people.

"You are right. To us Romans, no word is more hateful than 'king.' No Roman has dared call himself a king for hundreds of years. Even divine Tiberius, and the other Emperors, do not dare call themselves 'king.' For this is the title of tyrants, and the reason illustrious Julius Caesar was assassinated, out of fear he was making himself out to be a king.

"You indeed are right, my friends, no matter how ridiculous or mad this kingly imposter may be, anyone claiming to be a king is fit only to be impaled, that everyone may see what all kings deserve.

"Even though I do not believe this man is guilty of any crime, I will concede to your demand for Roman justice. I am the representative of divine Tiberius, and not ruled merely by my own conscience. It is for your sake, and for the sake of your own leaders the Sanhedrin, that I bow to your demands."

Pilate commanded his guards, "Bring out the Judgement Seat from the audience hall."

Setting it in front of the chief priests and the crowd, Pilate sat upon it and said, "Bring forth the prisoner for sentencing."

Jesus was dragged in front of Pilate's Judgement Seat, almost unable to walk, virtually carried by a huge Roman, Jesus' arm draped over the soldier's shoulder for support. With the legionnaire holding Jesus up, the Prefect sat down on the Judgment Seat, in the Praetorian courtyard called the Pavement, in Aramaic "Gabbatha." Noon was nearing when Pilate said to the crowd, "Behold! Your King!"

As one voice, they shouted, "Take him away. Take him away. Crucify this traitor."

"Should I crucify your King, then?"

The chief priests and Sadducees answered, "We have no ruler, but Caesar alone."

After pausing for a moment Pilate said, "I will demonstrate to you Rome's mercy. At Passover, it is the Prefect's custom to release a political prisoner of the people's choosing. I currently have in custody, three Zealot murderers, caught robbing and killing on the road to Jericho. The leader of the insurrectionists is named Bar-Abbas, Jesus Bar-Abbas." Pilate then ordered his guards, "Bring forth the prisoner, Bar-Abbas."

His hands and feet were shackled. A chain was fastened around his neck, by which he was led in front of the crowd. Bar-Abbas shouted. "I am the only free man here! The rest of you are sheep being led to slaughter."

The guard yanked his chain, chocking Bar-Abbas, and ordered, "Quiet, slave. Your spirit will be freed from its body soon enough."

Pilate continued, "To demonstrate Roman mercy, I will give you a choice. Whom do you choose for release, your king - Jesus Bar-David, or this Zealot murderer - Jesus Bar-Abbas?"

Holding his hand above my rabbi Pilate said, "Who desires your Messiah be set free, the wretch of Galilee?"

One or two spoke up for Jesus, but were quickly silenced by threats from the crowd.

Then Pilate raised his voice saying, "And how many desire Jesus, Son the of the Father, to be released (in Aramaic Bar-Abbas means "son of the father").

Even though the mob of Sadducees and Temple servants cared little for any Zealot, they all yelled, "Bar-Abbas...free Bar-Abbas."

Pilate sat back down on the Judgment Seat and asked yet again, "Whom do you wish me to release?"

They yelled as one voice, "Bar-Abbas."

"What then should I do with your Christ, King Jesus?"

"Crucify him."

"Why, what evil has he done?"

They cried out even more, "Crucify him."

Pilate ordered the washbasin be brought to him. In front of the crowd, the servants poured water over his hands as he said, "Look, I wash my hands of your king's blood. I have no part in him or his blood. His blood is upon you. You are washed in his blood. It is for you he dies, but not for me. He is your chosen victim. It is by your demand that your king is slain."

The crowd answered, "May his blood be on us, cover us, and be upon our offspring, for all generations to come."

Pilate then released Bar-Abbas, but delivered my rabbi, Jesus the Nazarene (the Branch), to be executed.

The Roman soldiers took Jesus into the assembly hall and encircled him. Caiaphas, Annas, and Pilate went to watch. I went with them. It was part the punishment I deserved for what I had done - to watch and see the terrible result of my betrayal. Caiaphas and Pilate wanted Jesus dead. But it was I who bore the greater guilt. They could not have arrested him without my help. If not for me, they would never have found Jesus in a secluded place. Everything Jesus was suffering, was my fault, and mine alone. Why did my mother give birth to me? It would have been better if I had never been born.

Wearing the crown of thorns that cut into his scalp, and Antipas' princely robe, the Roman legionnaires bowed before Jesus, as Antipas had done. They mocked Jesus by saying, "Hail, King of the Jews!" They all spat upon him, and beat him, yet again.

Then they stripped Jesus naked, and scourged him with a cat-of-nine-tails, each strip of leather having a piece of iron, glass, or sharp bone, tied tightly on the end. Oh, how I wished to take his place. I was the guilty one, not him.

The whipping began. One, two, three - Jesus' blood ran down his back. Four, five, six - the flesh began to flay. Seven, eight, and nine – Jesus' legs started to buckle. The only thing keeping him erect were the leather straps tying his hands tightly to a ring on the whipping post. Ten, eleven, and twelve - the blood ran down the back of his legs and onto Jerusalem's ground. Thirteen, fourteen, and fifteen - strips of flesh now dangled like strings. Sixteen, seventeen, and eighteen - the Romans took turns delivering the blows. Nineteen, twenty, and twenty-one - they laughed and drank, betting on whether Jesus would survive long enough to be crucified. Twenty-two, twenty-three, and four, the majority wagered that Jesus would die before being impaled upon the cross. Twenty-five, six, and seven - Jesus shrieked as only one tortured can do. Twenty-eight, twenty-nine, and thirty - the Romans began to complain about Jesus' silence, now only sporadically letting out a deep moan. Thirty-one, two, and three - the punisher yelled out, "Die already, you hated king of the hated Jews." Thirty-four, five, and six - even the cruel Romans began to pity this poor wretch. Thirty-seven, eight, and...nine - one short of forty, a death sentence few survived. Kidney's now torn apart, his body in severe shock, to the cohort's surprise, Jesus was still alive.

Pilate tired of the entertainment. No longer amused, he left his soldiers to finish the execution outside the city walls.

Roman Consul Sejanus hated Jews. He was the one who sent the Jew-hating, Jew-baiting Pilate to chastise and thoroughly Romanize Judea. Sejanus hand-picked Pilate as Prefect of our land.

While in the Praetorium, we heard news of Sejanus' fate. Because of that, I now understood the meaning of Roman justice, which is to say, no justice at all.

One day, Sejanus was ruler of the Roman Empire, in all but name, second in power only to the divine Emperor Tiberius, and heir apparent to Caesar's throne.

But the next day, the Roman senate received a letter from the Emperor. In it, Tiberius called upon the Senators, and all "friends of Caesar," to summarily execute Sejanus, without trial or defense.

Non-citizens, the vast majority of the Empire's residents, could be abused and crucified at will. But Roman citizens, it was said, must receive a trial, and can only be executed respectfully, by beheading with a Roman sword. That was Roman law. Tell that to the ghost of Roman citizen Sejanus.

After he was summarily killed, Sejanus' corpse was thrown down the Gemonian stairs to the Tiber River. But before it reached the water, the Roman mob grabbed his body, and tore it limb-from-limb in the streets of Rome, until only bits remained.

Sejanus's three citizen children: Strabo, Capito Aelianus, and Junilla, were likewise executed without trial.

Junilla was only a young girl. No virgin had even been executed in Rome. So her executioners raped her, before putting her to death.

Across the capital of Rome, rioting, terror, and a blood-bath ensued. The mighty city was plunged into chaos, as Tiberius' henchmen searched under every Roman rock for Sejanus' allies, that they might reunite them with their friend in Hades' domain. The Emperor was persecuting all who had ties to Sejanus - his associates, and those who had courted his patronage.

Pilate too, might soon be a fish caught in Tiberius' net, being an associate of Sejanus. But that was a fantasy too wonderful to imagine. And even if Pilate were to meet the same fate as his friend and patron, it would not save my rabbi.

The Roman soldiers took the wooden crossbeams, and placed them on the backs of the two Zealots. Lastly, they placed Jesus' cross upon him. Knees buckling, falling to the stone floor, the beam slammed hard on the pavement, making an echoing "thump." Jesus was forced to get up, leaving a large blotch of half-dried blood on the stone floor. Once again, the Romans placed the beam upon Jesus' bloody back. This time, he somehow remained standing. Going out the gate from the Praetorium, the procession through the streets of Jerusalem began, almost noon. The Passover would begin at sunset - in a little more than seven hours.

Two soldiers led the procession, making a hole in the crowds jamming Jerusalem's streets. Two more soldiers marched behind the three condemned men.

Caiaphas, Annas, and I, followed behind the execution squad. I marveled at the priests' hatred for Jesus. Even though Zealots are usually the focus of their ire, they took no notice of them. This day, it was the man from Galilee, the one who had never done anyone harm, he was the one they hated - because he represented a threat to their power, position, and profits. He was the one they truly hated. How could I have been so blind? How could I be so stupid?

Jesus had not walked far until he collapsed once again, the beam falling to the side of the street. Clearly too weak to carry the heavy weight any further, they grabbed a muscular young African man asking him, "What is your name?"

"Simon from Cyrene. I am here for the Passover."

The centurion said, "Simon of Cyrene, I hereby press you into service to the Legions of Rome. By law, you must help us carry our goods for a distance of one-mile. We will lift this crossbeam upon your back, and you will carry it to the place of execution, outside the city walls."

I remembered Jesus' teaching, "Whoever forces you to go one mile, go with him two."

The women from Galilee, joined the procession, mostly Jesus' relatives. I caught sight of Mary, Jesus' mother, but quickly turned away, afraid she would see me. I prayed, "Oh God, bring an earthquake. Make the stones of these buildings fall upon me. Hide me from Mary, and from You, O Lord."

Then Jesus turned to the women. Looking out from the eye that was not yet swollen shut, he said, "Daughters of Jerusalem, weep not for me, but weep for yourselves, and for your children. Behold, days are coming when people will say, 'Blessed are the barren, and the wombs that never gave birth, and the breasts that never fed.' Then the people of Jerusalem will say to the mountains, 'Fall on us;' and to the hills, 'Cover us.'"

The women were wailing. As the procession progressed, the number of mourners grew, until the entire city seemed to be weeping and wailing. I thought of the prophet Jeremiah who said, "I heard a voice in Ramah bitterly weeping. Rachel weeping for her children, refusing to be comforted, because they are no more."

Looking at me, face twisted, jaw ajar, unrecognizable, if I had not seen his transformation, Jesus said to me, "Judas…"

Before he could say another word, I ran away, the traitorous coward that I am. Pushing through the crowd, I ran as fast as I could. Halfway back to the Temple, covered in sweat and winded, I stopped. I had to go back. Don't ask me why. I was a rabbit, and Jesus the trap. I had betrayed him, and was responsible for his death, but couldn't keep away. My soul will go down to Gehenna, soon enough. But until that time, I had to be with my rabbi.

Running back, I reached the slow-moving procession, just as it was leaving the city gate. There the procession turned right, to climb the hill of exposed rock. It was an abandoned quarry, the stones used by Herod the Great for his massive monstrosities. It was called in Aramaic, Golgotha, the Place of the Skull.

ת

Chapter XI: The Tragedy

The legionnaires stopped everyone from coming close, making all of us wait by the road, until their gruesome task had been completed.

The African Jew seemed to have little trouble carrying Jesus' crossbeam up the steep incline, apparently used to carrying heavy burdens. Simon the Cyrene had truly done what Jesus said we all must do. Simon had taken up the cross and followed my rabbi. Jesus, almost unable see or walk, was helped to the top by one of the soldiers.

Straining to climb the embankment with their crosses, slowly the two Zealots trudged up the hill. At last, they also reached the crest. The soldiers made the Zealots lie down on their backs, with their shoulders and arms on the crossbeams. Then, the heavy nails were hammered, piercing first the skin, then the muscles, finally penetrating the bones of each wrist. Screams echoed against the city's nearby stone walls. Those passing by on the road below, jumped at each shriek.

When the Romans drove the nails into Jesus' hands, he was silent, quietly accepting the worst cruelties that one human being can inflict upon another.

Once the three men were securely affixed to their frames, ropes and pulleys were attached to each crossbeam. The men were then hoisted onto their respective posts, each permanently driven and mounted into the rock, reused for countless executions. The blood of past victims had been absorbed into each vertical post, making them look as though they had been generously slathered in brownish-red paint.

The three crossbeams now fastened in place, the men's feet were impaled. Jesus was in the center, the two Zealots on either side. Bar-Abbas, the ring-leader of the three highwaymen, was originally destined for the center position. But what importance is a mere rebel sergeant, in comparison to the King of Israel?

Each cross had the criminal offense nailed above. The Zealots' wooden plaques said, "rebel, murderer, and traitor to Rome," written in the Roman Empire's three most common and universal languages – Greek, Aramaic, and Latin. All three were tongues of cruel conquers who had defeated, oppressed, and abused the Jews: Alexander's Greek, Rome's Latin, and Assyria's Aramaic. Jesus' plaque of charges said, "Jesus the Branch, King of the Jews." The signs were hung for the benefit of passersby, because the place of execution was on a main highway leading into and out of Jerusalem.

Pilate wanted to teach all Jews a lesson - resist Rome, and you will die a cruel and ignoble death. After suffering eternal hours of unfathomable pain and suffering, you will welcome Death's arrival as a prayed for, begged for, and hoped for friend.

When the three condemned men were firmly affixed to their trees, those who wished, were allowed by the soldiers to draw near the condemned men. Jesus' mother, aunt, Mary from Magdala, and the mother of Zebedee's two sons, went to Jesus.

The only disciple present, was the youngest of our number, John, the one Jesus had a special affection for, because of his youth and playful good-hearted nature. None of the other disciples were anywhere to be seen. They were undoubtedly in hiding, afraid they might become next object lesson for Roman justice.

When Jesus saw Mary and John, standing in front of him, he said, "Mother, this is now your new son." To John he said, "This is your new mother." Jesus was Mary's only son. Joseph's children had become estranged from her, because she had chosen to remain with

Jesus, and his disciples. But the rest of Jesus' family had rejected him. They did not believe Jesus was the Messiah, or the Son of Man, and would not accept his teachings, content to remain Essene. John had lost his mother as a child. So, it made perfect sense for them to take care of one another. And in this way, perhaps one day, the division between Jesus' siblings, and his disciples, could be bridged and healed.

Then, John urged Mary and the other women to leave Golgotha, feeling as though the women had been through enough, wanting to spare them Jesus' agonizing end. I am sure John was also worried about the safety of the situation, not knowing what the authorities might do next. No doubt, he wondered how far Caiaphas' and Pilate's purge would reach. John led the women through the gate and back into the city.

I watched as the Roman legionnaires divided the condemned men's meager spoils. They took Jesus' garments and tore them into pieces, a part for each soldier. But his woven white tunic was seamless, the kind priests are required to wear by the Law of Moses, also the sort of garment Essene men wear, because most belong to the priestly Tribe of Levi.

The centurion said to his men, "Let's not tear this fine tunic into pieces. We will gamble for it by casting lots."

This made me recall the Psalm of David that says, "They divided my clothes between them, and cast lots for my tunic." Being a Levitical priest myself, I recalled the lots cast each year, on the Day of Atonement (Yom Kippur). The law states, "The High Priest is to cast lots for the two goats - one lot for the Lord and the other for the scapegoat. He shall bring the goat whose lot falls to the Lord, and sacrifice it as a sin offering."

I had complained to Jesus about wearing a seamless priestly tunic, uncomfortable with his family's heritage saying, "Rabbi, why do you wear such a tunic, when you are not a Temple priest? It makes you appear Essene."

He said, "Judas, how will you ever learn of heavenly things, while your mind is on earthly things? What difference does it matter, if I wear the garments of a shepherd, the tunic of a priest, or the crown of King David? I am descended of the tribes of Judah and Levi, and my mother and brothers are Essene. It is good and right that I wear the white robe of holiness. All who follow me will one day be given white robes of their own, not just priests, but also Judeans, Galileans, Pharisees, Sadducees, Essenes, men, women, and yes, even Samaritans and gentiles, both slave and free. All of them will receive white robes of righteousness, for they will all become part of the royal priesthood and a holy nation. They will also be given golden crowns, and rule with me for timeless ages, in the Kingdom of God."

When the crucifixion began, the skies started to darken. After the three men, had been hoisted up onto their "trees," it turned black as night. It was now past noon. Torches began to appear on the road, and at the gate leading into the city. The legionnaires had carried torches with them, knowing that those crucified, frequently linger in agony for days.

Even though it was now dark, it remained a hot and humid day. After carrying their crosses through the streets of Jerusalem, and losing a great deal of body fluid from blood loss, the crucified men were parched. One of the Zealots cried out to the Romans, "Water. Please friends, have mercy. Give me a drink of water."

One held up his leather canteen and said, "Do you want to drink from a Roman's canteen, Zealot? I thought you people hated everything Roman. What do you say, do you still want a drink, even though it has touched the lips of a pagan?"

The Zealot nodded and begged, "Yes, kind sir. I am dying of thirst."

"I don't think it is thirst you're dying from, my friend," the Roman laughed.

"Please, have mercy on me, kind sir. I beg you."

The soldier asked, "Tell me Zealot, when my fellow Romans were attacked by you and begged for their lives, did you have mercy on them?"

The Zealot didn't answer.

"Didn't you hear my question, Zealot? Have you become deaf? What did you and your rebel friends do to people on the road, when they begged for their lives?"

The Zealot still would not answer.

"I think someone has driven nails into your ears. Well, I will have mercy on you...of a kind. I won't give you my water. But we always offer condemned men as much vinegar as they want to drink. What do you say, Zealot? Would you like a drink of vinegar?"

"Please sir, have mercy. Please give me a drink of water."

The Roman dipped a sponge in rancid vinegar, placed it on a poll and held it up to the condemned man's lips. "What do you say, Zealot. Do you want the vinegar, or not?" If the man drank the vinegar, it would wet his mouth for a second, offering momentary relief. But then, it would make his thirst even worse than before, and turn his stomach. At first the prisoner would not drink. But unable to control himself or resist the temptation, he grabbed the sponge with his teeth, and sucked out as much vinegar as he could – a terrible mistake that would only make his suffering worse.

The process was repeated for each of the condemned men. The second Zealot also drank. When it was offered to Jesus, he turned his head away, and refused. One of David's Psalms came to mind, "My mouth is dried up like an earthen pot. My tongue sticks to the roof of my mouth, as you lay me in the dust of death."

Those passing on the road mocked Jesus, shook their heads, and said, "Aren't you the one who was going to destroy the Temple, and reconstruct again in only three days. Why can't you deliver yourself, and come down off your cross?"

The soldiers said, "Yes, if you are the King of the Jews, save yourself."

Caiaphas and Annas joined in, "He saved others. Let him save himself, if he is the Messiah, the king chosen by God. If he comes down off that cross, then we will believe in him. Let God deliver him, if he will have him. This Galilean said, 'I am the Son of Man."

One of the Zealots also joined in the mocking, yelling at Jesus, "If you are truly the Messiah, our king, then save yourself, and us also. For we fought as Zealots to establish the Kingdom of God. Come down off that cross, and make us your prime ministers."

The second Zealot yelled at the first, "Don't you even fear God? We are under the same judgement of condemnation. You and I deserve our sentence, for the crimes we did. But this man is innocent. He has done nothing deserving death." The man turned to Jesus and quietly said something to him. Then Jesus quietly answered him. But I could not hear what was said.

Some time passed. Then, Jesus cried out with a loud voice, "My God, my God, why have you forsaken me?"

When people heard this, they misunderstood and said, "He is calling for Elijah."

Others said, "Let's see, whether Elijah will come and save him."

But I knew what Jesus was saying, as his life and strength oozed out of his body. After all these months at his feet, as foolish and stupid as I had been, it was clear what he was saying. Jesus was quoting a Psalm of David that we sing in the Temple. And when I heard his words, my heart was broken anew. Jesus was quoting Scriptures, even while dying on the cross.

He continued to recite the Psalm, "Why are you so far from saving me, so far from my words of suffering? I am a worm, not a man, ridiculed by men and despised by all. Everyone who sees me mocks me. They hurl insults at me. Shaking their heads, they say, 'He trusts in God, let the Lord rescue him, if he is pleased with him.'

Unclean dogs have surrounded me. A gang of evil men have encircled me. They have pierced my hands and feet. They divide my garments among them, and cast lots for my tunic."

In response, I quietly recited the prophet Zechariah, "They will look on me, the one they have pierced. Yes, they will mourn for him, as one mourns for their only son, and grieve for him as a father grieves the loss of his firstborn child."

Jesus neared the end of the Psalm, "The whole earth will remember and turn to God. All nations will bow down before him. All authority belongs to God, and he rules over the nations... Future generations will serve Him, and be told about God. They will preach his holiness to a people not yet born – for He has accomplished this." Jesus mumbled again, "for he has accomplished this." Gathering all his strength he yelled, "It is accomplished!" After crying out in a loud voice, he died.

The ground shook, and the wind began to wail. Looking into the sky, the clouds started receding - but not in the usual way. An inverse tornado appeared above Jerusalem, as though sucking the clouds to its center. Light began to peak through at the horizons. Illumination increased as the dark clouds were drawn to the center, as though a drain had been drilled in the sky above Jerusalem, and the clouds were being sucked up into the drain.

Now sunny, the earth became quiet and still, like death, or when a total eclipse of the sun occurs. Not a bird, beast, man or woman was heard, silenced by the almighty power of nature. I whispered to myself, "Jesus commanded the winds and waves on Galilee's sea. Even though seemingly dead, was he also controlling the skies and earth in Jerusalem? Or was this God, showing his anger at what I, the Romans, and the Sanhedrin, had done to the prophet from Galilee?"

When the centurion witnessed how Jesus died, felt the earthquake, and saw the clouds disappear, he said, "Truly this must have been a son of the gods."

Standing next to Jesus' cross, I recited the prophet Isaiah, "He was hated and rejected by men, a man of suffering, no stranger to pain. Despised and rejected, he took our pain on himself and carried our suffering. But we regarded him as cursed by God, stricken by the Lord and afflicted. He was pierced for our sins, and beaten for our evils. The punishment that brought us peace was placed on him. By his wounds we are healed. We all, like sheep, have wandered away. Each of us has gone our own way. On him, God placed the sins of us all. He was persecuted and punished. But he did not open his mouth. He was led like a lamb to slaughter. Just as a sheep is silent before the priests when it is sacrificed, he too did not open his mouth. He was arrested by cruel tyrants and unjust rulers. But our people did not oppose his capture. And he was removed from the land of the living."

Then I said the Qaddish for my rabbi, "O Lord, holy and exalted is Your name. May Your Kingdom come quickly for all of Israel's children, bringing peace on earth, just as there is peace in heaven. Holy and praised is the Lord's mighty name, today, and for all eternity. Praised, honored, exalted, extolled, glorified, adored, and lauded is the name of the Blessed One, beyond what any earthly words or songs of praise can express. May the Lord who creates peace in heaven, also bring peace here on earth. O Lord, accept my prayers and the supplication of my heart. Amen."

A Roman soldier came from town, to speak with the centurion in charge. Then the centurion spoke to his men, "It is less than four hours before the Jewish Passover begins. Even though this means nothing to us, the Prefect has granted the High Priest's request, that the prisoners not remain on their crosses over their Sabbath. We have been commanded to mercifully speed the rebels' departure from this life, that they may descend to the shadows of hades, as is their destiny."

The soldiers went to the first Zealot. He was still alive. Taking the heavy hammer used to drive the nails, a "clump" pause "clump" was heard, along with screams of agony, because the man's legs had now been shattered. I became nauseous. The process was repeated for the second Zealot. With broken legs, the crucified men would no longer be able to push up and catch their breath. Hanging from their arms, hands above heart and lungs, they would soon suffocate, the cause of death for most who are crucified.

When they came to my rabbi, he was already dead. One of the legionaries took a hasta (spear) and plunged its iron head into Jesus' side to make sure. Blood and water flowed from the wound, proving he was dead.

Then I remembered another Psalm of David we sing in the Temple, "The Lord protects all his bones, not one of them will be broken."

I write these words, seated on a rock at the Place of the Skull, while all three bodies remain on their gallows. They are not the only dead in this place. Even though I still move and breath, I am dead inside. Soon I will join my evil brethren in dark Gehenna.

PART 3
ENDGAME

ל

Chapter XII: Final Curtain

Judas finished writing, and returned his diary to the leather knapsack he was carrying. As they waited for the two Zealots to suffocate, the Roman executions walked down the hill, to buy a drink from a wine merchant who had called to them from the road. While walking down the hill, they told mocking and obscene jokes.

Judas approached Jesus' body. Reaching up, he grabbed his rabbi's lifeless foot and wept bitterly. As he did, a stream of Jesus' blood oozed down his leg, and rolled upon Judas hand. At first he did not feel it. Then he recoiled, in horror. It burned - like acid. Staring at the blood, he grabbed an old rag lying at the foot of the cross, one left by the Romans. Hurriedly, he wiped Jesus' blood from his hand. Judas looked at it again, his hand still burning. Taking his cloak, he rubbed his hand a second time - hard. Looking at it yet again, it appeared clean, showing no hint of blood. But his hand did not feel "normal." Repeatedly Judas rubbed it, until the hand was raw.

Judas saw the spear used to pierce Jesus' side. It was lying beside the ropes and pulleys that had been used to hoist the crossbeams and victims into place. Hurrying to the items, he looked around to see if anyone was watching. No one was near. Judas grabbed the spear, and one of the ropes. A clump of bushes and rocks were nearby. Hiding the rope and spear behind them, Judas then left the Place of the Skull.

He returned to the city through the gate, the Gennath Gate. Walking quickly, he repeatedly glanced behind his shoulder, looking like a paranoid madman, as though he were expecting to see ghosts or demons chasing him in quick pursuit. Soon, Judas was running through Jerusalem's streets, as fast he could, shoving his way through the throngs of Passover pilgrims. Going past Pilate's Praetorium, then passing the theatre, and Caiaphas' house, Judas reached his own home. At least if would have been his home, if he had not been absent these many months. He knocked on the door, but no one answered.

Like any good Jew, Judas touched the doorpost, the Mezuzah that contained a small parchment. The parchment said, "Hear, O Israel: The Lord our God, the Lord is one. Love the Lord your God with all your heart, and with all your soul, and with all your strength. The commandments that I give to you today, are to be written on your hearts. Impress them on your children. Talk about them when you sit at home, and when you walk on the road, when you lie down, and when you get up. Tie them on your hands, and bind them on your foreheads. Write them on the doorframes of your houses and on your gates."

Judas then kissed the fingers that had touched the Mezuzah, and entered the house. He took out his diary from the knapsack and placed it on the table. Sitting down, he took out two sheets of papyri. On the first he wrote a note to his son, who was named Joshua. When translated into Greek, the name is Jesus.

My beloved son:

I write this last note to you with all my love and a final warning. Do not trust or follow the Sadducees, the Romans, or anyone hungry for power, money, or pleasure. Do not make the mistakes your father did.

Believe in God. Do what is right, and be faithful to all. And if you meet anyone like my rabbi, Jesus, who is humble, forgiving, and uncompromised by evil, follow such a one.

But do not follow your relatives - neither those related to your father or mother.

My son, I love you more than words can say, and hope you can understand why I cannot be with you.

There are some sins the blood of lambs and goats cannot atone for. Mine are unforgiveable sins. Only my own blood can pay the penalty due.

I will not be one of those who embrace evil, and then seek to escape the executioner's gallows. I will no longer be like the Romans or the God-accursed Sadducee priests, saying one thing but doing another. Playing the hypocrites, they condemn robbers, but use religious and government power to steal. Condemning murderers, they pervert the scales of justice, using the courts to murder their foes.

Your father is not innocent. I am guilty. And I will freely give my life, to repay my debt.

Your loving father,
Judas Bar-Simon

Taking the second sheet, Judas wrote a note to Rachel, his wife:

My precious little-lamb:

You deserve a man far better than me, and did not deserve what has happened these past months. I know you have been lonely, as I have been. But no matter what you think, or what anyone may say to you, know this - I love you!

One final request I make of you, my love. Keep this manuscript in a safe place for the day when our son is old enough to read and understand what it says. When he comes of age and has had his bar-

mitzvah, give him my last testament, that he might know his father, and learn from my mistakes. And give him my sword, that has been passed down for generations, from my fathers before me. May it keep him, and you, safe from Romans, Zealots, and even our own brethren.

I will always love you, my lamb. I wish I could promise we will meet again, either in Elysian bliss, or at the resurrection of all flesh. But we are Sadducees, disbelievers in an afterlife. The best our Sadducee families can hope for is shadowy Sheol.

Because of the evil I have done, if there is an afterlife, nothing but the fires of Gehenna await me. When you pass from this world, if by some pleasing happenstance you find yourself in heavenly bliss, do not search for me. You are better off without me.

Instead, may your joy be complete for all eternity, "May the Lord, bless you and keep you, the Lord make His face to shine upon you and be gracious unto you, the Lord lift up his countenance upon you and give you His peace."

Good-bye my love,
Your wayward husband, Judas

Judas, took the two letters and placed them on top of the scroll. Taking from his belt the short-sword, Judas put it on top of the sheets and the diary, to anchor them, leaving them for Rachel to find when she returned. Judas got up to leave. Opening the door, he stopped and looked back at the house one final time, tears filling his eyes.

Closing the door, he walked back to the hill where Jesus had been crucified - Golgotha. By this time, everyone had left, and the bodies had been removed from their gallows.

He looked around, making sure no one was near. Then he went to the clump of bushes and rocks, where he retrieved the hidden spear and rope, and hurried away. This time, he did not go back inside Jerusalem, but walked along the city's outer wall. Judas walked past the three tall towers of Mariamne, Phasaelis and Hippicus, and past the outer wall of the palace Herod the Great had built. He came to the Serpent's Pool. Then, he crossed underneath the new aqueduct - the one Pilate had erected with money confiscated from the Temple's treasury. Arriving at Jerusalem's southwestern gate, the Essene Gate, located near the upper room where Jesus shared his last supper, Judas arrived at the Valley of Hinnom (Gehenna).

There, Judas saw a large tree. It was growing in the middle of large boulders that sat beneath its branches. Taking the spear, he braced it between the boulders. Then he took the rope and tied the spear to the rocks, to firmly secure it. He climbed onto one of the tree's low lying branches, one located just above the spear, its point near.

Judas said, "Jesus, forgive me." Without hesitation or apprehension, he jumped off the branch, flinging his body onto the spear, impaling himself upon it. A deep "umph" came out of his mouth, as blood began to run down the spear's thick wooden shaft made of ash. Hanging there, Judas mumbled, "Oh Lord, may my blood atone for shedding Jesus' innocent blood, my rabbi, whom I have murdered."

Suddenly, a tall and thin man was standing in front of Judas. It startled him. Only a moment before, no one was within sight. Judas looked up at the man and said, "Rabbi…but…but I watched you die."

Jesus said, "Do you think your own blood will atone for your sin, Judas?"

"It's…all I have to give."

"It isn't enough," said the figure.

In pain, Judas spit out, "Then I have no way of paying my debt, to you or God."

"You were with me these many months, Judas. Don't you remember the Scriptures? Hosea spoke a prophesy about you. He said, "What am I to do with you Judas…I desire mercy, rather than sacrifice."

"I don't understand, Rabbi?"

"Your bloody sacrifice cannot atone for your sins. But my blood can. Your hand was covered with my blood at the Place of the Skull. Let my blood wash over all of you, not just over your hand. Let it cover all your sins.

"You were upset at the Passover meal, Judas, complaining there was no lamb to eat. But I was the Passover Lamb. Don't you remember what John the Baptizer said to you about me? He said, 'Behold, the Lamb of God that takes away the sin of the world.'

"Believe in me, Judas, even now. Believe in me. Believe in my blood."

"How can I, rabbi," Judas said bitterly, "I betrayed you to your enemies. I convinced myself I was serving my family and our nation. But it was the pagan Romans I helped. It's over now. It's too late for me."

"You are wrong, Judas. It's never too late. Two Zealots were crucified with me, murderers, highwaymen. Both deserved death. But even while dying on his cross, one of them believed in me and said, 'Jesus, when you come into your kingdom, remember me.' Do you know what I said to him, Judas?"

Judas shook his head no.

"I said, 'Today, you will be with me in Paradise.' It's never too late, Judas. Do you believe that? It's never too late."

Hesitantly Judas nodded, yes. It was now hard for him to speak. His intestines were oozing down the spear's shaft and onto the ground. Judas said, "Forgive me, Rabbi. I believe you are…" a spasm of pain made him pause. Gathering all his remaining strength, Judas muttered, "I believe you are the Lamb of God, who takes away the sins of the world…including mine." Then, Judas Son of Simon died.

FINI

Appendix 1: Dates of Jesus' Life and Death

What are the key dates of Jesus' life and death? Christian Scripture and history reveal much. Luke 1 and Matthew 2 tell us Jesus was born during the reign of Herod the Great. Herod died in 4BC. So, Jesus appears to have been born between 6 and 4BC.

Matthew 2 tells us Joseph, Mary and family, went to live in Egypt for a time. This is not surprising. There were one-million Greek-speaking Jews in northern Egypt, in and around Alexandria.

Jesus' family returned to the Promised Land after Herod's death. Matthew 2:22 says, "When he (Joseph) heard that Archelaus was reigning in Judea...he was afraid to settle there…and went to Galilee." Archelaus Bar-Herod (Herod Archelaus) reigned as Tetrarch of Judea from 4BC–6AD. So, Joseph, Mary and family appear to have moved to Nazareth before Jesus was eleven years old.

Luke's account of Jesus' conception, birth, and early years, appear to be recollections he gathered from Jesus' own family. They may have come directly from Jesus' mother, Mary. Luke 2 recounts Jesus' Bar-Mitzvah (Aramaic meaning "Son of the Law") at the Jerusalem Temple, when he was twelve-years old. This would be circa 8AD.

Luke 3:1-2 provides numerous historical references to the religious and political leaders during John's and Jesus' ministries. It says, "in the 15th year of Tiberius Caesars' reign, when Pontius Pilate was ruler of Judea, Herod (Antipas Bar-Herod) was Tetrarch of Galilee, his brother Philip (Philip Bar-Herod) Tetrarch of Iturea…while Annas and Caiaphas were high priests, the word of God came to John."

The fifteenth year of Tiberius' reign - circa 28AD
Pontius Pilate - Prefect of Judea, 26-36AD
Antipas Bar-Herod - Tetrarch of Galilee/Perea 4BC-39AD
Philip Bar-Herod - Tetrarch of Iturea, 4BC-34AD
Joseph Bar-Caiaphas - High Priest, 18-36AD
Annas Bar-Seth - High Priest, 6-15AD. Annas continued as the power behind succeeding High Priests for decades. Caiaphas was his son-in-law, and five of Annas' sons served as High Priest.

So, from Luke 3 we know that John's and Jesus' ministries took place between 26 and 34AD.

Luke 3:23 says, "Jesus was about 30-years old when he began his ministry." - circa 26-28AD.

John 2:20 says, "It has taken us 46-years to build this temple." Herod began to rebuilt the Temple circa 18-19BC. Therefore, John 2:20 takes place circa 28AD

The Gospel of John records three Passovers during Jesus' ministry. John the Baptizer and Jesus both appear to have begun their ministries circa 27-28AD. Jesus was baptized by John in the Jordan, likely taking place in January of 28AD.

During Pontius Pilate's term of office as Prefect of Judea, there were only two years when Passover fell on a Sabbath – the years 30 and 32AD. So, Jesus' crucifixion appears to have occurred on one of these two dates. Given the overall timeline, it is most likely that Jesus was crucified on April 7, 30AD.

Appendix 2: Cloud of God and Pentecost

There are numerous scriptural passages where God's presence is signified by a cloud, fire, and/or wind. The powerful significance of these epiphanies is frequently missed. To fully grasp what happens when Jesus dies on the cross, ascends forty-days after His resurrection, and at the arrival of the Holy Spirit on the Day of Pentecost, we need to connect New Testament events to ones that occurred in the Hebrew Scriptures.

Let us recall some of these Old Testament events: Genesis 15:17 says, "When the sun had set and darkness covered that place, a blazing firepot appeared." God first speaks to Moses from a "burning bush" in Exodus 3. Exodus 19:9 recounts, "The Lord said to Moses, "I am going to come to you in a heavy cloud, so that the people will hear me speaking with you and will always place their trust in you." Exodus 24:15-18 says, "When Moses went up the mountain, the cloud covered it, and God's glory was on Mt. Sinai. For six-days the cloud covered the mountain. On the seventh-day, God called to Moses from within the cloud. To the Israelites, God's glory appeared like an all-consuming fire, on top of the mountain. As he went up onto the mountain, Moses entered the cloud. And he remained on the mountain for forty-days and forty-nights." Exodus 33:9-11 tells of Moses meeting with God after Mt. Sinai, "When Moses went into the tent, the pillar of cloud would descend and remain at the entrance while God spoke to Moses...God would speak to Moses face-to-face, like one speaks to a friend." Exodus 40:34-38 says, "Then the cloud covered the Tent of Meeting. And God's glory filled the tabernacle. Moses could not enter the Tent of Meeting because of the cloud that had covered it, and God's glory filled the tabernacle. Throughout the Israelites' journey, whenever the cloud lifted from the tabernacle, they continued their journey. But if the cloud remained, they stayed there until it lifted. The cloud of God was on the tabernacle by day, and fire was in the cloud by night, seen by the Israelites during their journeys." Leviticus 16:2 recounts, "God said to Moses, 'Tell your brother Aaron that…I will appear in the cloud over the atonement cover.'" In 1 Kings 8:10-13, construction of the Jerusalem Temple had finished, and it is being dedicated when it says, "the priests left the Holy Place and the cloud filled God's Temple. The priests could not perform their services because of the cloud, because God's glory had filled His Temple. Then Solomon said, 'God told us he would dwell in a dark cloud.'" God speaks to Elijah at Mt. Sinai (Mt. Horeb) among the wind and fire in 1 Kings 19.

Remembering these and other passages in the Law and Prophets, we then turn to the New Testament. When Jesus was transfigured on the mountain (Mt. Hermon?) and met with Moses and Elijah, Mark 9:7 says about this event, "A cloud appeared and covered them. And a voice came from the cloud saying, 'This is my Son, whom I love. Listen to him.'"

When Jesus was on the cross, dying, the Gospels tells us, "Jesus cried out once again in a loud voice. Then he gave up His spirit. At that moment, the Temple's curtain was ripped in two, from top to bottom (Matthew 27:50-51)." What took place when the curtain separating God's presence in the Holy-of-Holies from the outside world was torn? Many have recognized that when Jesus died as the sacrificial lamb "the Lamb that takes away the sin of the world (John 1:29)," the tearing of the curtain showed that the barrier separating sinful humankind from God, was removed, once and for all.

However, there is a second significance to the rending of the curtain that is frequently missed. The cloud of God's presence that had been in the Holy of Holies, breaks out and leaves the Holy of

Holies and the Temple, just as the cloud of God's presence had entered the Temple during the dedication in 1 Kings 8.

What happens forty-days after Jesus resurrection, when he ascends? Where does Jesus ascend to? Acts 1:9 says, "he (Jesus) was taken up in front of their eyes, a cloud hid him from their sight." The same cloud that left the Temple's Holy-of-Holies on the day of Jesus' crucifixion, receives Him on the Day of Ascension.

A week later, when the Day of Pentecost comes, Jesus' followers (including his Mother, brothers, Mary Magdalene, Joanna and the other women) were gathered together in one place (possibly the Upper Room where the Last Supper was held, likely the Essene guest house next to Jerusalem's Essene Quarter, located on Mt. Zion, near the Essene Gate). Acts 2:2-3 says, "The sound of a blowing and violent wind came from the sky, filling the house where they were. They saw what looked like tongues of fire separating and resting on each of them."

The pillar of cloud and fire that left the Holy-of-Holies on the day of Jesus' sacrifice, and that received the resurrected Jesus on the day of his ascension, then returns and fills the Upper Room where Jesus had celebrated the Passover Meal, His Last Supper. There, the pillar of cloud and fire rests upon and enters those who have been washed clean of sin by the "blood of the Lamb." God's dwelling place is no longer a stone temple made by human hands, but is inside those who have been redeemed by the Lamb's sacrifice.

Appendix 3: The Jewish Race

Jews are the most persecuted people in human history. Countless other groups have also suffered oppression. But the persecution of Jews goes back at least 3000 years, and is more pervasive, persistent, and severe than for any other group.

In Jesus' day, there were as many as ten-million Jews. Today, two-thousand years later, there are still only sixteen-million. Since the end of World War II, because of the Holocaust, it has taken seventy-years for the world's Jewish population to recover its pre-war numbers.

Christians are the second most persecuted group in world history, suffering tens of millions of martyrs. Today, ISIS and other racist/terrorist groups are murdering still more Christians, Jews, and other minorities, such as the Yazidis and Zoroastrians. But no matter how many Christians have been persecuted, our suffering pales in comparison to what the Jewish people have suffered through the ages. Even though millions of Christians have been murdered over the centuries, there remain two-billion Christians today. But when Hitler tried to wipe out the Jewish people, the Nazis succeeded in eliminating almost half of all Jews in the world, reducing their number to a few million.

Christians and Jews must always remember the close symbiotic relationship between Christianity and Judaism. The Hebrew Scriptures form the foundation for both faiths. Jesus was a Jew, as were his twelve disciples. Even when Christianity began to expand outside the descendants of Israel, the Jewish/Christian evangelists first preached Jesus' message in the local synagogues. The earliest converts to the Christian faith were Jews, or converts to Judaism called "God-fearers." What resulted were two competing synagogues in each city - one believing Jesus was the Jewish Messiah, and the other remaining connected to the Pharisee school of thought.

Christians turned on Jews, and Jews on Christians. Eventually, racist anti-Semites began to take Scripture passages out of context, using them to justify persecuting their Jewish neighbors. The worst example of this is Matthew 27:25. During Jesus' trial before Pilate, the Jerusalem crowd calls for Jesus' crucifixion and says, "May his (Jesus') blood be on us and on our children." This statement has been used by racist anti-Semites to hold all Jews responsible for Jesus' death, to justify their persecution. However, Matthew 27:25, merely reaffirms the power and importance of blood atonement, which is the heart and soul of both Judaism and Christianity.

Exodus 24:8 says, "Moses took the blood, sprinkled it on the people and said, 'This is the blood of the covenant that the Lord has made with you.'" Rev. 7:14 says, "they have washed their robes and made them white in the blood of the Lamb." 1 Peter 1:1-2 says, "To God's elect…chosen according to the foreknowledge of God… sprinkled with his blood." The sprinkling of blood upon the people of the Covenant, in both the Hebrew and Christian Scriptures, is a good thing, a blessing, a cleansing, and a mark that we belong to God. When the Jerusalem crowd shouts, "May his (Jesus') blood be on us and on our children," this is a prophesy, and it is an affirmation of blood atonement, a statement that all Christians join the crowd in saying, "May his (Jesus') blood be on us and on our children," because if Jesus' blood is not upon us, then we have no salvation. It was Pilate who washed his hands of Jesus' blood, which means he has no part in Jesus' atonement for sins.

Who is guilty of killing Jesus? You and I are! It was my sin, and yours, that killed him. If I were alive and standing in the crowd on the day of Jesus' trial, I am under no delusion. Would I be on Jesus' side and cry out for His release? As a sinner, I likely would have cried out, "Crucify him." And yet, it is through this terrible act, the sacrifice of the Lamb of God, that my sins are atoned for, enabling me to receive forgiveness.

This is one of my motivations for writing this novel. Judas is an accursed figure. And yet, if I were in his place, would I have done better? I doubt it. Jesus' other disciples didn't do much better than Judas. Not only that, the man many consider to be the greatest Christian of all time, the Apostle Paul, was a murderer, a man who hated Jesus' followers and sought their death. But then, he was given unearned, unmerited grace and forgiveness by Jesus. I am no better than Judas, the crowd, or Paul. Undeserved mercy and forgiveness is the central message of the Christian Gospel. And yet, too often this essential foundation of our faith is forgotten, traded for a foolish self-righteousness that proclaims, "I am better than you – I am saved and you are not."

As for the question of "race" – scientifically there is no such thing. Race is an artificial construct. Science has shown through analysis of mitochondrial DNA that all human beings originated from a single mother. The biblical account says the same thing - that all human beings are ultimately related to one another.

Not only that, but if one counts back twenty-generations, roughly five-hundred years, at the twentieth-generation each of us has more than one-million great…grandparents. This is not the combined number of ancestors, but merely the number of ancestors each person has at the twentieth-generation. If one counts back ten more generations, each person has more than five-hundred-million great…grandparents, at the thirtieth-generation. As descendants of primordial Adam and Eve, we are all connected to and related to one another.

Many enjoy tracing their genealogy, to see what famous ancestors are in their family tree. But it is not unusual to have a George Washington, a Benjamin Franklin, or a thousand other famous figures in our family tree. Some fifteen generations later, those who are direct descendants of American's Founders, number in the millions.

Likewise, "Jewish blood" has likely been passed down to you from your recent ancestors. This is particularly true for those with a European, Middle eastern, Persian, Indian, or North African heritage – those places where diaspora Jews lived, beginning 2800 years ago. I have not tested my DNA to see what "Jewish blood" I may have flowing through my veins. Even if there is none, I still affirm and honor my Jewish heritage. All Christians share in the Jewish heritage, through the Scriptures, and through Jesus. We too are Children of Israel, grafted into the Root of Jesse.

NOTES:

Chapter I

Page 3

Via Maris – Latin for: "Way of the Sea" or "Road by the Sea." In Hebrew: "Derech Ha Yam" (Isaiah 9:1). It is also called the "Coastal Road," "Way of the Philistines," and "Great Trunk Road."

Armageddon – Hebrew: "Har Megiddo" (Rev. 16:16), meaning "Place of troops." The Valley of Megiddo was where Barak defeated the King of Hazor (Judges 4:15), King Hezikiah died (2 Kings 9:27), and where King Josiah died trying to stop the Pharaoh Neco (2 Kings 23:29, 2 Chron. 35:20-24, Zechariah 12:11).

Simon – See JN. 6:71

Bar – Aramaic for "son of" equivalent to "Ben" in Hebrew. Aramaic was an official language of the Assyrian Empire. Following their conquest of the Northern Kingdom of Israel, c.720BC, Aramaic became increasingly common among Israelites. Later, it was also an official language of the Babylonian Empire. Following the Babylonian conquest of Jerusalem and Judah in the sixth-century BC, and Israel's "Babylonian Exile", Aramaic was increasingly dominant in Israel. Parts of the Bible are written in Aramaic, such as Daniel 2-7. Over time, Aramaic's square letters replaced Hebrew's original Paleo-Hebraic script. In Jesus' day, Galilean Aramaic was a distinct dialect from Judean Aramaic.

Azazel – In Hebrew "Azaz" means "power" and "el" God. The phrase "lekh le'Azazel," in modern Hebrew means "Go to hell." Azazel occurs in Leviticus 16:8, and is often translated "scapegoat." "Azazel" also appears in the ancient Jewish book "Enoch" which says, "The whole earth has been corrupted through the works that were taught by Azazel: to him ascribe all sin." (1 Enoch 10:8). Azazel is also mentioned in the Dead Sea Scrolls. Azazel is often equated with Satan, or regarded as one of the most important fallen angels.

Angel names and archangels – Only two angels are named in the canonical biblical books recognized by protestant Christian denominations: Gabriel (meaning voice of God), and Michael (meaning might of God). Both are archangels. Eastern Orthodox, Coptic, and Roman Catholic traditions suggest there are seven archangels. The Apocrypha mentions two other archangels by name: Raphael (Tobit chapters 1, 3, 5, 6, 7, 8, 9, 10, 11, 12), and Uriel (2 Esdras chapters 4, 5, 10). These examples suggest that all angel names (or at least archangels) may end in "el." Enoch lists the names and descriptions of other angels and fallen angels.

The Sadducees – See Josephus' writings about the four Israelite schools of thought or parties in: *Jewish Antiquities*, XVIII.1, and *The Jewish War*, II.117. Also, see *With Jesus through Galilee*, by Pixner, pgs. 25-27. "Sadducee" is derived from the word "Zadok". It was the smallest and least popular Israelite party. But they controlled the High Priesthood, the Sanhedrin, and the Temple. Hellenized priests, they believed only the Torah was authoritative, discounting the prophets and other Scriptures. They did not believe in angels, demons or an afterlife. Sadducees were the wealthiest Jews in Judea, collaborating closely with the Roman authorities. When the Temple was destroyed in 70AD, the Sadducees lost their power base and ceased to exist.

The Pharisees - Hebrew: "Perushim" meaning "the Separated," largest and most popular Israelite school of thought. They revered the writings of the prophets, believed in angels, demons, and the resurrection of the dead at the last day. Central to the Pharisees was their "Halakhah" (oral traditions and interpretation of the Torah), which they believed back to Moses. In a sense the oral tradition formed a protective wall around the Torah. Rabbinical Judaism developed out of Phariseeism after the Temple's destruction.

The Essenes – originated as a group of priests who withdrew from the Temple during the Hasmonean (Maccabean) reign, c.150BC, rejecting the Hasmonean priesthood as illegitimate. This is the group that wrote the Dead Sea Scrolls. Essenes focused on ritual cleansing and purification, righteous living, prophesies concerning the coming Messiah/Son of Man, and the End Times. Jesus' and John the Baptizer's teachings share similarities with the Essenes. It is likely that John the Baptist was connected to the Essenes, given the location of his preaching on the Jordan near the Dead Sea (Salt Sea) was near Qumran (Secacah). Also, John was of the Levitical priestly line, since his father Zechariah was a priest. There are also indications Jesus' family may have been Essene.

<u>The Zealots</u> - a radical nationalist movement coming out of the Pharisees. Founded by Judas the Galilean, the Zealots violently rejected Roman rule and taxation, seeking to restore an independent Kingdom of Israel. They led the revolt against Rome that resulted in the Temple's destruction in 70 AD. Josephus had been a rebel commander in Galilee during the war, although he was not a Zealot. Josephus came from a priestly Sadducee family, and at points in his life appears to have studied Essene and Pharisee teachings.

Notes: Page 4
<u>Levi Bar Simon</u> – See LK. 1. It was a common among Israelites to have a set progression for naming children after their relatives. The firstborn son was often named after the paternal grandfather. If Simon were the son of Levi, it would be normal for his firstborn son to be named Levi Bar-Simon.

<u>Zechariah the priest</u> – See LK. 1:5-25

Notes: Page 5
<u>Nazareth</u> - The name comes from the word, "Netzer", meaning shoot, branch, or root, as in "root of Jesse," or "David's branch." See *With Jesus through Galilee*, by Pixner, p.14. Nazareth was likely settled by a clan from the Tribe of Judah that returned from Babylon c. 100 BC, during the Hasmonean reign. It was a village of some two-hundred Israelites. Situated near the Jezreel Valley, Nazareth was 3 miles from Sepphoris, Galilee's capital and largest city. Sepphoris was rebuilt by Antipas' following its destruction during the Zealot uprising that occurred when Jesus was a small child. Some traditions say Sepphoris was the birthplace of Mary's parents, Joachim and Anne. It is likely Jesus' step-father, Joseph,

helped construct buildings in Sepphoris during Antipas reign. The abundant construction work at Sepphoris may be part of the reason Joseph decided to settle his family in Nazareth when returning from Egypt. Jesus may also have done construction in Sepphoris.

Valley of Hinnom – Hebrew: "Ge Hinnom", in English, "Gehenna." It was the site of a Jerusalem garbage dump. Smoldering trash burned continuously, among decaying animal carcasses, and reeking smells. It is a fitting image for hell. Jesus frequently used this term, such as in the Sermon on the Mount.

Notes: Page 6
Solomon's death - c.931 BC

Kingdom of Israel divides – 1 Kings 12 and 2 Chronicles 10

Elijah and the prophets of Baal - 1 Kings 18

Distance from Mt. Carmel to Jerusalem – approx. 75 miles

Notes: Page 7
YHVH – personal name for the God of Abraham, Isaac, Jacob and Moses. In Exodus 3:14, when Moses asks what God's name is, he is told, "I am who I am (or I will be who I will be)," in Hebrew YHVH (Yahweh). Composed of the four Hebrew letters: Yod, Hey, Vav and Hey, it is also called the "Tetragrammaton" (four letters). It is unspoken among Jews, so as not to break the command against misusing God's name, or using it in vain. In reading the Hebrew Scriptures aloud, when YHWH occurs in the text, "the Lord" is said in its place.

Golden calf in the wilderness – See Exodus 32.

Notes: Page 8
Israel's Disobedience – See 1 and 2 Kings.

Assyria's conquest of the Northern Kingdom - c.720 BC. See 2 Kings 17.

Assyrian brutality – inscription by Ashurnasirpal II. See article, "Grisly Assyrian Record of Torture and Death" by Erika Belibtreu, Jan/Feb 1991, *Biblical Archaeology Society*. Today, ISIS displays a remarkably similar cruelty, on the same piece of land that the Assyrian Empire occupied.

Notes: Page 9
Holocaust – Greek word: "holocaustos," meaning burnt sacrifice.

Hellenization – the spread of Greek language, culture, and religion. Hellenization in Israel began when Alexander the Great conquered the region in the 4th century BC. During the next two-centuries of Greek rule, Hellenic culture and language increased and spread. Rome itself had been Hellenized at an early date in its history. In turn, Rome continued the process of Hellenization across its Empire. A sharp conflict raged between Hellenized Jews and those wanting to expunge Greco-Roman influences in the Promised Land. Pharisees, Essenes, and Zealots resisted Roman rule and culture. But the Sadducees were Hellenized Jews who supported Greco-Roman culture and Roman rule.

Notes: Page 10
Caesarea Marittima – Hellenistic Greco-Roman city constructed by King Herod the Great to be the new capital of Israel. Later it became the Roman Capital of Judea. Pontius Pilate ruled from it.

The Decapolis - Greco-Roman cities founded after Alexander's and Pompey's conquests of Israel. Located southeast of the Sea of Galilee, in Jesus' day, they belonged neither to Judea or Galilee, but enjoyed semi-autonomous self-governance as Roman city-states.

Sepphoris – See Note for p.5 "Nazareth"

Caesarea Philippi – Greco-Roman capital of Philip's tetrarchy, north of Galilee.

Notes: Page 11
Sanhedrin – meaning council. It was the highest Jewish ruling body in Judea. Having both Pharisee and Sadducee members, it governed religious matters, the Temple, but also operated like a combined city council/criminal court. The Sanhedrin had considerable power over local affairs, which was typical of Roman rule. The one power the Sanhedrin could not wield was capital punishment. The Torah requires stoning for capital offenses. Roman modes of execution were primarily beheading, crucifixion or death in the arenas, depending on the offence and citizenship of the offender. The primary task Rome required of the High Priest and Sanhedrin, was to maintain peace and order in the Temple and Jerusalem. If the current High Priest failed to meet expectations, he was replaced. Numerous high priests served only one-year. Annus Bar-Seth and his son-in-law, Joseph Bar-Caiaphas (Caiaphas), are the biggest exceptions. Annus was high priest from 6–15AD, and Caiaphas from 18-36AD. Annus had five sons who also served as high priest. Annus and his family controlled the office for more than a half-century. When Jesus was tried, Caiaphas was High Priest. But Annus was the power behind the throne. Both Caiaphas and Annus were involved in Jesus' trial, appearing almost as co-high priests. By controlling the Temple, its offerings, money-changing (currency exchange), and sale of sacrificial animals, Annus and his family were the wealthiest Jews in Judea.

Rome seized control of Israel – Pompey, 63BC.

The Roman Peace – Latin: "Pax Romana," began in 27BC.

Notes: Page 12
Rome's elite and leadership – See *Money Changes Everything: How Finance Made Civilization Possible* by William N. Goetzman, p.105.

Notes: Page 13
King Herod the Great - ruled Israel 37-4BC, as Rome's puppet.

Jerusalem Temple Built by Herod the Great – Herod completely rebuilt the Temple, making it the largest and most grandiose in the world. Herod enlarged its platform (the Temple Mount) to the size of twenty football fields. Jerusalem had been the capital of Judah/Israel since the time of King David. When Herod the Great built the thoroughly Greco-Roman city of Caesarea Marittima on the coast, it replaced Jerusalem as the seat of government. From that time on, Jerusalem became a "one-industry town," dependent on the Temple and religious "tourism.". Beginning in the eighth-century BC, large numbers of Jews had been scattered in a diaspora around the world. The vast majority of Jews lived outside Israel. Three times each year, Jews returned to worship God at the Jerusalem Temple. This was impossible for many who lived far away. Distant Jewish Communities sent representatives to worship on their behalf. Jews from around the globe flocked to Jerusalem to observe the required festivals, swelling the city's population from 50,000 to more than 500,000. Jerusalem was a city of stark contrasts. The wealthiest inhabitants were the chief priests and Sadducees. A small middle class consisted of scribes and Temple bureaucrats. The vast majority of Jerusalem residents were tradesmen, servants, slaves, and disabled beggars.

Notes: Page 15
Delilah – meaning delicate or dainty. See Judges 16.

Kerioth – small southern Judean town, where Judas is believed to be from, origin of the term "Iscariot."

The 9th day of Av – day on the Jewish calendar when Solomon's Temple was destroyed by the Babylonians; also, the day when Rome destroyed Herod's Temple in 70AD

Chapter II

Notes: Page 17
Sabbath begins at sunset - for the Children of Israel, each day began at sunset, not midnight.

Notes: Page 18
Sheol – Hebrew term for the place where the dead dwell after death, in shadows. Sheol shares some similarities to the Greek concept of Hade's domain.

Hell - an English word derived from Norse myths concerning the goddess Hel and her domain in the underworld.

The Pit – also called Abyss, where Satan is thrown in Rev. 20.

Gehenna - See Note for p.5 "Valley of Hinnom".

Heaven – from Middle English meaning: "sky," "firmament," "realm where angelic beings dwell with God," and so on.

Paradise – garden. The biblical concept of returning to the perfection of Genesis 1. See LK. 23:43.

Bosom of Abraham - another term for "Paradise". See LK. 16:22

Notes: Page 19
Firstborn son – The Torah says the firstborn male of every womb belongs to God. To redeem a firstborn son, a lamb is sacrificed to God (if poor, a dove) in substitutionary atonement. This recalls the prophetic act carried out by Abraham when he was commanded by God to take his firstborn son, Isaac, to Mt. Moriah (where Solomon would later build the Jerusalem Temple), and there sacrifice his son. Isaac asked his father, "Where is the lamb for the burnt offering?" Abraham said, "God himself will provide the lamb for the burnt offering, my son (Genesis 22:7-8)." God provided a lamb on Mt. Moriah, in place of Abraham's first-born son, Isaac. Two-thousand years later, God provided the "the lamb who takes away the sin of the world" (John 1:29).

Memorizing the Torah – few "books" were available in ancient times. An Israelite village commonly had one copy of the Law and Prophets (TANAHK). Before the advent of the printing press, each "book" had to be copied by hand. The writing materials were costly, as was the labor, expertise and intensive effort required to make each copy. In Jesus' day, the best and brightest students of the Torah often had the Torah memorized. Some students even had the entire TANAHK memorized. This was the only sure way for a person to have constant access to the Scriptures.

Greek language – Alexander the Great conquered a vast domain in the 4th century BC, from Macedonia to India, including Israel, the Middle East and Egypt. The Greek language became increasingly important as Greek rule continued for the two centuries, becoming the language of government, trade, commerce, philosophy, and education. The Jewish diaspora began with the eighth-century BC Assyrian conquest, continuing with the sixth-century BC Babylonian exile. Expatriate Jewish communities greatly increased during the Greek and Roman Empires, reaching as far as India, North Africa, and Spain. In the first-century AD, perhaps ten-percent of the Roman Empire's population was Jewish, as many as ten-million Jews. One-million Jews lived in northern Egypt, providing insight for why Joseph and Mary fled there with Jesus. But few Jews in the diaspora knew Hebrew. The greatest Israelite mind of the first-century, Philo (4BC–60AD), lived in Alexandria and wrote exclusively in Greek. Jews living in Israel, spoke Aramaic. Scribes and religious leaders knew Hebrew. But the dominate language of governance and trade in Israel was Greek. The Hebrew Scriptures were translated into Greek by the second-century BC. Called the Septuagint, this became the dominate version of Scripture among the Jewish diaspora, which is why the Christian Scriptures were also written in Greek. The Gospels, however, retain some Aramaic words Jesus spoke, such as: "talitha cumi" ("Little girl get up." Mark 5:41), "ephaphatha" ("Be opened." Mark 7:34), and "Eloi lama sabachtani" ("My God, My God, why have you forsaken me?" Mark 15:34). And there is an ancient tradition that the Gospel of Matthew was originally written in Hebrew/Aramaic. Also, see Note for p.3 "Bar".

Sadducees - See Note for p.3 "Sadducees"

Notes: Page 20
Dagger – Zealots were called by the Romans "Sicarii," Latin for "daggermen." They were known for having daggers hidden beneath their garments to stab unsuspecting Romans or collaborators when passing them on the street.

Rachel – in Hebrew it means ewe or lamb.

High Priest – See Note for p.11 "Sanhedrin."

Joseph Bar-Caiaphas – High Priest officiating at Jesus' trial. The discovery of his bone box is one of the great archeological discoveries in recent decades. His ossuary is one of twelve ossuaries or bone boxes, discovered in a burial cave in Jerusalem in 1990. This ornate ossuary is twice inscribed "Joseph, son of Caiaphas," and it held the bones of a 60-year-old male.

Insula – traditional Israelite family home, a multi-generational stone dwelling situated around a central courtyard.

Notes: Page 21
Palace of Caiaphas – High Priest's opulent insula in Jerusalem.

Priestly blessing – See Numbers 6:24-26.

Notes: Page 23
Talent of gold – approx. 110 pounds, $2 million on today's market. See "The Parable of the Talents," MT. 25:14-30.

Notes: Page 24
Bride-price – until the bride-price was paid, the betrothal was not binding. When the bride-price was paid, the couple was considered married, even before they came together for the wedding celebration. Any babies conceived during the betrothal were recognized as legitimate. After the bride-price was paid, a divorce would be necessary to break the betrothal.

Surprising the bride and her maids – See MT. 25:1-13.

Notes: Page 26
Killing of Zechariah – See MT. 23:35, and the Protoevangelicum 16:12-25.

Annus' five sons – also became High Priests: Eleazar 16-17AD; Jonathan 36-37, 44; Theophilis 37-41; Matthias 43; Ananus 63AD.

Birth and prophesy of John the Baptizer – See LK. 1

Notes: Page 27
David in En-Gedi – See 1 Samuel 23 and 24

Notes: Page 28
Rabbi - Hebrew meaning: master, great one, teacher

Disciples – students or learners

Chapter III

Notes: Page 33
Pontius Pilate – Roman Prefect of Judea under Tiberius, 26-36AD.

Valerius Gratus – Roman Prefect of Judea 15-26AD. He deposed Annus as High Priest, appointing Ishmael Bar-Fabus, then replaced him with Eleazar Bar-Annus, then Simon Bar-Camith, each serving only one-year. Lastly he appointed Joseph Bar-Caiaphas.

Notes: Page 34
Antiochus Epiphanes– See Josephus' *Antiquities of the Jews*, XII, 5-6

Notes: Page 35
Mikveh - Hebrew, small pool of water for ritual immersion.

Messiah – from the Hebrew Mashiach meaning "anointed one." Messiah translated into Greek is "Christos" or Christ, both mean "anointed one." The kings of Israel were "anointed ones." The prophet Samuel anointed both Saul and David as kings of Israel. The term does not carry with it a suggestion of divinity. It does however, confer a sense of God's approval, in that the person anointed has been selected by God to be the king over God's Kingdom (Israel). Likewise, the term "son of god," does not necessarily carry with it a strictly divine meaning either, in that the Roman Emperors of Jesus' day were called "son of god." The Latin term "Divi Filius" was used by the Emperor Augustus, first conferred on him in 27BC. It commonly appeared on Roman coins with the Roman Emperor's image. The term suggesting divinity that Jesus used most often is: "Son of Man" - in Greek. "huios (tou) anthrōpou," in Aramaic, "bar enos." "Son of Man" is derived from prophesy in the Book of Daniel. The Essenes focused on the "Son of Man" concerning the End Times and the Messiah. The other divine term Jesus used in referring to himself was "I am" - in Greek, "ego eimi," harkening back to Moses at the burning bush.

<u>Zoroastrian priests</u> – See MT. 2:1-12. The term "magi" specifically means Zoroastrian priests from Persia. Zoroastrianism is regarded as the oldest monotheistic religion. It was the dominant religion of Persia until the Muslim conquest. Jews were first exiled to Zoroastrian/Persian lands in the 8th century BC. There was a great deal of interaction between Zoroastrians and Jews, particularly during the Babylonian Exile and afterwards. There continues to be a Jewish community in Iran (Persia) today, even though they have suffered persecution and discrimination. The term "magi" is the origin for English words such as "magic" and "magician."

Notes: Page 39
<u>Repent, for the God's Kingdom is near</u> – See Daniel. 2:44, MT. 3:2-3, MK. 1:2-3, Malachi. 3:1.

<u>Kohanim</u> – from the Hebrew meaning "priests." Kohen is the singular. It is thought that people today with the last name Cohen likely means they are descendants of the Levitical priesthood.

Notes: Page 40
<u>Pharisees began to question John</u> – See JN. 1:19-28, MT. 3:1-12, MK. 1:2-8, LK. 3:1-8.

<u>Make your paths straight</u> – See Isaiah 40:3 and Proverbs 3:6.

Notes: Page 41
<u>Take on the mantle Elijah</u> – See 1 Kings 17 and Daniel 7.

Notes: Page 42
<u>Tax-collectors</u> – were hated and regarded as evil for several reasons. They engaged in "tax farming" which meant the authorities told them how much they would have to give to the government, and anything they collected above that amount they could keep. Imagine what it would be like if the IRS agent auditing your taxes could keep anything he pressured out of you. Another problem: taxes were pervasive and odious, even apart from "tax-farming." On the Sea of Galilee, a fisherman would be taxed by Antipas' tax-collectors as soon as they reached shore with their catch. Furthermore, tax-collectors were hated as Roman collaborators.

Notes: Page 43
<u>One more powerful than I is coming</u> – See MT. 3:11-12.

<u>Holy Spirit and fire</u> – God's Spirit is frequently represented and/or displayed as fire, wind and cloud, in both the Hebrew and Christian Scriptures. The Hebrews were led by a "pillar of cloud" by day and a "pillar of fire" by night (Ex. 13). See "Appendix 1: Cloud of God's Presence and Pentecost."

<u>Threshing-floor/Temple</u> – Jerusalem's Temple was built on the threshing floor, at the summit of Mt. Moriah, that King David had bought. See 2 Chronicles 3:1.

Notes: Page 45
<u>Yoke</u> – See MT. 11:29-30. A yoke was used on beasts of burden, to employ them in labor. It was also a symbol of submission or servitude. Each rabbi had a set of doctrines he taught to his disciples, his "yoke." A person agreeing to be a rabbi's student, agreed to serve the rabbi until his "yoke" of teaching was fulling learned. Then disciple could become a rabbi and gather his own students.

Kissed the tassel of his shawl – God's people were commanded to wear tassels. See Numbers 15:37-39 and MT. 23:5. Today Jews still wear tassels. Example: this was prominent in the play and movie *Fiddler on the Roof.*

Notes: Page 46
Man from Galilee - See MT. 3:13-14, LK. 3:21-22, JN. 1:29-34.

Chapter IV

Notes: Page 47
My Son, in him I am pleased – See MT. 3:15-17.

I saw Jesus coming from the wilderness – See JN. 1:29-40.

What were you doing in the desert? – See MT. 4:1-11, MK. 1:12-13, LK. 4:1-13

Notes: Page 52
Builder – in Greek "tekton" from which we get such English words "architect" meaning: chief builder, and technician. Joseph and Jesus have wrongly been called carpenters. Israel has few trees and little wood. Homes and buildings have always been made of stone. A "tekton" is a builder, especially in stone. It would be more accurate to call Joseph and Jesus stone-masons.

Notes: Page 53
We have found the Messiah – JN. 1:40-51, MK. 1:16-20, LK. 1:16-20

Notes: Page 54
Rock – in Aramaic "Cephas" or stone, such as the stone in the Holy-of-Holies at the top of Mt. Moriah, the threshing floor.

Bethsaida - a fishing town on the Eastern side of the Sea of Galilee, in Herod Philipp's domain, only a short distance from the founding city of the Zealots, Gamla, where Judas of Galilee was from.

Notes: Page 55
Wedding at Cana – See JN. 2:1-12.

They have run out of wine – A wedding banquet continued as long as a week. To run out of wine was embarrassing and a disgrace.

Ceremonial washing – The Essenes and Pharisees both had extensive ceremonial washing and cleansing rituals as part of daily life. To all Jews ceremonial washing and cleansing is of central importance, derived from the commandments God gave to Moses.

Chapter V

Notes: Page 57
Zebulun and Naphtali – See Isaiah 9:1-2, JN. 2:12, MT. 4:15.

Peter's House (insula) – was located near the synagogue and close to the Sea. It was a large insula made of black basalt stone. Today a church is built over it, but the foundations can still be seen.

Notes: Page 58
Joseph, Mary and their family - See *With Jesus in Jerusalem* by Pixner, pgs.15-24; and the P*rotoevangelium of James.*

Joseph's betrothal – See MT. 1:18-25, LK. 1:26-38.

Righteous man – in Hebrew: "Tzadik Ha-Dor," in Greek: "dikaios"

Notes: Page 60
Jesus, save his people from their sins – Jesus (Yeshua) means "Yahweh saves"

Moved to Egypt – See Hosea 11:1, MT. 2:13-15.

Septuagint – Greek translation of the Hebrew Scriptures completed some 200 years before Jesus.

Notes: Page 61
Nazareth – in Hebrew "Netzer" meaning "branch,: as in "branch of David." See Isaiah 11:1, 15:19, 60:21, Daniel 11:7.

Sepphoris - See Josephus, *Antiquities* 18.27.

Notes: Page 62
Jesus at twelve - See LK. 2:41-52.

Bar-Mitzvah – Aramaic meaning "son of the commandment" or "son of God' Law."

Father's House – in Hebrew, "Bet Av," what the Temple was called, the Father's House (God's House).

Notes: Page 63
Passover Festival – God commanded the Jews to worship him at the Jerusalem Temple at least three times each year, at the three major festivals – "Pesach" (Passover), "Shavuot" (Pentecost), and "Sukkot" (Tabernacles). At these times, Jerusalem would swell, while whole villages across Israel would become deserted.

Notes: Page 64
Stone signs – one of these signs from the Temple's separation wall (soreg) can been at the Istanbul Archeological Museum.

Cleansing of the Temple – See JN. 2:13-25.

Notes: Page 65
Tassels – God commanded His people to wear tassels in Numbers 15:38-39, "Throughout the generations to come you are to make tassels on the corners of your garments, with a blue cord on each tassel. You will have these tassels to look at and so you will remember all the commands of the Lord." See Matthew 9. When the woman touched the edge of Jesus' garment and was healed, she almost certainly touched his tassel.

God's House – or the Father's House, in Hebrew "Bet Av"

Mikvehs and ritual cleanness – ritual cleanliness was a crucial part of all the directions given to Moses for worshiping God in the right way at the tabernacle/temple. The commotion, animal stench, noise of commerce and cheating of pilgrims were making the Temple "unclean".

Notes: Page 66
Zeal for your house - Psalm 69, "God of Israel…I endure ridicule for your name, and shame covers my face. I am a foreigner to my own family, a stranger to my mother's children. Zeal for your house consumes me - and the insults of those who insult you fall on me."

Notes: Page 67
Destroy this Temple and I will rebuild it in three days – double meaning: Jesus being God in human flesh, he is the Temple of the Lord. When his body is destroyed on the cross, it is rebuilt on the third day. Also, this is a prophesy about the coming destruction of Jerusalem's Temple that will take place in 70AD.

Forty-six years to build this temple – Herod the Great began rebuilding the Temple in circa 19BC. That would make the year of this event circa 28AD.

Jewish calendars – most Jews in Israel followed the lunar calendar. The Essene's followed a solar calendar much like the one we use today. The Essene's rejected the lunar calendar, saying it was a pagan, brought back from Babylon, but that the one the Essene's used was the original Hebrew calendar. For his reason Essenes celebrated the Jewish Feasts on different days than everyone else.

Notes: Page 69
Daggerman – "Sicarii" is what the Romans called the Zealots. Sica" is Latin for dagger. "Sicarii" means "daggermen." Also, see not for p.20 "dagger."

Notes: Page 72
Nicodemus in the Garden – See JN. 3:1-21.

Notes: Page 73
Spirit – in Hebrew and Aramaic "ruach," in Greek "pneuma," it is also the word for wind.

Son of Man – this is the term Jesus most often used in referring to himself, rather than Messiah, or Son of God. It harkens back to Daniel 7, "In my vision I looked, there before me was one like a Son of Man, coming with the clouds of heaven. He approached the Ancient of Days and was led into his presence. He was given authority, glory and royal power. All nations and peoples of every language worshiped him. His kingdom is an everlasting kingdom that will never pass away - his kingdom is one that will never be destroyed." Son of Man may also reference the ancient Jewish book of Enoch. The Essenes especially focused on Daniel in their messianic expectations of the End Times. Copies of the ancient Jewish book of Enoch were found among the Dead Sea Scrolls. Enoch also focuses on the Son of Man.

Snake on the pole – See Numbers 21:4-9.

Notes: Page 75
Jesus on banks of Jordan – See JN 3:22-36.

Elijah at Aenon – See 1 Kings 17:2-6.

Notes: Page 76
John's arrest – See MT. 4:12, MK. 1:14-15, LK. 4:14-15, JN. 4:1-4.

Sychar in Samaria - See JN. 4:1-42.

Samaritans desecrate Jerusalem Temple - See Josephus, Antiq. 18.29-30.

Notes: Page 77
No one will be worshiping in Jerusalem – Jesus' prophesy of event that will happen within the next 100 years. The Temple will be destroyed by the Romans in 70AD. Some seventy-years after that, following the Bar-Kokhba Revolt, the Romans will remove all Jews

from Jerusalem, rename the city, and erect a statue of Jupiter/Zeus where the Temple's Holy-of-Holies had been. Even more important, and immediate, Jesus is prophesying that after his death, resurrection, ascension, and the pouring out of God's Spirit on the Day of Pentecost, there will no longer be a need for people to worship at an earthly Temple made of stone, but people will worship God "in Spirit and in Truth."

Notes: Page 80
<u>Fishermen in Capernaum</u> – See LK 5:1-12, MT. 4:18-22, MK. 1:16-20.

<u>Sea of Galilee</u> – 12-miles long, it is the lowest freshwater lake in the world, 700 feet below sea level. It was also called Lake Tiberias (see JN 6:1) in honor of the Roman Emperor, and Lake Gennesaret (see LK 5:1). Antipas built his new Greco-Roman capital for Galilee on its shores (supplanting Sepphoris) around 20AD, also naming the new capital for Emperor Tiberius.

Notes: Page 81
<u>Calling of Matthew</u> – See MT. 9:9-13, MK. 2:13-17, LK.5:27-32.

Notes: Page 83
<u>I desire mercy rather than sacrifice</u> – See Hosea 6:6.

Notes: Page 84
<u>Capernaum</u> – See MK. 1:21-27, MT. 8:14-17, LK. 4:31-41.

<u>Preaching in Galilee</u> – See MK. 1:35-39, MT. 4:23-25, LK 4:42-44.

Notes: Page 85
<u>Mary of Magdala</u> – See LK. 8:1-3.

<u>Seven</u> - 7 is a holy number, the number of perfection. Jesus' number is 777, three 7s. The "mark of the beast" is 666. Six is the number for sin, or falling short. So, 666 is perfect sin. The numbers 3, 12 and 40 are also holy. Multiples can be holy, such as 144 (12 time 12) or 24 (2 times 12).

Notes: Page 86
Crowds came from across Galilee – See MT. 5:1-42.

Notes: Page 88
An eye for an eye – the punishment in the Law of Moses for certain offenses. For instance: Exodus 21 provides that a person who harms a pregnant woman be harmed to the same amount as their just punishment, "an eye for eye". Leviticus 24 says that if someone harms their neighbor, the offender is to be harmed in the same way, 'an eye for eye." Deuteronomy 19 states that if a person gives false testimony intending to harm the defendant, the false witness is to receive the same punishment they intended the defendant to receive, "an eye for an eye."

Forces you to go a mile – refers to the Roman army's right to force civilians to carry their equipment for a distance of one-mile. Jesus telling people to freely carry their equipment a second mile, would be a controversial statement, especially to Zealots or those opposing Rome. But by telling his followers to "go the second mile" this would spare another person from having to carry the burden. This ties into Jesus teachings: "do to others as you would have them do to you," "love your enemies," and "love your neighbor as you love yourself."

Notes: Page 89
Love your enemies – See MT. 5:43-6:4.

Love one another; as I have loved you – See JN. 13:34-35.

Notes: Page 90
Love is from God – See I JN 4:7.

Love covers a multitude of sins – See Proverb 10:12.

Love God – See Deuteronomy 6:5, Leviticus 19:18, MT. 22:34-40.

Rabbi, teach us how to pray – See MT. 6:5-15, LK. 6:1-4.

Qaddish – from the Aramaic meaning "holy" one of the central payers of Jewish worship. See Ezekiel 38:23, Job 25:2, I Kings 8:45

Notes: Page 91
House upon a rock – See MT. 7:24-29, LK. 6:47-49.

Abraham on Mt. Moriah - See Genesis 22:1-18.

Notes: Page 93
I am the Rock – See LK. 20:17, MT. 21:42.

I am – in Greek "ego ami." When Moses asked God what his name was he replied "I am" (Yahveh - I will be who I will be). See Exodus 3:14.

Stone the builders rejected – See Psalm 118:22.

Multiplication of loaves – See JN. 6:1-14, MT. 14:13-21, MK. 6:30-44, LK. 9:10-17.

Notes: Page 94
Wanted to make Jesus king (Messiah) – See JN. 6:15.

Judas the Galilean – founder of the Zealots, also known as Jehuda of Gamla.

Quirinius – See Acts 5:37, LK. 1.

The Zealots continued - In 66AD, Judas the Galilean's son, Menachem, let the Zealot revolt against Rome. Judas' grandson, Eleazar, commanded Masada, when it was besieged by the Roman legions, and the entire Zealot community committed suicide.

What sign will you do – See JN. 6:30-59.

Notes: Page 95
I am – See note for p.93 "I am."

Son of Man – See note for p.73 "Son of Man."

Notes: Page 96
Many no longer followed Jesus - See JN. 6:60-71.

Chapter VI

Notes: Page 97
We went to Nazareth – See MK. 6:1-6, LK. 4:16-30, MT. 13:53-58. Also, see note for p.15 "Nazareth."

Sat in the Moses Seat to teach – in synagogues the one teaching sat on a stone chair called the "Moses Seat" and teach from there.

Notes: Page 99
Peter's home in Capernaum – See MK. 2:1-14, MT. 9:1-8, LK 5.

Insula – multigenerational home. See note for p.20 for "insula."

Blasphemy – in this case, it is claiming power and authority God alone has. God alone can forgive sins. Therefore, they believe Jesus is guilty of blasphemy, a capital offense in Mosaic Law. This is ultimately what the Sanhedrin find Jesus guilty of in his trial.

Notes: Page 100
Why don't Jesus' disciples fast? – See MK. 2:18-22, MT. 9:14-17, LK. 5:33-39.

Notes: Page 101
Show us a sign to prove you are from God – See MT. 12:38-41, LK. 11:24-32.

Jonah – was from Gath Helpher, virtually the same spot as Jesus home village, Nazareth. There is a close connection between Jonah and Jesus, similar to the close connection between Elijah and John the Baptizer. Jonah had the unique call of God to go to the pagan city of Nineveh, a capital of the cruel and ruthless Assyrian Empire, the ones who would eventually swoop down and destroy the Northern Kingdom of Israel. Jonah was sent to the gentiles, just a

Jesus' message is to be spread to the gentiles. Jesus goes to the pagan cities of the Decapolis, Caesarea Philippi, Tyre and Sidon. Jesus also compares Jonah's time in the belly of the fish, to his time in the tomb.

Jesus' brothers want to speak with him - See MT. 12:46-50, MK. 3:31-35, LK. 8:19-21.

Roman centurion – See MT. 8:5-13, LK. 7:1-10. This centurion commanded the small garrison located on the eastern side of Capernaum. The troops were there to protect the Via Maris, tax-collection in the area, and to keep the Zealots at bay. The birthplace of the Zealotry, Gamla, is only a few miles east of Capernaum. A centurion commanded about 100 men, and there were 60 centurions in a legion.

Notes: Page 102
Roman bath house – There is archeological evidence of a Roman bath at the garrison east of Capernaum, measuring 24 feet by 60 feet in size.

Not yet fully a Jew - This would seem to indicate the centurion was a "God-fearer" a gentile who worshiped the "God of the Jews," but had not been circumcised, or fully obey Jewish dietary restrictions. There were many "God-fearers" across the Roman Empire in the 1st Century AD.

Notes: Page 105
John executed – See MT. 14:1-12, MK. 6:14-29, LK. 9:7-9.

Teacher of Righteousness – the Dead Sea Scrolls call their leader this.

Zechariah – See note for p.26 "Killing of Zechariah."

John imprisoned at Machaerus in Perea - Josephus *Ant.* XVIII 119.

Notes: Page 106
Daggermen – See p.20 and p.69 notes for "daggermen."

Notes: Page 108
Several Pharisees arrived from Jerusalem – See MK. 7:1-23, MT. 15:1-20.

Notes: Page 109
Hypocrites – from Greek word "hypokrites" for actor. Actors wore masks on the stage, so they were "two-faced," hiding their true selves behind a mask.

The Pharisees tried to trap him – See MK. 10-12, MT. 19:1-12.

What God joins together, must not be separated – See Genesis 2:24.

Notes: Page 110
Because you say "I see," your guilt remains – See JN. 9:40-41.

Jesus preached in Capernaum synagogue – See JN. 6:25-71.

Father's seal – It was normal to have a signet ring that acted as one's seal or signature. To be able to use a person's seal, was to have a person's full authority in all important and financial matters. Likewise, the Scripture often speaks of God's people having God's sign or seal on them. The primary seal or sign for the Hebrews was circumcision. The primary seal for Christians is baptism.

True manna that gives life to the Cosmos – manna in the wilderness only satisfies physical hunger for a short time. But Jesus is calling himself the Bread of Heaven that gives eternal life.

Notes: Page 112
Man/Adam – Adam means man, and vice versa. Adam also means red dirt, recalling "ashes to ashes, dust to dust."

Breath/Spirit - Wind (breathe) and Spirit are the same word. See "Appendix 2: The Cloud of God and Pentecost."

Antipas is searching for you – See LK 13:31-33.

Chapter VII

Notes: Page 113
Crossing the Sea of Galilee – See MK. 4:35-41, MT. 8:23-27, LK. 8:22-25.

Tiberias - Antipas' new capital, built circa 20AD. The city was built on a graveyard. This made it an unclean place to live for devout Jews. Antipas had to give away free land and have numerous inducements to get Jews to live and stay there because of its uncleanness.

Notes: Page 114
The Decapolis – See MK. 5:1-20, MT. 8:28-34, LK. 8:26-39.

Legion – a Roman legion had between five to eight-thousand men. The Judean Prefect, Pontius Pilate, did not have a whole legion under his command, just a few cohorts.

A herd of pigs – devout Jews did not keep or eat pigs. They were an unclean animal in Mosaic Law. Pigs, however, were a sacrificial animal of choice for pagan worship. It is likely these pigs were to be sacrificed in the Greco-Roman temples in the Decapolis. The pigs' death would have been very costly to the owners. Being a "holy" animal to the pagans, their death was a bad omen.

Notes: Page 115
When we reached Bethsaida – See MT. 11:16-24. Bethsaida was the birthplace of Jesus' fishermen disciples. It was on the eastern side of the Sea of Galilee.

Notes: Page 116
Abyss – See notes for p.28 concerning "Sheol," "Hell," "The Pit" and "Gehenna."

Sackcloth and ashes – is a sign and symbol for mourning, grief and repentance. One took off their normal clothes and put on sackcloth garments, and sat in ashes. See Jonah 3:6.

Yoke – See note for p.45 "yoke."

Notes: Page 117
Tyre and Sidon – See MK. 7:24, MT. 15:21.

Return to the Decapolis – See MK. 7:31-37, MT. 15:29-31.

The Decapolis countryside – See MK. 8:1-10, MT. 15:32-39.

Notes: Page 119
Seven baskets of leftovers – in the first miracle of the loaves, twelve baskets of leftovers signified the Twelve Tribes of Israel, since it was a Jewish crowd. This multiplication happens in the Decapolis among gentiles. Seven is symbolic of the surrounding "non-Jewish" or Seven Canaanite nations - "Hittites, Girgashites, Amorites, Canaanites, Perizzites, Hivites and Jebusites." See Deut. 7:1.

Yeast of the Pharisees – See MT. 16:5-12, MK. 8:13-21, LK. 12:1.

Notes: Page 120
Magdala - Aramaic meaning: tower, great or elegant.

Healing blind man – See MK. 8:22-26.

Notes: Page 121
Caesarea Philippi – See MT. 16:13-23, MK. 8:27-30, LK. 9:18-21.

Grotto of Pan – at Caesarea Philippi there was a Grotto of Pan that had a cave leading to the "underworld" which was believed to be a path to "Hades" called "the Gates of Hell (Hades)." Pan did not usually have "temples" but was "worshiped" outdoors around such places as this grotto. Located at the same place in Caesarea Philippi as Pan's Grotto, there were also temples to Zeus (Jupiter- king of the gods), and to the Roman Emperor.

Notes: Page 122
Messiah, the Son of the living God – whenever reading the Gospels we must be careful. When people called Jesus "Messiah" or "Son of God" they likely do not understand the full meaning of these terms. In Jesus' day, both "Messiah" and "Son of God" are terms for human beings, not YHVH. Caesar was called "Son of God," and any rightful king of Israel would be called "Messiah." Peter likely do not understand the fullness of what he is saying. It is not until Jesus' resurrection, ascension, and then the pouring out of the Holy Spirit at Pentecost, that Peter and the disciples fully understand who Jesus is and his divinity.

Peter – is Greek meaning "stone," in Aramaic "Cephas." "Upon this stone I will build my Church" also references back to the "Rock" in the Holy-of-Holies in the Temple. Also, throughout the Torah and Prophets YHVH is constantly referred to as the "Rock".

Take up their cross – MK. 8:34-38, MT. 16:24-27, LK. 9:22-27.

Notes: Page 123
All who acknowledge me to men – MT. 10:32-39.

Enemies will be the members of their household – See Micah 7:6.

Mt. Hermon – MT. 17:1-9, MK. 9:2-13, LK. 9:28-30.

God called to Moses from within the cloud – See Exodus 24.

Elijah on Mt. Horeb/Sinai - See 1 Kings 19, also see "Appendix 2: Cloud of God and Pentecost."

Notes: Page 124
Came Again to Galilee – See MK. 9:30-35.

Notes: Page 125
Tax-collectors and sinners gathered – See LK. 15:1-2, 11-32.

Notes: Page 128
Benefits of serving Caesar, full citizenship in Rome - the Apostle Paul was a Citizen of Rome, through his father. One likelihood is that his father obtained Roman citizenship as a soldier in service to Rome. See Acts 22:27-28.

One such Jewish prodigal - Tiberius Julius Alexander was a Jewish contemporary of Jesus, about ten-years younger, nephew of Philo of Alexander. Tiberius Julius Alexander was Jewish, but turned his back on his people and faith, by joining the armies of Rome. Eventually he became part of the equestrian class, like Pontius Pilate. Alexander was appointed Procurator of Judea in c. 46AD. In May 66AD, he was appointed Prefect of Egypt. When Roman legions laid siege to Jerusalem, during the Jewish Revolt, Vespasian sent Tiberius Julius Alexander to serve as Titus' Chief of Staff, making him second-in-command to Titus. So, when Jerusalem fell and the Temple decimated, it was a prodigal Jew who helped to destroy the center of Jewish life, faith, and national identity.

Cautioned Jesus to leave – See LK. 16:1-13.

Notes: Page 130
Parable of rich man – LK. 16:19-31.

Buried - not Caesar or a Roman, because they would be cremated on a funeral pyre. Jews (and then Christians) were buried.

Hades – See note for p.18 for "Sheol" "Hell" "Pit" and "Gehenna."

Lazarus - meaning "without help."

Dogs licked his sores – In the Law of Moses, dogs are an unclean animal. To have one's sores licked by dogs, is to be doubly unclean, and refused entrance to the Temple.

Paradise – See note for p.18 "paradise."

Five brothers - Antipas' had numerous "brothers," mostly half-brothers. Several were killed by his father, Herod the Great. It is likely there were other "sons of Herod" we are not now aware of. But it is not clear how many of Antipas' brothers were alive during Jesus earthly ministry when he told this parable.

Chapter VIII

Notes: Page 134
Jesus teaching in the Temple – See JN. 7:7-18.

Water flowed from the rock – See Exodus 17:1-7.

Notes: Page 135
Broken cisterns unable to hold water – See Jeremiah 2:13.

Lord will be king over the whole earth – See Zechariah 14:1-9.

Notes: Page 136
Roman short sword – Called a Gladius, 2' long. See JN. 18:10-11.

Zealot – also called Canaanian, or Sicarii.

Notes: Page 138
Jonah's hometown – See note for p.101 "Jonah."

Notes: Page 139
Went to Bethany – See LK. 10:38-42.

Be fruitful and multiply – See Genesis 9:1.

Wandered in the hill country of Judea – See JN. 8:1-11.

Feast of Dedication- also called Feast of the Maccabees/Hanukah.

Notes: Page 140
A people with no understanding come to ruin - See Hosea 4:14.

I desire mercy and not sacrifice – See Hosea 6:6.

Notes: Page 141
Man blind from birth – See JN. 9:1-8.

Siloam - means "to send."

Bethesda – See JN. 51:14.

Notes: Page 142
Went into Solomon's Porch – See JN. 10:22-42.

The Shepherd of Israel – is God. See Genesis 49:24.

Notes: Page 143
You are gods - See Psalm 82:6.

Notes: Page 146
Aristophanes - the greatest comic playwright of ancient Greece.

Notes: Page 148
When we came to Jericho – See LK. 19:1-10.

Notes: Page 149
Lazarus – See JN. 11:1-57.

Notes: Page 152
Statue of Zeus placed in Temple's Holy-of-Holies – what the Greek (Seleucid) ruler Antiochus Epiphanes did. The Romans did the same thing following the Bar Kokhba Revolt.

Notes: Page 153
Better that one man die - See JN. 11:20. Unknowingly the High Priest was prophesying what would take place, that one man would die for the salvation of many.

Notes: Page 154
Chief priests – when this term is used in the Gospels, it may refer to Caiaphas and Annas. It may also include the other former high

priests, who end up serving an "executive committee" for the Sanhedrin.

Notes: Page 155
Six days before Passover – See JN. 12:1-11.

Chapter IX

Notes: Page 157
Setting out from Lazarus' house – See MK 10:35-45 MT. 20:20-28.

Near to Jerusalem – See MK. 11:1-11, MT. 21:1-9, LK. 19:28-44, JN. 12:12-19.

Notes: Page 159
The king rode on a donkey – See 2 Samuel 16:2 "The donkeys are for the king's household to ride on." Also, see Zechariah 9:9 "See, your king comes to you, righteous and victorious, lowly and riding on a donkey, on a colt, the foal of a donkey."

Notes: Page 160
Hosannas from the crowd – Hosanna means "save us" in Aramaic/Hebrew. The crowd is shouting or singing the Psalms 118:26 and 148:1.

Notes: Page 161
Going into the Temple – See MK. 11:15-19, MT. 21:12-17, LK. 19-48.

Notes: Page 162
Lamb Selection Day – See MK. 11:27-33, MT. 21:23-27, LK. 20.

Notes: Page 164
Cry havoc and let slip the dogs of war - Shakespeare's Julius Caesar, Act 3, Scene 1. Mark Antony reacts to the assassination of Caesar.

Object lesson for all who dare oppose Rome - this is what happened when Israel revolted in 66AD.

Notes: Page 165
Pharisee teachers came to Jesus – MK. 12:13-17, MT. 22:15-22, LK. 20:20-26.

A denarius - typical pay for a day's labor.

Notes: Page 166
Most important commandment – See MK 12:28-34, LK 10:25-37, MT 22:34-40.

These are more important than all burnt offerings – See 1 Samuel 15:22, Psalm 40:6.

Notes: Page 167
Why do the rabbis call the Messiah David's son – See MK. 12:35-37, MT. 22:41-46, LK. 20:41-44.

Sit at my right hand til I put your enemies under your feet – Ps. 110.

Two men went up to the Temple to pray – See LK. 18:9-14.

Notes: Page 168
God's Kingdom like a king who arranged a marriage for his son – See MT. 22:1-14, LK. 14:15-24.

Notes: Page 169
Parable about Herod the Great – See Josephus, *War* 1.12.3 240-241, and 1.17.8 244.

A prince went to a distant country – See LK. 19:11-27, MT. 25.

Achelaus – See List of Characters.

Minas - was about three-month's wages – about 100 denarii.

Notes: Page 170
Landowner leased a vineyard – See MT. 21:33-46, MK. 12:1-12, LK. 20:9-19.

Notes: Page 172
God loved his creation so much – See JN. 3:16.

Woe to you Pharisees – See MT. 23:13-36, MK. 12:40, LK. 20:47.

Notes: Page 174
How magnificent is the Temple – See MK. 13:1-2, MT. 24:1-2, LK. 21:5-6.

The Christ will be put to death – See Daniel 9:26. Although this prophesy it translated as Anointed One or Messiah in most English translations, in the Septuagint, the ancient Greek translation of the Hebrew Scripture, the word is Christ (Christos).

Notes: Page 175
I am the light of the world – See JN. 8:12:59.

I am – See Exodus 3:14. Also see note for "I am" on p.103. Jesus is ultimately condemned to death by the Sanhedrin on the charge of blasphemy, claiming to be God.

Notes: Page 176
Not bastards born out of wedlock, like you – may refer to their poor view of Galileans, in that most were not "full-blooded" Jews, but were of only partially of "Jewish blood." Many of their ancestors had converted to Judaism some one-hundred years before, under Hasmonean rule. And/or this may be a reference to rumors of Jesus' unusual conception.

Notes: Page 177
You are a Samaritan and demon possessed – Galileans were often not regarded much higher than Samaritans by elitist Judean religious authorities. Also, it should be noted that Jesus began ministered among the Samaritans early in his ministry; and they eagerly accepted his message. The Pharisees also often made the charge against Jesus that he did his miracles by the power of Satan. (Whereas, Sadducees did not believe in demons, so they would not have accused Jesus of this.)

Abraham rejoices at my arrival and prophesied about it – The story of Abraham taking Isaac to Mt. Moriah for the sacrifice is a prophesy of the coming Lamb of God who will be sacrificed. See Genesis 22. Also, see note for "firstborn son" p.29.

I am – in Hebrew: YHVH. See Exodus 3:14 Also see note for "I am" on p.93.

Now only two days before Passover – See MK. 14, MT. 26:1-5, LK. 22:1, 2.

Notes: Page 179
Make preparations for the Passover meal – See MK. 14:12-16, MT. 26:17-19, LK. 22:7-13.

Essene calendar – a 365-day solar calendar similar to the one we follow today, whereas most Jews followed a lunar calendar. Essenes believe the lunar calendar was of pagan origin, from Babylon, and therefore improper. They held their calendar to be the one Jews originally had. On the Essene Calendar, Passover begins on the same day of the week every year, a Wednesday.

Notes: Page 180
Kill the shepherd, the sheep will be scattered – See Zechariah. 13:7.

Notes: Page 183
Took Jesus to Caiaphas' palace – See MK. 14:53-72, MT. 26:57-75, LK. 22:54-62, JN. 18:13-27.

You are a Galilean - Galileans spoke a different dialect of Aramaic than people in Judea.

Notes: Page 184
Jesus' trial - should have been held in daytime and with adequate notice of the proceeding for those who might wish to offer testimony in defense of the accused.

Notes: Page 185
I am – in Greek: "ego ami" - in Hebrew: YHVH. See Exodus 3:14 Also see note for "I am" on p.93.

Notes: Page 186
Take him to the pit - Caiaphas' palace had cell to hold prisoners. There is historical and archeological evidence for this pit.

Chapter X

Notes: Page 195
Thirty pieces of silver – See Zechariah 11:12-13.

Notes: Page 196
Hosea's harlot wife - See Hosea 1:2-3.

Notes: Page 197
Darkness covered Egypt for three days – See Exodus 10:22.

Notes: Page 198
He brought me up out of the pit – See Psalm 40:2.

No pit is so deep, that God is not deeper still – a quote from Corrie Ten Boom.

Notes: Page 200
Led him to Pilate – See JN. 18:28-40.

Notes: Page 201
Goy – from Hebrew, a non-Jew, a pagan, non-Jewish nations.

Notes: Page 202
Are you the King of Israel – See LK. 23:2-5.

Have you no defense at all – See MT. 27:11-14.

This man is a Galilean – See LK. 23:6-16.

Notes: Page 207
Wove together a crown of thorns – See JN. 19:1-16.

Notes: Page 209
Release a prisoner of the people's choosing – See MT. 27:15-31.

Notes: Page 210
His blood be on us – the blood of the sacrificial animals was upon the people. By it came remission/atonement of sins. Likewise, as Christians we join in this statement with the crowd, for if Jesus' blood is not upon us, we are not saved. Who is to blame for Jesus' death? All of us are to blame. It is for our sins Jesus died. See "Appendix 3: The Jewish "Race."

Notes: Page 213
They placed Jesus' cross on him – See LK. 23:26-32.

Notes: Page 214
Forces you to go one mile – See MT. 5:41.

Weeping for her children – See Jeremiah 31:15.

Fall on us, and to the hills cover us - See Hosea 10:8.

Chapter XI

Notes: Page 215
To Golgotha - See JN. 19:17-37.

Notes: Page 217
Divided my clothes, cast lots – See Psalm 22:18.

Goat whose lot falls as a sin offering – See Leviticus 16:8-9.

Page 218
White robes - See Revelation 7:9.

Crowns – See Revelation 2:10.

Crucifixion – See MT. 27:33-56, MK. 15:22-41, LK. 23:33-45.

Notes: Page 219
My mouth is dried up – See Psalm 22:15.

Notes: Page 220
My God, my God, why have you forsaken me - Jesus said this in Aramaic: "Eloi, Eloi, lama sabachthani?" See Psalm 22:1, and MK. 15:34.
He continued to recite the Psalm – See Psalm 22.

Notes: Page 221
They will look on me, the one they have pierced – See Zechariah 12:10.

Truly this must have been a son of the gods – See MK. 15:39. The concept of "sons of the gods" is common in pagan Roman culture. On Roman coins was the inscription for Caesar, "Son of God" (Divi Filius). So, this is probably a statement of faith in YHVH, or that Jesus is God in human flesh. See note on "Messiah" for p.35.

I recited the prophet Isaiah – See Isaiah 53:3-8.

Notes: Page 222
Qaddish – in Aramaic means "holy". See Ezekiel 38:23, Job 25:2, and I Kings 8:45.

Notes: Page 223
Hasta - a Roman spear about six-feet long, having a shaft usually made of ash, with a heavy iron head.

Not one of his bones will be broken – See Psalm 34:20.

Chapter XII

Notes: Page 228
Mezuzah Scripture, "Hear, O Israel" - See Deut. 6:4-9, 11:13-21.

Notes: Page 230

The Lord bless you and keep you – the priestly blessing. See Numbers 6:24-26

Valley of Hinnom. See note on "Valley of Hinnom" p.5.

Notes: Page 231

How did Judas hang himself? – MT. 27:5 says, "he (Judas) went away and hung himself." In the modern age, when we hear of someone hanging themselves, we think of hanging by a rope. In the ancient world "hanging" usually meant some form of impalement. In Acts 10:39, Peter preaches the Gospel to the Roman Centurion in Caesarea. Of the crucifixion, he says, "They killed him (Jesus) by hanging him on a tree." In Acts 5:30, Peter and the Apostles are before the Sanhedrin and say, "whom you killed by hanging him on a tree." In Esther 7:10, it says, "So they impaled (hung) Haman on the pole he had set up for Mordecai." Joshua 8:29 says, "He impaled (hung) the body of the king of Ai on a pole, leaving it there until evening." I know of no instances in the Bible where someone was executed or killed themselves by hanging from a rope. This helps explain the seeming discrepancy between MT. 27:5 and Acts 1:18 which says, "Judas bought a field and there fell headlong, his body burst open and all his intestines spilled out." If one is impaled, it is not unusual for one's intestines to spill. Conclusion: Judas hung (impaled) himself on a pole (spear) and his intestines spilled out.

Notes: Page 232

I desire mercy, rather than sacrifice – See Hosea 6:4, 6.

Behold, the Lamb of God – See JN. 1:29.

When you come into your Kingdom, remember me – See LK. 23:42-43.

69288964R00162

Made in the USA
Columbia, SC
16 April 2017